Prayer in Counselling and Psychotherapy

of related interest

The Challenge of Practical Theology
Selected Essays
Stephen Pattison
ISBN 978 1 84310 453 7

Spirituality, Ethics and Care
Simon Robinson
ISBN 978 1 84310 498 8

Medicine of the Person
Faith, Science and Values in Health Care Provision
Edited by John Cox, Alastair V. Campbell and Bill K.W.M. Fulford
Foreword by Julia Neuberger
ISBN 978 1 84310 397 4

In Living Color
An Intercultural Approach to Pastoral Care and Counseling
2nd edition
Emmanuel Y. Lartey
Foreword by James Newton Poling
ISBN 978 1 84310 750 7

Spiritual Caregiving as Secular Sacrament
A Practical Theology for Professional Caregivers
Ray S. Anderson
Foreword by John Swinton
ISBN 978 1 84310 746 0

Making Sense of Spirituality in Nursing and Health Care Practice
An Interactive Approach
2nd edition
Wilfred McSherry
Foreword by Keith Cash
ISBN 978 1 84310 365 3

Prayer in Counselling and Psychotherapy

Exploring a Hidden Meaningful Dimension

Peter Madsen Gubi

Foreword by Brian Thorne

Jessica Kingsley Publishers
London and Philadelphia

The author and publisher are grateful to the proprietors listed below for permission to quote the following material:

R.D. Dobbins (2000) 'Psychotherapy with Pentecostal Protestants.' In P.S. Richards and A.E. Bergin (eds) *Handbook of Psychotherapy and Religious Diversity.* Copyright © 2000 by the American Psychological Association. Reproduced with permission.

H.G. Koenig and J. Pritchett (1998) 'Religion and Psychotherapy.' In H.G. Koenig (ed.) *Handbook of Religion and Mental Health*, pp.323–336, copyright © Elsevier (1998).

M.E. McCullough and D.B. Larson (1999) 'Prayer.' In W.R. Miller (ed.) *Integrating Spirituality into Treatment – Resources for Practitioners.* Copyright © 1999 by the American Psychological Association. Reproduced with permission.

S.-Y. Tan (1996) 'Religion and the Clinical Practice: Implicit and Explicit Integration.' In E.P. Schafranske (ed.) *Religion and the Clinical Practice* of Psychology. Copyright © 1996 by the American Psychological Association. Reproduced with permission.

First published in 2008
by Jessica Kingsley Publishers
116 Pentonville Road
London N1 9JB, UK
and
400 Market Street, Suite 400
Philadelphia, PA 19106, USA

www.jkp.com

Copyright © Peter Madsen Gubi 2008
Foreword copyright © Brian Thorne 2008

Library of Congress Cataloging in Publication Data
Gubi, Peter Madsen, 1963-
    Prayer in counselling and psychotherapy : exploring a hidden meaningful dimension / Peter Madsen Gubi ; foreword by Brian Thorne.
        p. ; cm.
    ISBN 978-1-84310-519-0 (alk. paper)
    1. Psychotherapy--Religious aspects. 2. Counseling--Religious aspects. 3. Prayer. I. Title.
    [DNLM: 1. Psychotherapy--methods. 2. Counseling--methods. 3. Faith Healing. 4. Pastoral Care. WM 420 G921p 2007]
    RC489.S676G83 2007
    616.89'14--dc22
                                                        2007026574

British Library Cataloguing in Publication Data
A CIP catalogue record for this book is available from the British Library

ISBN 978 1 84310 519 0

Printed and bound in Great Britain by
Athenaeum Press, Gateshead, Tyne and Wear

This book is dedicated to my parents, Joyce and Peter Gubi, who have always loved me, stood by me and believed in me. Thank you.

Acknowledgements

I wish particularly to acknowledge Dr William West, Reader in Counselling at Manchester University, and Canon Professor Dr Brian Thorne, Emeritus Professor in Counselling at the University of East Anglia, whose wisdom, encouragement, writing and teaching have contributed much to my personal, spiritual and professional development. I am grateful to my colleagues for their support and to my students for their encouragement. I am also grateful to St Deiniol's Library, Hawarden, Flintshire, for awarding me scholarships that have ultimately enabled this book to be written.

Peter Madsen Gubi
University of Central Lancashire
December 2007

Contents

Foreword

For a profession which produces an ever more abundant supply of literature, it is perhaps surprising that certain aspects of what happens behind the closed doors of the therapeutic encounter have remained comparatively unexplored. Until fairly recent times this has included the spiritual dimension of the counselling interaction, especially where this takes place within the context of a secular counselling agency with no affiliation to a religious institution or a particular faith community. Indeed, it is still not uncommon to discover agencies where spiritual issues and concerns are deemed to be inappropriate and where clients quickly receive the message that their spirituality – however they conceptualise it – should be left firmly outside the counselling door.

Fortunately the situation has begun to change – in some cases dramatically – during the last decade and there is now an increasing willingness on the part of practitioners and their trainers to consider spirituality as a legitimate area for therapeutic exploration. This shift in attitude has been driven partly by the increasing number of clients seeking help for spiritual matters but is also the outcome of significant innovations in the educational sphere where schools are now specifically required to foster the spiritual development of their pupils. The recognition, too, that religion and spirituality are not the same, although often related, has made it possible for spirituality to enter the therapeutic agenda without the fear that counsellors will be tempted to plug a particular value system, let alone to seek converts to a particular faith.

It is in this changing context that Peter Madsen Gubi has taken the audacious step of exploring the place of prayer within therapeutic processes and in the lives of clients and therapists. That this is a somewhat risky undertaking is underlined by the fact, revealed by his own researches,

that although many practitioners claim to integrate prayer into their therapeutic work, almost all are reluctant to discuss this aspect of their practice
with their supervisors. There is clearly a fear of being adversely judged or
even of being considered to be acting irresponsibly or unethically.

Peter Madsen Gubi, with great clarity and no little scholarly application, brings prayer out of the counselling closet and makes a strong case for
its rightful inclusion in the armamentarium of the therapist's skills and
helping strategies. He shows that this can be done with the utmost respect
for the client's autonomy and without inappropriate imposition or coercion. With meticulous attention to the various objections to prayer within
therapy, on the one hand, and careful exposition of the different modes of
prayer, on the other, he has produced a book which will be experienced by
many practitioners as immensely liberating. They will be encouraged and
supported by his reasoned and sensitive insistence on the appropriateness
of incorporating into the therapeutic process a response to pain and suffering and a mode of comfort and healing which have characterised the
spiritual and religious lives of human beings from time immemorial. At the
same time, those who might be tempted to manipulate clients or engender
passivity through the invocation of an all-powerful deity will find no
encouragement in these pages. Peter Madsen Gubi holds no brief for those
who would seek miraculous cures or divine intervention. For him, prayer
which finds its rightful place in the counselling room honours the client's
autonomy at all times and is the outcome of the relational depth which
both client and counsellor have dared to enter. What is more, like all therapeutic practices and experiences, it must be subject to analysis and
reflection and not confined to a 'sacred' arena which prohibits or restricts
full discussion and exploration.

It is clear that for Peter Madsen Gubi his book is the result of a lengthy,
and at times arduous, personal journey. In the process he has been forced to
question some of the cherished beliefs and assumptions acquired from his
training as a therapist and often reinforced by the 'norms' of the therapeutic professions. At the same time, many of his theological constructs have
come in for rigorous scrutiny and, as a result, dogmatic religion no longer
finds a place in his response to reality unless it is buttressed by his own
experience and insight. The book is a challenge to all therapists to examine
their own presuppositions and prejudices and to discover, in so doing, an
enhanced flexibility without losing their integrity. It is not recommended

reading for those settled in their ways or unwilling to acknowledge their own spiritual yearnings or their lack of courage in the face of another's spirituality. Prayer can be a tough discipline and Peter Madsen Gubi demonstrates that its incorporation into the work of the therapist requires no little courage and a willingness to explore afresh what constitutes ethical behaviour as opposed to following the rule book.

Brian Thorne,
Professor Emeritus, University of East Anglia, and Honorary Lay Canon,
Norwich Cathedral

Introduction

Why write a book on 'prayer in counselling and psychotherapy'? In some sense the journey began sub-consciously with having a mother whose response to almost every problem is to pray about it. Whilst her process is often a reaction to helplessness – a 'holding on to hope' – I have always appreciated her sincerity even when I have been critical of her. She has been a strong believer in intercessory prayer for others. Whilst I have often been cynical of the fact that many people on her prayer-list seem to die, there have been examples of unexpected healing. I have wondered how much intercessory prayer has helped. How does one measure 'helped'? Perhaps people have been helped in ways that are immeasurable (e.g. gaining peace of mind and a greater acceptance of their condition). Maybe death is a form of healing, so through death the prayers have been answered. In spite of my own questioning I have felt upheld by my mother's prayer.

My father's approach to prayer has been very different. Rather than seek to make demands on God, he adopts a quiet, reflexive and thoughtful manner to prayer. His prayer is largely non-verbal and contemplative. His attitude is one of submission to the will of God, and personal growth can be seen in adopting an attitude towards acceptance of that will (destiny). He is more at peace in himself, content with life, enjoys his own company and enjoys being with nature. For him, existential aloneness does not exist because God is all 'around' him and 'in' him. He is never alone. This way of thinking has impacted deeply on me and is one I strive to live.

Both parents represent something of the range of views that exist about prayer. In my journey moments of profound connection and intimacy with some clients, or silences in which intensity of emotion is being experienced, have felt prayerful and spiritual. The same is true of those times sitting in my garden or on a mountain experiencing deep anguish or profound peace and connectedness; those times of intimate loving or being with death have felt like prayer. I have noticed that separation is often accompanied with such expressions as 'I'll be thinking of you' which is akin to 'distant prayer' – 'I'll pray for you'. So my research into prayer in counselling and psychotherapy continues to be a personal journey to discover where I am with prayer. What is it? What does it mean to me as a counsellor and spiritual pilgrim?

At times in my life, when emotional despair has occurred, along with personal therapy I have sought solace in deep personal prayer where I have poured out my inner thoughts and feelings to 'Other' (which I call 'God') and have received a great depth of release and comfort with an accompanying difference in perspective on life. During the course of my research I suffered some kind of breakdown (breakthrough) or 'dark night of the soul' experience in which I questioned the purpose of life, felt bereft of faith, and utterly alone in the cosmos. Through prayer I experienced being bathed in inner light, and experienced intense warmth, love and forgiveness, which were crucial to my recovery and which made my research heuristically 'real' at a level that I have never engaged with before.

Although the constructs of my faith have altered during the course of my life, my sense of the spiritual dimension to life has emerged as highly important and vital. I would describe myself as a broadly liberal Christian, in that I strive to live closely to the spirit of Jesus Christ as it is presented in the Gospels. By 'spirit' I mean a 'presence' and a 'way of being' that is characterised by love, a deep connectedness with the source of being, and a valuing of others and environment. It is the same 'spirit' that I see in some people from many spiritual traditions, e.g. Gandhi, the Dalai Lama, Basil Hulme, Rowan Williams, Jonathan Sacks and in many who do not reach the ranks of societal greatness.

I do not subscribe to the dogma of institutionalised religion except that which I have thought through for myself and find personally helpful because I recognise the emotional and psychological destructiveness that some religious dogma has had on many. For historical and ancestral reasons, and because of issues of 'needing to belong', I associate with the Moravian denomination of the Christian Church. I come from a religious background and upbringing with my grandfather having been a Bishop of the Unitas Fratrum (Moravian Church) and my father and uncle being retired Moravian ministers. I myself have studied counselling at masters and doctorate level, theology at masters degree level, world religions at graduate degree level, and spiritual accompaniment at diploma level. I have found 'God' (relational connectedness with that which is bigger than me) in the mosque and the gurdwara, in the countryside, the church and the Hindu temple, in loving others/self and in life, and in experiencing death situations. I have a deep interest in, and I am profoundly influenced in my thinking and my relating to God, life and others, by Celtic Christian spirituality (O'Donohue 1997, 1998; Simpson 1995). I use the language of Christianity in my relating to 'prayer' but I recognise that what I understand in certain ways can be understood using language from other spiritual and religious traditions and from the psycho-philosophical genre. I find some Christian language difficult because of the oppressive values it has come to represent and I confess to not understanding some Christian concepts and ways of thinking.

Like many of the experienced counsellors that I have met on the journey of my research I have questioned why something that is so important to my personal and psychological well-being should be left out of counselling if it could be of help to others. Does prayer have a place in counselling? As prayer has many attributes that are similar to other accepted therapeutic interventions (e.g. relaxation techniques, visualisation, mindfulness) why cannot prayer be considered? Where are the boundaries between prayer and therapy? What do other counsellors do with similar faith/professional questions? Can I be a person of integrity if an important part of me feels like it is left out of my practice in which the greatest asset is my investment of self – even though at some level it is present, whether it is articulated or not, because 'I am'?

These questions led to some initial research (Gubi 1999, 2001) that explored some of these questions with experienced counselling trainers from British universities, whom I respected and whose opinions I valued. My sense was, and is, that I am uncovering an aspect of counselling that people want to talk about and feel is valuable but who are reluctant to 'come out' about their practice in order to protect their professional credibility. Certainly, the uncomplimentary responses that were sent to the *British Medical Journal* in reply to Leibovici's (2001) research, the unusual need for editorial justification (Browner and Goldman 2000) preceding the publication of Harkness, Abbot and Ernst's (2000) work, and the initial rejection of my book review of *Sharing Spaces? Prayer and the Counselling*

Relationship (Rose 2002) by the editor of the *Counselling and Psychotherapy Journal* on grounds of insufficient practitioner relevance and interest (although the book review was later published after a change of editor) (Gubi 2003a) indicate the depth of criticism that can be directed at those who dare to research areas of work like prayer that are deemed by some to be superstitious, unscientific and culturally unacceptable.

Yet the subject of prayer in relation to counselling feels too important to my own personal and professional curiosity and spiritual growth to leave uncovered and unacknowledged, and I hope that I can offer some contribution to the increasing interest in the spiritual dimension of counselling as the counselling profession embraces multi-culturalism, working at relational depth and integration. I believe that I, as a counsellor and trainer, have a responsibility to be receptive to new ideas and that humility and open-mindedness in that process are essential. However, I know from my experience of research, and the depth of reflection that has been involved, just how scary it is to have my sacredly held assumptions and beliefs challenged, to be stripped bare of things that I have held dear, and almost to start again in my understanding of, and relating to, spirituality. I accept that fear may preclude others from reflecting on their spiritual and counselling constructs in order to embrace this work openly. Yet the growth that has been engendered from the experience has been enormous and precious to me. I also need to acknowledge my own scepticism that leads me to question and reflect on the implications of prayer for good counselling practice. I too am wary of unscrupulous practitioners who may use prayer to evangelise and proselytise, or in a routine, mechanical, unthinking way; but mostly I have not met them in my research journey. Instead I have largely met practitioners whose spirituality is evident from the warmth in their eyes, and from their deep and calm way of being – a profound stillness of presence and love that I admire. I have been struck by their sense of integrity and desire for professionalism which are demonstrated by reflexive, safe, ethical practice that puts the clients' needs and safety first, and which fosters autonomy, trust and respect. Where I have met ways of expressing concepts, thinking and practice that I have instinctively felt uncomfortable with, I have tried to stand back and bracket my constructs in order to enter their frame of reference. In so doing I have been able to appreciate that much of what I have felt uncomfortable with can often be 'reframed' into more acceptable concepts that are meaningful for both me and for the counsellor who was being interviewed. When that has not been possible, I have simply registered my discomfort to myself and reflected on it away from the interview process, being careful not to let those difficulties prejudice my approach to the research as far as is humanly possible. All of these experiences and constructs have an influence on my ability, as researcher, to hear the voice of others, to interpret the data, and to present my findings in this book.

As well as being a spiritual pilgrim, I am a BACP Accredited Counsellor and a BACP Accredited Supervisor who works as a person-centred counsellor in a private practice setting (Sanctum Counselling) and as a counsellor trainer within various settings. I have never explicitly used prayer with any of my clients (or have I?) in over 21 years of counselling-related work, and part of my journey has been to ask myself 'why not?' – given that prayer has been so cathartic for me. As I bring to this work a background of learning and reflection in the disciplines of theology and mainstream counselling, I bring a dual ability to appreciate the alienated voices of counselling and prayer. My hope is that I can do justice to both through this book. My assumption that underpins this book is that they are not that far apart.

Throughout the text I refer to my sense of encounter, connection or communication with 'transcendent otherness' as 'prayer' but I realise that the word 'prayer' may inhibit many people from reading on because of what they bring to the word. If you are struggling with the word 'prayer' please give yourself time to overcome this hurdle and feel free to replace the word 'prayer' with whatever feels meaningful for you and encapsulates your existential awareness of 'connection with otherness'. Likewise, I will often refer to the 'transcendent otherness' as 'God'. These are words from my frame of reference but I am happy to embrace other words that enable the concepts being discussed to make sense to the reader and ask the reader again to embrace their own language to make meaning of what follows.

Aims of this book

This book is not intended as a vehicle to promote the use of prayer in counselling and psychotherapy. Rather it is intended to be a forum of exploration by which practitioners can be informed in their relational encounters with clients of faith and when working with their spiritual dimension. It is my contention that prayer has similar properties to some psychotherapeutic interventions so arguably prayer might be used when working with the spiritual dimension of the client. Earlier research that I have carried out (Gubi 1999, 2000, 2001) has demonstrated something of how prayer can be psychologically understood, how prayer might be used in mainstream counselling when working with Christian clients, and what the ethical implications might be. Based on the findings of my doctoral research (Gubi 2003b) for which I conducted 19 in-depth interviews with mainstream counsellors whose work includes prayer, with the data being analysed using interpretative phenomenological analysis (Smith 1996; Smith, Jarman and Osborne 1999), the intention of this book is to provide insight into the use of prayer in mainstream counselling and psychotherapy and enable the voices of those mainstream counsellors whose work includes prayer to be heard and validated.

What is in the book?

Chapter 1 sets the context for subsequent chapters by exploring changes in professional attitude that potentially enable a greater openness to prayer being considered in the therapeutic relationship. It defines spirituality and prayer, examines the relationship between prayer and counselling and surveys the extent of the use of prayer in psychotherapy. Chapter 2 asks if prayer is beneficial and proceeds to explore some of the research that has been conducted into the value of prayer on health and psychological well-being. Chapter 3 looks at what the literature says about the potential ethical difficulties that may be faced when integrating prayer in counselling. Chapter 4 gives some thought from the literature about how prayer might strategically be integrated. Based on the experiences of counsellors whose work includes prayer, Chapter 5 examines how prayer philosophically and supportively influences counselling and practitioners. Chapter 6 continues with these counsellors' experiences to explore how prayer can form an explicit part of the therapeutic process. Chapter 7 concludes with some thoughts as to a possible way forward for practice, supervision and training.

Throughout the text I have used the concepts of 'counselling' and 'psychotherapy' interchangeably. I have also used she/he interchangeably. I make reference to BACP Accredited Counsellors and CMCS Approved Counsellors. The British Association for Counselling and Psychotherapy (BACP) accredits counsellors who fulfil a criterion of training, client experience, personal development and continuing professional development. BACP Accredited Counsellors are arguably representative of counsellors who have attained a high degree of training and experience in mainstream counselling. The Churches Ministerial Counselling Service (CMCS) is a group of mainstream counsellors to whom clergy and their families are referred. The CMCS maintains a register of 'approved counsellors' whose training and experience equates to that of a BACP Accredited Counsellor.

Although the book is primarily written from a Christian perspective for mainstream and pastoral counsellors and psychotherapists, my hope is that the insights can be considered in a multi-faith, multi-spiritual, multi-cultural and multi-agency context. I am extremely grateful to those counsellors who 'came out' to speak to me about their experiences during my research for this book. I have their agreement to utilise their experiences in publications but I have protected their identity for reasons of confidentiality.

CHAPTER 1

Setting the Context

Recent developments in counselling

Recent practitioner-led research and philosophical debate within counselling and psychotherapy have brought the profession to a point where there is now a greater openness among some practitioners to embracing the inclusion of carefully considered 'unorthodox practices' like prayer. As the profession grows to maturity in a climate of openness and risk-taking where practitioners are expected to develop their own internal frames of evaluation, more experienced therapists tend to depart from the norms and conventions of their previous training to put themselves out on a limb to work in original, innovative and intuitive ways (Wosket 1999). However, Wosket acknowledges that 'there is a whole vital area of counselling and psychotherapy practice [that] is not openly discussed and infrequently finds its way into books, journals and research studies' (p.1). This is true about the practice of prayer in counselling. As the profession slowly journeys to that place of maturity and acceptance, it is wrestling with the tensions of regulation and accountability and by traditional frames of reference that inhibit progress.

One such development in more recent research and philosophical thinking has been the emergence of 'integration', not as the development of a new model created out of the drawing together of elements from other theories to create a new modality in therapy, but integration as a way of thinking about how we as individuals, responsibly, ethically and with integrity, integrate 'self' and all that makes us who we are into the thera-peutic relationship in relation to existing theories, and in response to client needs (Worsley 2004). This way of working gives us permission as thera-pists to be appropriately more of 'ourselves' – to be freer to take responsible and appropriate risks in the therapeutic relationship and to be less inhuman, rigid and incongruent.

Furthering this development has been the work of Mearns and Cooper (2005) who have written a seminal in-depth exposition of what it means to work with clients at relational depth. Their work invites us to consider, and if necessary to revise, our modes of relating to enable us to encounter our clients at a more meaningful relational level within a good working alliance which Mearns and Cooper argue increases the effectiveness of therapy. This includes being open to ways of being that increase appropriate levels of congruence, risk-taking, intimacy, mutuality, tenderness and relational connection without losing sight of appropriate and ethical practice. Thorne (1991, 2002) gives this sense of deep relational connection a 'spiritual' context.

Mearns and Thorne (2000) have also strongly argued for recapturing the essence of humanity in therapy that has got lost in the fear of accountability which can motivate therapists to work defensively and self-protectively, with the potential consequence that we do not meet our clients at (or are not truly aware of) their point of need – rather we meet them at our place of safety which, they argue, is less effective. Mearns and Thorne encourage us to be ethically and responsibly 'freer' in our humanity and in our responses with our clients.

Other developments in research and thinking that I believe impact on the use of prayer in counselling and psychotherapy have been the increasing recognition of the spiritual dimension of counselling, an interest in the integration of spiritual 'interventions' in mainstream counselling (King-Spooner and Newnes 2001; Moore and Purton 2006; Richards and Bergin 1997, 2003; Schreurs 2002; Sperry 2001; West 2000, 2004) and an acknowledgement that spirituality forms an important part of maintaining many people's psychological well-being (Bearon and Koenig 1990; Ellinson and Taylor 1996; Moss 2005). Yet within the mental health professions, clients' spirituality is often a neglected part of mental health care (Swinton 2001), or one which is 'ring-fenced' as being not appropriate for discussion, or psychopathologised or labelled and treated as 'psychosis' (Jenkins 2006). Research undertaken by the Mental Health Foundation (Nicholls 2002), conducted among users of mental health services, illustrates the importance of taking clients' spirituality seriously in promoting or working with mental health, of valuing clients' spiritual experiences, and of understanding and supporting clients in their spiritual journeys whilst respecting the uniqueness and individuality of each person's spirituality. Jenkins (2006) too has offered disturbing evidence of the impact of denying the client's spiritual experience and of excluding spirituality from counselling and psychotherapy which is the antithesis of healing.

Richards and Bergin (1997) state that because of the growth in spiritual interest within the general population there is a need for counsellors and psychotherapists to challenge the historical alienation between religion and psychotherapy and increase their awareness of religious and spiritual issues. They argue that more successful outcomes are achieved when spiritual issues are worked with sensitively and competently within counselling. West (2000, 2004) challenges us as therapists to be open to our clients' spirituality and to recognise counselling as a spiritual space in which clients can be spiritually present. This means being receptive to, and aware of, spiritual issues and practices. Moss (2005) argues for a celebration of diversity, and Moodley and West (2005) have offered a forum for us to consider how traditional healing practices might be integrated into counselling and psychotherapy, including some spiritual practices such as prayer. Hay and Nye (2006) have argued for spirituality and relational consciousness to be taken seriously as they are implicit in human need. Tacey (2004) states that spirituality is crucial to addressing the yearning for a deeper connection with meaning and purpose in life which, if not met, leads to alienation, disempowerment and disillusionment which are implicit in much of the suicide, depression and psychological suffering that we as therapists work with on a daily basis.

Whilst openness to the client's spirituality is often a part of counselling that is explicitly associated with a religious context, e.g. pastoral counselling (Foskett and Lynch 2001; Lyall 1995; Lynch 1999, 2000; Wimberly 1990), Jenkins (2006) suggests that such openness is not always found in mainstream counselling. I would argue that to engage in that process of openness, mainstream counselling needs to consider if spiritual interventions, like prayer, can appropriately engage with the therapeutic relationship and be enhancing of the counselling process, when working with clients of faith and spiritual belief; and if so, how it can be ethically implemented. Whilst some research has been carried out in this field (e.g. Gubi 1999, 2001, 2003b, 2004; Lange 1983a, 1983b; Rose 1993; Ten Eyck 1993; Webster 1992), it is largely unpublished and limited in its findings and methodology. Prayer is regarded as being important to psychological well-being (Maltby, Lewis and Day 1999) so it is important that we as counselling practitioners are aware of its use and informed in our consideration of how it can be ethically integrated into our counselling practice, if and when it is necessary and appropriate to do so.

There is a burgeoning interest in the relationship between spirituality, religion, pastoral care and mental health that is increasingly reflected in the literature (e.g. Head 2002; May 1993; Miller 1999; Pargament 1992, 1997; Rose 2002; Schreurs 2002; Schumaker 1992; Shelly 1983; Swinton 2001; White and MacDougall 2001; Willows and Swinton 2000). This is evident in the promotion of research into the relationship between prayer and well-being using scientific methodology that attempts to understand, and make credible, the experience of prayer and to determine its efficacy (e.g. Astin, Harkness and Ernst 2000; Byrd 1988; Dossey 1993; Leibovici 2001; Matthews 1998), although there are difficulties with researching prayer in this way.

Defining spirituality

Spirituality has many meanings and interpretations that are difficult to encapsulate in a common definition (Barnum 1998). Spirituality has been described as 'breath' (Latin root *spiritus* meaning breath of life) – the essence of life or life force. This essence of life '…infuses human beings with qualities such as inspiration, creativity and connection with others…' (Fukuyama and Sevig 1999, pp.4–5). O'Murchu (1994, pp.169–170) defines spirituality as the human search for meaning and fulfilment in life. Spirituality is our ability to make sense and meaning out of life, to discover one's ultimate true nature and relationship to the universe. Shafranske and Gorsuch (1984) define spirituality as the courage to look inside one's self, and as trust and openness to the infinite. Thorne (2001) defines spirituality as, 'the yearning within the human being for meaning for that which is greater than the encapsulated individual, for interconnection with all that is. It is an expression of the whole person, physical, emotional and intellectual' (p.438).

Within these definitions the relevance of spirituality to counselling is clear. Like spirituality, the purpose of counselling is to make life meaningful and become more in tune with one's 'authentic self' in relation to others and to the world through awareness. The difference seems to be in the sense of 'openness to the infinite' and in 'the interconnection with all that is', which seems to indicate something beyond 'self' that is experienced through an awareness of the limitation of self in the cosmos. Yet, there is a sense of connection and relationship (interconnection) with all that is (creation), which can give meaning and purpose to life. This sense of interconnectedness with creation and 'all that is of life' is certainly inherent in some forms of spirituality, e.g. Celtic spirituality (O'Donohue 1997, 1998). This awareness of our place in creation leads some to create a system of relating (personal/communal/religious) that leads to the development of a way of being and experiencing that is characterised by beliefs about self, others, nature and life (Elkins *et al.* 1988), often created through an awareness of a transcendent 'Ultimate' which is the object of relating (connection) and from which meaning and purpose comes. Hardy (1979) concludes that for many, that sense of relating in spirituality is characterised by a felt sense of 'Something Other' that has been traditionally characterised as a deity with whom one can have a personalised 'I–Thou' relationship, with prayer being the means of communication. So spirituality is that which involves the transcendent self, or that part of one that is more than any role or action one is engaged in; that part of one that is engaged in relationship with the ultimate mystery who is greater than the self (Shea 1991). This 'ultimate mystery' or 'transcendent other' has many ways of being understood and related to – God, Higher Self, Inner Light, Cosmos; one's sense of inner love, wisdom, and compassion; one's connectedness with the world, the cosmos and the creative energies that run through it (Gubi 2002).

Within each of these definitions spirituality is encompassed with the characteristics of transcendence of otherness with which/whom one has connection that enable a deeper sense of awareness and communion with life, resulting in purpose and meaning. These definitions show spirituality to be a very natural process rather than a paranormal or supernatural process. Goddard (1995) argues that 'the human spirit is the dynamic force that keeps a person growing and changing, continuously involved in a process of emerging, becoming and transcending self…it is through this process that life is imbued with meaning and a sense of purpose for existence… Spirituality pervades, unites and directs all human dimensions

and, therefore, constitutes the internal locus of natural health…'
(pp.809–813).

The difficulty with definitions is that they have to be communicated
through language that is intrinsically reductionist (Watts and Williams
1988). The phenomena of spirituality cannot be wholly understood in
these terms but has to be a 'lived experience' to become real. Swinton
(2001, p.13) argues that to understand spirituality it is necessary to let go
of our desire for absolute certainty, neat definitions and universally applicable categories in order to enter into an aspect of human experience that
transcends final categorisation. He states that it is difficult to capture spiritual experience in words. It is tantamount to expressing the inexpressible
(Hay 1982).

Defining prayer

Like the word 'spirituality', prayer is a difficult word to define because
through defining it something of its profound essence is also lost. Prayer is
the word that describes that process of being in touch with a sense of
transcendent inter- (or intra-) connectedness. Prayer is an encounter and
communion with God (Bloom and LeFebvre 2002). Prayer is 'I'
connecting with 'Other', where 'Other' relates to a non-physical object or
being (Gubi 2000). In the Christian experience of prayer, that sense of
connectedness with 'otherness' (or God) can have the qualities of
tenderness, warmth and intensity, which can be experienced over and
above that which might be experienced in many human relationships. So
God can be sensed as personal and close, with the intense 'I/Thou' quality
of the relationship (cf. Buber 1970) feeling cathartic, wholesome and, in
some way, healing. At other times prayer can be experienced as an absence
of God which can lead to an inner search or journeying of the psyche or
soul. Prayer can also be experienced as simply waiting in silence (Gubi
2002) providing that the purpose of silence is waiting in relationship to
the transcendent 'other'. Prayer can also be defined as a reaching into the
spiritual centre within each individual. This centre can be described as
'Centre', 'Self', 'Soul', 'Atman', 'the chief motivating and co-ordinating
energy within us'. Within the Christian tradition, such prayer is
contemplative and meditative in nature (Finney and Malony 1985b).

Sperry (2001, p.152) states that prayer is probably the most distinctive and characteristically spiritual of all activities associated with the spiritual dimension and it is the spiritual phenomenon that is central to most seekers' spiritual journey. Johnson (1953) describes prayer: '…as in love, life is devoted to life, so in prayer I seek Thou trusting that Thou is seeking me, and through this conscious effort to establish an I–Thou relationship, we may experience a deepening sense of integration and communion' (Johnson 1953, p.35). Prayer offers an opportunity for a relationship of dynamic wholeness with the Universal Thou and the transpersonal. O'Donohue (1998, pp.262–270) captures the relationship between prayer and spirituality in the following quotation: 'When the body gathers itself before the Divine, a stillness deepens. The blaring din of distraction ceases and the deeper tranquility within the heart envelops the body… A person at prayer evokes the sense of vulnerability and fragility… Prayer is an ancient longing; it has a special light, hunger and energy…it is an attempt to enter into harmony with the deeper rhythm of life… Prayer issues from that threshold where soul and life interflow…' In this beautiful, poetic way, O'Donohue is able to capture the interconnectedness within and without of self that comes through prayer. Prayer assumes the existence of an 'other', however that other is defined (God, Higher Self, Inner Light, Cosmos etc.), with whom one has a dialogue or connectedness, and is a response of gratitude for the gift of life. It is a process, rather than a content, that, like counselling, is rooted in incongruity (Rose 2002, pp.3–4). 'Prayer is a matter of taking what is there, taking ourselves, taking our world, and making what we can of both with the help of a magnificent tradition and a newness of insight' (Ulanov and Ulanov 1982, p.viii).

Prayer and the spiritual dimension of counselling

All of these definitions are clumsy, yet they each speak a profound truth. It is especially difficult to define spirituality within the profession of counselling (Maher and Hunt 1993) because of the different ways that the spiritual dimension of counselling is understood. Some argue (e.g. Rose 1993; Thorne 2002; Webster 1992) that the therapeutic process, in itself, can be regarded as a spiritual journey, with spirituality being claimed to be the very essence of, and an inseparable part of, the counselling process.

This is manifest in the quality of attention present in the counselling relationship (Rose 1999, 2002) and in the way that the counselling process is conceptualised, e.g. the belief that, bidden or not bidden, 'God' is present in the counselling relationship, and the belief that the counselling process is when the counsellor's 'god-centre' is in contact with the client's 'god-centre' (Gubi 1999), or the belief that counselling is a spiritual space (West 1998). In these ways, spirituality defines the counselling process without being necessarily explicit. Others (e.g. Richards and Bergin 1997; Sperry 2001; West 2000) have claimed that spirituality can be a clearly recognisable and definable dimension of counselling and of the client's being which needs to be assessed, strategically accommodated and facilitated in the session. For others (e.g. Thorne 1998), spiritual practices influence their vocation to be counsellors and their ability to cope with the demands of counselling.

Why has the spiritual dimension of counselling become of interest to practitioners? The literature suggests a variety of reasons for this growing phenomenon. Whilst acknowledging the inherent components of spirituality in the counselling process, many practitioners have argued that because of the historic alienation between psychology and religion, the spiritual dimension has been undermined and needs to be rediscovered (Swinton 2001) and made more explicit through the development and integration of spiritual strategies (Richards and Bergin 1997; West 2000). Counselling has its roots in spirituality and religion: 'psyche' meaning 'soul' or 'breath of life', and 'therapeia' meaning 'attendant', are Greek words at the root of the word 'psychotherapy'. Even though counselling has grown away from its spiritual antecedents in an attempt to make our understanding of the human psyche and the therapeutic process more scientific, at heart it can never really shake off its spiritual essence. This needs to be recaptured and reintegrated into theory and practice.

There is an acknowledgement in the literature that counselling often involves aspects of intimacy, mystery and unknowingness that are difficult to capture in existing psychological terms (e.g. Thorne 2002). This dissatisfaction with language to articulate the 'beyond words' has led to the borrowing of genres from other 'spiritual' approaches that seem to capture practitioner and client experience more fully. As the counselling texts have hinted at this, so interest among practitioners has grown. West (2000) argues that as many prominent counsellors have got older they have been more willing to write about a more mystical and spiritual view of life (e.g. Rogers 1980; Rowan 1993; Thorne 2001, 2002). This has influenced the thinking and exploration of practitioners. An increase in reflexive research that details practitioner and client experience has encouraged counsellors to come out from behind closed doors and talk about their faith, their sense of vocation and their spiritual experience in relation to their counselling work (Gubi 2001; West 1995). Steere (1997) argues that many clients are 'spiritually homeless' because of a sense of feeling less 'at home' with organised religion. The search for wholeness and healing which might at one time have brought them to religion now brings them into counselling and psychotherapy. This search for meaning, purpose and inner fulfilment means that the counsellor cannot avoid encountering the client's spirituality. Counsellors have taken on the role of 'secular priest' (London 1985; Thorne 2002) by default. There is a greater awareness of spiritual practices and multi-cultural philosophies that have been incorporated into western societies as alternative life-styles. Spirituality is often an integral component of culture and in many cultures spiritual concerns are not separated from physical, mental or health concerns (Fukuyama and Sevig 1999). These are increasingly being brought to practitioners for exploration.

There is a growing awareness, through research, that spirituality can make a significant contribution to personal health and well-being and may even be at the heart of personal health and well-being. This is especially so of prayer (Baines 1994; King and Brunswick 1994; Koenig, Cohen and Blazer 1992; Lindgren and Coursey 1995; Maltby et al. 1999; Poloma and Pendleton 1991). Swinton (2001, p.7) points out that whilst it may appear that the spiritual dimension to people's lives has been superseded by humanity's technological and scientific prowess, there is still a strong quest for the transcendent that has given rise to an increased interest in spirituality, in spite of diminishing institutionalised religion. This quest is of importance to those who are struggling with the pain and confusion of mental illness, as well as to the 'worried-well', even though it is not much acknowledged in research and practice. Swinton states that 'The dimensions of emotion, feeling, intuition and a sense of something beyond what there is are not illogical irrelevancies in the process of care. If we exclude hope, meaning, purpose and transcendence from the heart of our caring practices, what type of care are we going to offer?' (Swinton 2001, pp.8–9). He argues that if mental health practitioners (including counsellors) truly listen to the actual experience of their clients and see their world through their eyes, then they discover that spirituality is central to enabling mental health. However, he warns that doing so will challenge assumptions about both mental health and spirituality that will lead to a modification of caring responses that is truly person-centred and genuinely therapeutic.

Swinton alerts us to the need for thoughtfulness, imagination, creativity and flexibility when seeking to address the spiritual needs of people. To make sense of spirituality only from a religious framework is to miss out on the significant spiritual needs that are expressed by people with no formal religious interest. He stresses that if mental health practitioners are to develop a therapeutic understanding of spirituality, it is necessary to learn to be comfortable with uncertainty and mystery, and to be with it in ourselves. Where and how are we 'held' in this as counsellors and psychotherapists?

Practitioner vulnerability may be a good reason why spirituality has not been encompassed more readily. Many counsellors also experience this quest for meaning in their professional and personal lives (Sperry 2001) and are questioning the historical alienation from the spiritual dimension that has traditionally existed in psychology. Some already privately engage in spiritual practices like prayer and meditation as a way of helping them cope with the demands of the work (Gubi 2001; Sperry 2001; Thorne 1994). Some are motivated to practise counselling through a sense of vocation that they feel is spiritually directed or inspired (Gubi 1995). Many professionals are exploring how these spiritual practices, which are so important in sustaining their own well-being, can be sanctioned professionally and incorporated appropriately and ethically (Gubi 2001, 2002; Richards and Bergin 1997; Rose 1996, 2002; West 2001). Indeed, more and more professional counsellors of standing in Britain are prepared to acknowledge publicly their thinking on the spiritual dimension of counselling (Rowan 1993; Thorne 1991, 1994, 1998, 2001; West 1998, 2000).

Whilst some writers have argued that counselling and spirituality are not the same (West 2000, p.50) it is clear that there are many commonalities. Counselling and spirituality can be described as a quest for wholeness, although how the concept of 'wholeness' is qualified is different between spirituality and counselling, and within different spiritual and counselling approaches. Counselling is a practical, spiritual discipline that attends to, and develops, a client's capacity to accept and live the truth. Counselling attends to the whole person in order to assist in the discovery of how the client relates to reality, to self and to others, including God (transcendent other) (Webster 1992, p.44). In his doctoral research, West (1995) gives examples of clients who experience some kind of 'quantum leap' in their therapeutic process that they describe as 'healing', and where the therapists feel part of something bigger. West (2000, p.68) states that it is possible to describe such encounters in non-spiritual language, e.g. empathy (Rogers 1951) and tenderness (Thorne 1991), but it is equally possible (and perhaps more meaningful for some) to describe the qualities of such encounters as 'spiritual'. This evokes a greater sense of intimacy and can give the encounter greater meaning. The quality of attention evident in counselling can be described as spiritual and prayerful (Rose 1993, 1996, 1999, 2002). Indeed, the integration of psychology and spirituality provides more wholeness than either alone, and because there is a need for counsellors to address diverse cultural needs, spirituality must be included, for spirituality transcends culture (Ten Eyck 1993, p.112).

Spirituality can influence the counselling session in overt ways. Prayer is explored in this book as one of those ways. Other ways involve embracing concepts like forgiveness, religious imaging, etc. Spirituality also influences counselling in covert ways, e.g. many practitioners use spiritual resources (e.g. prayer, meditation, silence) to cope with the demands of counselling practice. In this way, spirituality is brought into the counselling relationship through the counsellor's way of being. Simon (1989) recommends that all counsellors should practise a programme of authentic spirituality if they choose to work with the spiritual dimension of counselling.

Thorne (1994, 1998) likewise encourages counsellors to develop a spiritual discipline that is akin to prayer. He incites counsellors to practise: (a) self-exploration and self-acceptance, and (b) a focused holding of the absent client (Thorne 1998, p.87). This greatly increases the likelihood of therapeutic relationships where the transcendent core of the counsellor and client come together, resulting in a release of healing energy. For *self-exploration and self-acceptance*, Thorne recommends four elements to spiritual practice for counsellors. The first is to attend prayerfully to the body, reflecting on thoughts and feelings, particularly self-deprecatory ones, paying attention to how the body is cared for. The second is to reflect prayerfully on the counsellor's relationships with others (non-clients) and how loving of others and self the counsellor is. The third is to reflect prayerfully on the use of time. The fourth is to reflect prayerfully on the created order of which the counsellor is a part. Finally, Thorne puts himself 'in the presence of God' (higher power or influence irradiated by destiny). This enables total surrender so that the counsellor is immersed in God, and enables the counsellor to experience her unique and absolute value without hindrance or self-recrimination (Thorne 1998, p.88). For *focused holding of the absent client*, Thorne recommends that the counsellor focuses on each client in turn, bringing them to mind and having an image of the person in mind. The counsellor then holds the client in a metaphorical embrace of acceptance and understanding for a minute or two. Thorne argues that this practice strengthens the relationship between counsellor and client because it taps into the forces that become powerfully operative in the transcendent encounter. If clients know that the counsellor does this, it adds to their sense of being cared for, and can reduce the sense of abandonment and separation the client may feel between sessions. However, Thorne warns against the unhealthy preoccupation with a client in the counsellor's inner life (Thorne 1998, pp.98–99). Practices like these described above act as a way of maintaining balance in the counsellor's life, preventing burnout (Shelly 1983). Even for a counsellor with no spiritual belief, such practice is beneficial.

Although prayer can be regarded as the antithesis of counselling (Rose 2002) there are also many commonalities between counselling and prayer. Webster (1992, pp.42–46) states that prayer and counselling become means by which human beings search for, and relate to, what is ultimately trustworthy. Both prayer and counselling develop the capacity for mature dependence; they create a transitional space in which persons can discover their uniqueness; they encourage symbolising the true self to an 'other'. Prayer and counselling create an intermediate space for experiencing, to which both inner reality and external reality contribute. Authentic prayer and counselling create a transitional space in which the client's projections are at play with reality, in the effort to encounter and internalise a trustworthy other. Prayer, like counselling, exercises a person in relation to another. Both prayer and counselling are efforts towards being human, towards making contact with the deepest sources of human life. Both prayer and counselling attend to those matters of the heart where the initial impulse of life (physical, psychological, emotional and spiritual) is experienced. One's wounds can become a doorway through which life is rediscovered. When a client engages with a counsellor, together they walk a spiritual path that passes through the realm of pain towards the realm of divine healing and acceptance. Prayer links with counselling in the internal realm of self–other relations that counselling attempts to acknowledge and understand. Rose (2002, p.5) states that both disciplines have consequences for those who participate in them. Both prayer and counselling can provide insights. 'Something appears to happen which the participants regard as significant, but the how or why cannot definitely be stated...' (Rose 2002, p.6). In both disciplines, certain practices are helpful, and both are subject to the unexpected and inexplicable. Both are concerned with nourishing the person and about becoming more authentic. Both can be accused of seeming strange and cultic, or a means of avoiding the real world (Rose 2002, p.12). Both involve taking time to set aside the distractions of everyday life. Both involve reorientation, a conscious attempt to listen and to participate at a deeper level than the everyday (Rose 2002, pp.15–16). The relationship between prayer, spirituality and counselling is multifaceted, but ultimately the relationship is not purposeful if it is not beneficial. The benefits of prayer will be the focus of the next chapter.

The extent of the use of prayer

It would seem to be pointless to write a book about prayer in counselling if prayer were not happening in the therapeutic arena. Shafranske and Malony (1990), through a mail survey of 1000 clinical psychologists in the USA, found that 24 per cent reported praying privately for their clients. Lange (1983a, 1983b) carried out a survey of the 1284 members of the Christian Association for Psychological Studies. Based on a return of 335 questionnaires, Lange discovered that 53.1 per cent of therapists felt that prayer was an important agent in therapy, 53.4 per cent strongly felt that therapeutic outcome was affected by prayer, 93.4 per cent felt that audible prayer should be allowed in therapy, and 79.4 per cent felt that therapists should pray regularly for their clients. Bullis (2001) presents limited empirical data that are based on counselling practitioners' reports of professional ethics and personal comfort with the use of religious or spiritual interventions in practice. From this study he found that 83.5 per cent feel that praying for their clients is ethically appropriate, and 70.5 per cent feel comfortable in praying privately for their clients. He also found that 37.1 per cent felt that it was ethically appropriate to pray with a client in the session, but only 24.5 per cent felt comfortable in doing so.

Research that I conducted (Gubi 2004) revealed that prayer influences the work of a significant number of mainstream counsellors. Nearly half of the British Association for Counselling and Psychotherapy (BACP) Accredited Counsellors (49%) who were surveyed had prayed for their clients (Christian or otherwise) away from the counselling session; over half of the BACP Accredited Counsellors (51%) had used prayer as a means of preparing themselves to work with clients and 37 per cent had prayed for guidance during a counselling session. Only 6 per cent used overt prayer in their current practice, whereas 11 per cent had used overt prayer in the past; 24 per cent had discussed the use of prayer in supervision.

The number of Churches Ministerial Counselling Service (CMCS) Approved Counsellors whose work is influenced by prayer was also significant but less surprising considering that they needed to have a religious affiliation in order to belong to the organisation. The assumption here is that because they have a religious faith they will be more open to the use of prayer in counselling. However, that is an assumption that cannot be substantiated and the reverse attitude (i.e. that prayer should not have a place in counselling) might have been the case. Among CMCS Approved Counsellors, 41 per cent had used prayer in their past work; 16 per cent were using prayer overtly with current clients; 65 per cent had prayed for guidance; 54 per cent had prayed for their client during the session without their client's knowledge; 80 per cent had interceded for their client away from the session; 82 per cent had used prayer to prepare for their counselling work; and only 46 per cent had discussed the use of prayer in supervision.

Even though these surveys are limited, they indicate that prayer is clearly a part of mainstream and pastoral therapeutic practice so there needs to be an informed debate about its value and limitation (Feltham 2005; Foskett and Lynch 2001). The remainder of this book is devoted to that task. The following chapter examines how prayer might be beneficial to health, psychological well-being and to counselling.

CHAPTER 2

Is Prayer Beneficial?

The psychological impact of prayer

Although prayer at its essence is existentially meaningful rather than merely functional, some have attempted to offer psychological perspectives on prayer (e.g. Ames 1910; Beck 1906; Brown 1994; Capps 1982; Coe 1916; Doniger 1953; Francis and Astley 2001; Goehring 1995; Hood *et al.* 1996; Stolz 1923; Strong 1909) and to prove the efficacy of prayer (e.g. Astin *et al.* 2000; Leibovici 2001). In most spiritualities prayer exists for the purpose of developing and deepening a personal relationship with God (Richards 1991) rather than as a psychological intervention.

> [Prayer] is a conversation between desire and reality... Prayer awakens the soul and opens doors of possibility... It is the only refuge of belonging in extreme times... Real prayer is the liberation of that inner voice of the eternal... It always brings transformation... Prayer refines you so that you may become worthy of your possibility and destiny... Prayer helps you to clearer vision. It opens you up to experiences you would never otherwise entertain. It refines your eyes for the unknown narrative which is quietly working itself through your words, actions and thoughts. (O'Donohue 1998, pp.270–310)

In the development of a psychology of religion James (1902) is widely credited with being the instigator for the exploration of religious experience from a psychological perspective (Brown 1994; Cox 2000; Dmochowski 1991) of which prayer is 'the very soul and essence'. Prayer is suggested by James to be 'every kind of inward communion or conversation with the power recognised as divine' (James 1902, p.464); an act that elicits, in consciousness, a 'conviction that something is genuinely transacted' that results in the setting free of energy (James 1902, p.466), bringing about 'a new reach of freedom', 'an added dimension of emotion', 'a new sphere of power', 'an absolute addition to the subject's range of life' and 'a happiness in the absolute and everlasting' (James 1902, p.48). From these comments, prayer can be regarded as liberating and conducive to happiness.

Freud (1927), however, believed religion to be infantile and foreign to reality, a manifestation of obsessive and compulsive actions, with God as the illusory object of wish-fulfilment, making prayer into an empty, irrational act that led to unhealthy deception, and crooked cure (Freud 1963). Freud and James represent the polarity that is the psychological truth about prayer. Prayer can be used as a form of wish-fulfilment (sometimes referred to as 'cosmic ordering' or 'asking the universe') and be demonstrative of infantile regression, but it can also transform and transcend experience, enabling the pray-er to cope with, and experience, reality more fully. These polarities are now explored and a consideration made of the work that examines the psychology of prayer.

The heart of Freud's reductionist thesis is that religion, and thus prayer, is an immature response to an awareness of helplessness. Prayer, and its implicit belief, provides an illusion that is created as a way of coping with unpleasant reality, thus reducing fears of helplessness. This, however, does not explain why people pray at times of contentment, except perhaps as a way of ensuring God's benevolence at times of crisis. Freud also reduced the notion of God to that of the projection of an ideal father figure, much as a child relates to a teddy bear. This view is valid if prayer is characterised by supernatural assumptions, magical ideas and egotistical notions (Macquarrie 1972). Freud's view of religion can also be seen in prayer that is regarded as routine and mechanistic, through which the pray-er attempts to cheat the laws of nature, or prayer that is construed as a form of begging favours of a benevolent Divinity.

Other ways in which prayer can demonstrate immaturity are when prayer is used as a way of reminding God that he has neglected his/her duties, telling him/her what s/he ought to know, with petitions on behalf of various people and situations (Johnson 1953). These forms of prayer are considered to be psychologically unhealthy (Pargament 1997; Ulanov and Ulanov 1992), although Schreurs (2002, pp.234–237) points out that not all religion based on magic is destructive, and that there is potential for therapeutic change in impersonal spiritual relationships and determinism.

Other psychologically unhealthy forms of prayer are when prayer is used as a powerful defence, creating barriers to self-discovery, relationship and responsibility (Rose 1996, p.9). Prayer can be a means of avoiding unresolved and painful emotional difficulties and of avoiding direct communication with others (Gubi 2000).

There is a fine line between psychologically healthy and unhealthy prayer. Phillips (1965) suggests that confession and petition are forms of prayer that enable insight and awareness to grow. However, they can easily stray into desire for magical intervention and superstition. Macquarrie (1972, p.95) defines the main difference between psychologically healthy and unhealthy prayer as the ability to use prayer not as a means of bending the divine will in accordance with our desires but rather in bending our will to God's will, enabling God to transcend us. Johnson (1953) states that prayer is a 'dynamic experience of harmony within and without that heals conflict and loneliness in renewing one's sense of belonging to a larger wholeness' (p.35), enabling psychological benefits which promote a sense of being unconditionally loved and accepted that is profoundly growthful (Gubi 1999).

Prayer can be an important mover in one's locus of evaluation, fostering authenticity and self-worth. Prayer can be a means by which unfinished business can be expressed and 'contact' met through communication with God (Gubi 2000). Prayer can be a place of forgiveness and confession – the place where I have to face my true self (Ulanov and Ulanov 1982, 1992). Leech (1980) describes prayer as a process of opening ourselves out to God from which we gain liberation and awakening: 'At heart prayer is a process of self-giving and of being set free from isolation. To pray is to enter into relationship with God and to be transformed by him' (p.6). Johnson (1945, pp.122–123) states that prayer results in an awareness of needs, emotional catharsis, peace of mind, broader perspective on problems, decisions, emotional renewal, social responsiveness, joy, gratitude, acceptance of one's losses, loyalty, perseverance, and integration of personality. Prayer has been viewed simply as an expression of need (Heiler 1932; Hodge 1931; Johnson 1945; Pratt 1930; Selbie 1924) and as an affirmation of faith (Ellens 1977; Phillips 1965).

In terms of psychological process, prayer can involve hypnotic suggestion (Coe 1916; Cutten 1908; Hodge 1931; Horton 1931; James 1902; Pratt 1930; Relton 1925; Selbie 1924; Strunk 1959; Thouless 1923;

Valentine 1929), regression (Allinson 1966; Arieti 1967; Fingarette 1958; Freud 1963; Kris 1936; Maupin 1965; Prince and Savage 1972), a de-automatisation of perception and cognition (Carrington 1977; Deikman 1966; Goleman 1971; Ornstein 1971), a lowering of arousal through the induction of relaxation (Shapiro 1980) and desensitisation (Carrington and Ephron 1975; Goleman 1971; Otis 1974).

McDonald (1999, pp.36–37) states that breath control (breathing in the spirit of God) alongside a basic religious mantra enables 'the spirals of anxiety to be put to one side, and a deeper awareness of "body and spirit" to emerge, facilitating a deeper integration of self'. Bernardi et al. (2001) have found that the recitation of yoga mantras or the rosary prayer has a significant impact on respiration and induces physical and psychological changes that can be viewed as good health practice as well as good religious practice. This is a similar psychological process to that which is found in meditative practice, the very activity of which, some argue, is prayer (e.g. Helminiak 1982), especially contemplative prayer (Finney and Malony 1985a, 1985b) – the essence of the practice of mindfulness which is helpful in managing depression (Segal, Williams and Teasdale 2001). Brown-Saltzman (1997) also argues that meditative prayer and guided imagery replenish the spirit, enabling us to receive and to let go.

Prayer satisfies the need for an experience of the numinous, the need for a sense of meaning, purpose and value to one's existence, and the need for a feeling of deep trust and relatedness to life (Clinebell 1963). O'Connor's (1975) research into Christians' motives and expectations in prayer revealed that Christians pray out of a recognition of personal need for development and growth, and they expect a sense of security or assurance, and the gaining of insights or help in decision-making. Kaye and Robinson (1994) state that prayer enables the perception of forgiveness from God, and the reframing of experience. Gay (1978) states that prayer promotes both interpersonal and intra-psychic adaptation that can foster readjustment and coping behaviours. Crocker (1984) argues that prayer can foster better communication. Prayer is a complex entity that can encompass all of human experience. It can be experienced as a deep search and be characterised by genuine openness and honesty, or be a playground of games with God. It can involve the revelation of insight and spiritual connection, or be a shallow duty with empty words. It can encompass the experiencing of great love and security, or be a place of abandonment by

IS PRAYER BENEFICIAL? / 39

God. It can be a place where one has a fuller awareness of the world, of 'self' and of others; a place of connectedness with 'otherness'; a place of letting go and reframing of experience (Gubi 1999, p.25). Woodmansee (2000) concludes from her research that prayer provides the pray-er with peace, connectedness with God, an increased ability to trust, increased feelings of closeness, and a deepened sense of faith. Other research (e.g. Bunker 1991; Clarke 1983; Duncan 1993) indicates that greater psychological benefit can be had through prayer if there is a greater affinity between the different ways of praying and the different functions within the Jungian personality types. Cox (2000) also concludes that certain prayer types may be more associated with certain types of difficulties than others, e.g. someone suffering from stress may seek solace in contemplative prayer which reduces anxiety. Cox argues that counsellors need to investigate and use the type of prayer that best enables a client to remove the obstacles that stand in the way of their happiness and well-being.

Prayer can be said to be mainly of psychological benefit in bringing about shifts in psychological well-being (e.g. reframing experience, feeling loved, feeling forgiven, feeling more at peace, feeling more connected and less isolated). The relationship of prayer to counselling is clear in that prayer can be transformational and promote psychological well-being.

Prayer and mental health well-being

There is much empirical evidence that suggests that prayer is beneficial to mental health well-being (e.g. Davis 1986; Lawrence 1993; Tuckwell and Flagg 1995) but however rich its content may be, and however persuasively written, it is not sufficient to determine the credibility of prayer, according to some, e.g. Dossey (1993) and Matthews (1998). For them, prayer needs to be researched using methodology that proves the efficacy of prayer beyond doubt. Although it is sometimes the case that with prayer no change can be measured or observed yet those directly involved will feel that something significant has taken place, there can be a sense of emotional well-being that does not necessarily correlate with the healing of emotional pain (Rose 2002, p.6). Furthermore, when prayer is subjected to analytical study to see if it works, it ceases to be prayer (Carr 1997). There have, nevertheless, been a number of research studies that examine the influence of prayer on well-being and there have also been a number of reviews of these studies.

Mental health well-being can be defined as the ability to cope with depression, anxiety and low self-esteem. Prayer has been used by many people throughout history to cope with life's problems (Hawley and Irurita 1998; McCullough 1995). There is certainly no shortage of research in the last 20 years to support that (e.g. Ai et al. 1998; Armer 1994; Bearon and Koenig 1990; Cronan et al. 1989; Dunn and Horgas 2000; Ellinson and Taylor 1996; Fry 1990; Gass 1987; Harvey et al. 1995; Kaplan, Marks and Mertens 1997; Kaye and Robinson 1994; Leyser 1994; Neser et al. 1989; Ohaeri et al. 1995; Potts 1996; Saudia et al. 1991; Sodestrom and Martinson 1987; Stern, Canda and Doershuk 1992; Stolley, Buckwalter and Koenig 1999; Sutton and Murphy 1989; Zeidner 1993). However, if one examines the lives of many of the mystics of what-ever faith who lived their life through contemplative prayer (e.g. Julian of Norwich and John of the Cross) it is common for them to have experienced a 'dark night of the soul' episode in their life, which suggests depressive symptoms (Yarnold 1992). Within the Judeo-Christian scriptures 'the Psalms' in particular are associated with the expression of deep depression, hopelessness and rage, as well as fervent celebration. They enable others to identify with and express their feelings, perceptions and convictions (Webster 1992) and are an assurance that prayer does not deny deepness or censure human experience that is cathartic and liberating (Brueggemann 1993). There is also some research that indicates that prayer can be a maladaptive strategy in relation to pain (e.g. Ashby and Lenhart 1994; Keefe and Dolan 1986) and be symptomatic of mental health problems (Greenberg and Witztum 1994). Where prayer is associated with worsen-ing mental health it is often because prayer is underpinned by an insecure religious attachment, an imbalance between religion and other aspects of life, religious rigidity, and religious deception (Pargament 1997).

However, most of the reviews of the research on prayer suggest that the research is either in favour of prayer as being beneficial to well-being or is at least ambivalent about it. Finney and Malony (1985c) carried out a review of the literature on empirical studies into Christian prayer. Their review was focused on what was written about contemplative and verbal prayer since 1872 (the birth of psychology). The review included research by Carson and Huss (1979), Elkins, Anchor and Sandler (1979), Galton

(1872), Mallory (1977), Parker and St John (1957), Sacks (1979), Sajwaj and Hedges (1973), Surwillo and Hobson (1978) and Welford (1947). Galton (1872) tested the hypothesis that prayer would enhance the well-being of those who pray as well as those being prayed for. He looked at the average lifespan of the monarchy, missionaries and the clergy – three groups which were regularly prayed for – on the presumption that they would live longer than the average person and enjoy better health. Because the mortality rate of missionaries was no better than the population average, the monarchy enjoyed modest life-expectancy with a high rate of insanity among the nobility, and the clergy of the day had a less-than-average life-expectancy, Galton concluded that there was little statistical evidence for the efficacy of prayer. However, he concluded his article by saying that prayer is of subjective value as a means of venting emotional pain and as a way of experiencing the comforting sense of communion with God.

Finney and Malony (1985c) state that Galton's work can be criticised because his evidence does not justify his conclusion. There is hard empirical evidence missing, and where statistics are provided, they are open to various interpretations. Chamberlain and Hall (2000) state that Galton's work raises a number of questions about the possibility of studying prayer empirically. Although long life and good health were not above average, the participants might have experienced healing, inner peace, and a sense of deeper spirituality, so a gain could have been made in other ways than were measured. This gives a picture of the difficulties of measuring the efficacy of prayer. Chamberlain and Hall (2000) also raise other difficulties.

> Should prayerful people expect a response to all petitions? Indeed, what constitutes a positive response? If people do not receive what is construed to be an immediate positive response to petition, should they immediately deduce that prayer was ineffective or unanswered? Is the intensity of a prayer or its repetition or duration related to its efficacy? What theological considerations enter into the question of efficacy? Is the righteousness of the intercessor related to the efficacy of the request? What criteria are to be employed in determining efficaciousness? Can the intricacies and complexities of God's responses to prayer be adequate, and accurately observed and measured? What kind of experiment would

effectively control for all variables involved? (Chamberlain and Hall 2000, p.31)

Finney and Malony (1985c) provide fuller details in the review of each of the other studies than can be afforded here. Finney and Malony conclude their review by stating that research by Elkins *et al.* (1979), Parker and St John (1957) and Sacks (1979) is significant. Elkins *et al.* found that verbal intercessory and reflective prayer are probably not effective in reducing anxiety – a finding that Schneider and Kastenbaum (1993) have subsequently disputed by demonstrating how being in contact with a higher being, gained through prayer, can enable a letting go of one's self and anxiety. Parker and St John's research raised the possibility that verbal positive petitionary prayer could form an effective core for group therapy. Sacks' research infers that contemplative prayer may facilitate integration of the self-system.

Poloma and Pendleton (1991) based their research on a 1985 Akron area survey that focused on religiosity and subjective perceptions of well-being by measuring the frequency of prayer, prayer experience, and different forms of prayer, together with more standard forms of religiosity. From a sample of 560 telephone interviews, Poloma and Pendleton concluded that meditative prayer moderately, but significantly, related to improved quality of life and deeper religious satisfaction. Those who used ritual prayer were more likely to be sad, lonely, depressed or tense; and those who used colloquial prayer (prayer that includes informal petition such as asking for guidance, blessing, forgiveness, thanksgiving and love) were found to be more likely to be happy. Many other questions and conclusions arise from this research. However, the effect of prayer (especially meditative and colloquial prayer) on well-being is clear.

Dossey (1993, pp.97–100) points to the Spindrift experiments as showing conclusively that prayer works. Through many simple laboratory tests in which moulds were grown in adverse conditions – one group of moulds being prayed for and the other group not – non-directed prayer (where there was no goal in the mind of the pray-er) produced the best results, whereas directed prayer was not very productive. The Spindrift experiments conclude that, based on the evidence of a large number of tests, when non-directed prayer is answered, the outcome is always in the direction of what is best for the organism, where the organism moves towards those states of form and function that are healthiest for it . Dossey

(1993, p.100) states that the Spindrift experiments suggest that it is not always necessary to know how the body (and mind) ought to behave for healing to occur. One need only pray for what is best: the 'Thy will be done' approach. However, research carried out by O'Laoire (1997) into the effects of distant, intercessory prayer on self-esteem, anxiety and depression indicates that there is no difference between directed and non-directed prayer with regard to psychological well-being.

McCullough (1995) reviewed empirical literature from 35 research investigations into the relationship between prayer and health, from which he drew four tentative conclusions:

- Prayer, especially prayer that is rich in mystical and religious experience, appears to be related at least to some measures of well-being.

- Prayer is popularly relied on for coping with difficult life circumstances and may serve a stress-deterrent effect during such circumstances.

- The relationship between prayer and psychiatric circumstances remains unclear, although several investigations yielded promising preliminary results.

- Although the empirical investigations are plagued with methodological flaws, Byrd's (1988) well-designed study shows how we can investigate how God heals through intercessory prayer.

This last conclusion is disputed by O'Laoire (1997, p.40) who berates Byrd's methodology by claiming that there was no standardisation of prayer technique in either quality or quantity. There was no mention of feedback from the intercessors, e.g. how often did they pray? What if two or more patients had the same first name? Dossey (1993, p.180), however, states that the research by Byrd (1988) would have been heralded as a 'breakthrough' if the technique being studied were a new drug or surgical procedure rather than prayer. Byrd's research involved a randomised, double-blind study of 393 patients in a coronary care unit. The research took place over ten months. Patients were divided into two groups. One group was prayed for using distant prayer. The other group was not prayed for (although this is acknowledged as a methodological weakness as there could be no guarantee that no-one was praying for any member of the control group). However, there was a significant improvement in the group that was prayed for, which was over and above the control group, thus Byrd concludes that intercessory prayer is important in healing. This can include healing of the mind. In spite of these difficulties, McCullough concludes overall that prayer may be beneficial to psychological well-being. It is interesting to note that Byrd's research was modified and replicated by Harris *et al.* (1999) using a randomised, controlled, double-blind, prospective, parallel-group trial, involving 990 consecutive patients who were newly admitted to a coronary care unit, to determine whether remote, intercessory prayer for hospitalised cardiac patients would reduce overall adverse events and length of stay. They concluded that remote, intercessory prayer was associated with lower scores, which suggests that prayer may be an effective adjunct to standard medical care.

Matthews (1998) reviewed 325 studies, of different types, into the relationship between religious involvement, health and well-being, and claims that over 75 per cent of these studies have produced findings that indicate that religious involvement (including prayer) is of benefit to well-being (psychological and physical). Maltby *et al.* (1999) conducted research among 474 students using a questionnaire to measure frequency of personal prayer (intrinsic) and church attendance (extrinsic), alongside measures of depressive symptoms, trait anxiety and self-esteem (Quest). The aim was to examine the role of religious acts within the relationship between measures of religious orientation and psychological well-being, and to examine the theoretical view that religion can act as a coping mechanism. Correlational statistics, principal components analysis with Oblimin rotation and multiple regression were used to examine the relationships between a number of religiosity and psychological well-being measures. The results suggested that: (1) the correlations between a number of measures of religiosity and psychological well-being may be mediated by the relationship between frequency of personal prayer and psychological well-being, and (2) personal prayer may be an important variable to consider within the theory of religious coping.

Chamberlain and Hall (2000) conducted a substantial review of the literature on the relationship between religion and health. They concluded that the majority of studies presented and analysed in their survey affirm the positive effect of religious belief and practice on significant health issues, including mental health well-being. In particular, they highlight the work of Larson (1993) who carried out a systematic review of 16 studies into the relationship between religion and mental health. Larson concluded that religious people who live out their faith (including praying) are more likely to say that they are enjoying life, and that they like their work, their marriage and their family (p.20). Having an honest commitment to God, a moderate flexibility, an openness to change, and a willingness to acknowledge the need or assistance of others, raises levels of health (p.22). All of these factors that aid mental health can be achieved through prayer.

Although not strictly relevant to psychological well-being, the conclusions of Roberts, Ahmed and Hall (2001) have relevance to research on prayer. Roberts *et al.* conducted a Cochrane Review into the effectiveness of intercessory prayer as an additional intervention for those with health problems who were already receiving standard medical care. Studies were extensively selected using a number of electronic databases and assessed for methodological quality. Seven studies were excluded because of methodological issues (Galton 1883; Greyson 1997; Lilliston and Brown 1981; Lilliston, Brown and Schliebe 1982; Sicher *et al.* 1998; Wirth and Barrett 1994; Wirth and Cram 1994). Four studies were included in the review (Byrd 1988; Collipp 1969; Harris *et al.* 1999; Joyce and Welldon 1964). Roberts *et al.* concluded that the link between prayer and the alleviation of ill-health is not conclusive because of the limited number of trials that have been conducted into the efficacy of prayer. However, they state that:

> If prayer is seen as a human endeavour it may or may not be beneficial and further trials could uncover this. It could be that any effects of prayer are due to elements beyond present scientific understanding that will, in time, be understood. If any benefit derives from God's response to prayer it may be beyond any such trials to prove or disprove. (Roberts *et al.* 2001, p.11)

These conclusions are important in that intercessory prayer, if beneficial for health, could also be beneficial for psychological well-being.

Astin *et al.* (2000) conducted a systematic review of randomised trials into the efficacy of distant healing. A total of 23 trials involving 2774 patients were included and analysed. Five studies examined intercessory prayer as a distant healing intervention, 11 studies assessed non-contact therapeutic touch, and seven trials examined other forms of distant healing (e.g. paranormal healing, psychokinetic influence, remote mental healing). Astin *et al.* (2000) found that 57 per cent (13 of 23) of the randomised trials showed a positive treatment effect – evidence that merits further study. They concluded that:

> No experiment can prove or disprove the existence of God, but if mental intentions can be shown to facilitate healing at a distance, this would clearly imply that human beings are more connected to each other and more responsible to each other than previously believed. That connection could be actuated through the agency of God, consciousness, love, electrons, or a combination. The answers to such questions await further research. (Astin *et al.* 2000, p.909)

Whilst some of the more recent randomised trials have demonstrated that prayer has no effect or does show some, but not a significant, benefit (e.g. Aviles *et al.* 2001; Harkness *et al.* 2000; Palmer, Katerndahl and Morgan-Kidd 2004), others (e.g. Leibovici 2001; Matthews, Marlowe and MacNutt 2000) demonstrate that prayer can have a significant effect on illness and that it should be considered for use in clinical practice. Leibovici (2001) carried out a double-blind study to determine whether remote retroactive intercessory prayer, said for a group of patients with a bloodstream infection, had an effect on outcomes. He randomly divided 3393 patients into two groups. A remote, retroactive intercessory prayer was said for the well-being and full recovery of the intervention group. The control group was treated in the same way, except for the intercessory prayer. Levels of mortality in hospital, length of stay in hospital, and the duration of fever were measured and compared between the two groups. The level of mortality between the two groups was not significantly different, but the length of stay in hospital and the duration of the fever were significantly shorter in the intervention group than in the control group. Whilst this research raises many philosophical, theological, methodological and ethical issues, it (along with Harkness *et al.* 2000 and others) does demonstrate a growing, but tentative, interest and openness within conventional medical science towards addressing the empirical truth of others, in order to try and make sense of their experience using scientific methods. Pearsall (2001, p.255) draws attention to the work of Benor (1993) whose studies into prayer and intentionality show 'statistically significant results of the power of prayer'.

Although researching the efficacy of prayer in relation to psychological and health well-being is intrinsically flawed in relation to how outcomes are determined, qualified and measured, it is interesting to notice that although many of the reviews that have been carried out to determine the efficacy of prayer have proved inconclusive, prayer has not been dismissed as ineffective by any of the reviews. All the reviews conclude that the benefits are significant enough to warrant further research. So, if the benefits are significant enough to include prayer for consideration in therapeutic practice, what might hinder its use? This is the focus of the next chapter.

CHAPTER 3

Reflecting on Potential Problems

Potential ethical issues

Before we consider the use of prayer in counselling and psychotherapy it is important to explore what the potential problems might be. Research by Lindgren and Coursey (1995) concluded that spirituality can be an appropriate topic for therapeutic discussion and can be of therapeutic value in supporting clients with psychological difficulties. However, all therapeutic interventions and strategies need to be carefully considered before they are practised (Richards and Bergin 1997). 'Any relationship between human beings carries potential for healing, but at the same time the possibility for damage; and to enter into any relationship involves taking a risk' (Rose 2002, pp.6–7).

The British Association for Counselling and Psychotherapy (BACP) provides an ethical framework with fundamental values that:

- respect human rights and dignity
- ensure the integrity of the practitioner–client relationship
- believe in the enhancement of the quality of professional knowledge and its application
- alleviate personal distress and suffering
- foster a sense of self that is meaningful to the person concerned
- increase personal effectiveness
- enhance the quality of relationships between people
- appreciate the variety of human experience and culture
- strive for the fair and adequate provision of counselling and psychotherapy services.

These values are underpinned by the ethical principles of fidelity, autonomy, beneficence, non-maleficence, justice and self-respect (BACP 2002). It is within such a framework of ethical values and principles that the use of prayer must be considered if prayer is to be part of ethical, mainstream counselling and psychotherapy practice. These values inform the counselling practitioner of the most appropriate, helpful and therapeutic way of working with the people whom she encounters (Lynch 2002, pp.9–10). Rose (2002) states that counsellors have to be committed to providing a safe and accepting environment in which clients can explore their story without being judged or told what to do, to enable them to find a way through that is authentic for them. The use of prayer is not exempt from this, neither is any practice exempt from the requirements of the law (Bullis 2001).

Webster (1992) asks the question, 'Why might a therapist be reluctant to pray in psychotherapy?' In response to this question he offers a number of reasons. Prayer involves being transparent before God, which can be frightening for both therapist and client. Facing God can mean embracing that fear. Such authenticity may involve inappropriate self-disclosure from the therapist which will intrude into the client's space. Because of the power differential in the therapeutic relationship, the therapist may have concern about how prayer will impact on the client. Will the words spoken by the therapist benefit or burden the client?

Because of the transference phenomena, the therapist must seek to understand the hidden, unconscious meanings of prayer with a client. 'If a client sees the therapist as an authority figure, or as God's broker in prayer, subtle, unintended nuances of the therapist's prayer can suggest adaptation rather than discovery of the client's unique self and so have great influence upon the client' (Webster 1992, p.14). There may be a fear of colluding with a client's inauthentic prayer. The practice of prayer creates potential for denial or distortion of the client's truth, e.g. a client may pray for his wife to change rather than for an awareness of how he himself contributes to the dysfunction of the marriage. Prayer can be formulated to ask God's help in avoiding painful symptoms rather than actively relating to them and understanding their importance. Prayer can express the expectation that God will answer in the way one wishes (wish-fulfilment) rather than with divine wisdom.

When a false notion of God is projected in prayer, one can become alienated from genuine experience and one's true self. The words of prayer may disguise a manipulation – if I am good to God, God will be good to me. A therapist who is overly eager to pray with a client may believe that good will be achieved if one prays, rather than using prayer as a recognition of God's freedom and transcendence. Prayer may be an egotistic expression striving towards perfection without a recognition of one's dependency upon an 'other' who is trustworthy.

Prayer can be used to avoid listening, to avoid awareness of the unfamiliar, to avoid becoming conscious of the truth, and to avoid the challenge of living one's life. The pretence of prayer can be used for promoting one's own agenda rather than being open to authenticity. Prayer can be a play-act to comply with another's expectation. This can be revealed by either client or therapist praying for positive things to happen and for good feelings to be experienced, rather than for support in experiencing difficult pain and for the ability eventually to transcend it. It is relatively easy for the client or therapist to initiate or join in prayer to remain in the good graces of each other by loosening conscious boundaries and creating opportunity for collusion, merging and fusion. Prayer may divert the therapist's attention away from the client to God.

> Incorporating prayer in one's psychotherapeutic repertoire, a therapist risks being co-opted by false consciousness, idolatry, superstition, hypocrisy, and legalism. Prayer may divert awareness from one's immediate experience of oneself with another and shift responsibility for one's choices in life to another. Praying risks evoking motives for inauthentic prayer, just as speaking risks misuse of language. If the risk is to be taken, it must be a considered risk, born in the hope that good can result in the process when appropriate choices are made. (Webster 1992, p.28)

Reluctance may also stem from the therapist's experience of God, or lack of experience. As in the person-centred relationship, some therapists may find difficulty in coping with the level of transparency which prayer demands of them. Webster (1992) concludes that although prayer can be motivated by a fear of truth, it is the task of the therapist to bring these attitudes into awareness. Clients do not act consistently from 'true self' in psychotherapy. Indeed, enormous pressures are transferred to the therapist to avoid awareness of one's true feelings, thoughts and inclinations. This is no different in prayer. It is for the therapist to address their reluctance, and to work with these transferences. Webster illuminates the reflexiveness of all good counsellors as they attempt to get inside their own, and their client's, frame of reference to understand the process. The difficulties that Webster highlights are similar to all good therapeutic interventions which in themselves are neither good nor bad – only potent (Rose 2002, p.7). Any strategy that involves self-disclosure, or any approach that requires an authentic way of being (e.g. the person-centred approach), involves a high degree of congruence and risk-taking. So prayer is not unusual in this respect, and demands the same degree of reflexivity and care that is required of all good practice.

Ten Eyck (1993) warns against two limitations that might cause ethical problems. The first involves the therapist's limitations – primarily misusing, abusing or having inadequate training or personal growth and insight in the use of prayer. The second involves those that the client brings to prayer. If the client is not open about conflictual issues with God, then these may affect prayer in the session. These need to be addressed first so that they do not constrict the use of inner healing prayer (IHP). Although none of the respondents from her research had ever had any negative consequences as a result of using IHP, Ten Eyck emphasises the need for the therapist to be trained and be accountable in the use of IHP. This raises issues about what training is appropriate to enable a counsellor to use prayer, where such training can be accessed, and the nature and adequacy of supervision – issues that Ten Eyck does not address in her research. Again, the issues raised here are no different from those required of all good counselling practice. Accountability and adequate training to ensure competent practice is a minimal expectation of all mainstream counselling practice. This raises the question of how acceptable the use of prayer, as being good therapeutic practice, is in supervision. West (2000), Rose (2002) and Gubi (2002) suggest that it is problematic.

McMinn (1996), writing from a Christian counselling perspective, states that prayer can be a frequent part of counselling but it should never be routine. The use of prayer depends on the theoretical orientation of the counsellor. Prayer is a good thing that can also be misused, so its use needs careful monitoring. McMinn states that religious practices can be used as a defence against insight and self-understanding. Praying aloud can also weaken the client's sense of direct accountability to God. Praying may introduce a form of interpersonal intimacy that may not be wise in every counselling situation. Praying may also inhibit the disclosure of important information, particularly if routine prayer promotes the counsellor to 'spiritual-giant' status in the eyes of the client. Some clients will hesitate to share what they consider to be 'sin' for fear of a judgemental response. If prayer is used insensitively, or as a perfunctory part of treatment, it can be spiritually or emotionally harmful. McMinn identifies six challenges that face the integration of prayer in counselling. They are:

- *Competence:* Counsellors must be aware of issues related to theological perspectives on prayer, the psychological implications of using prayer in counselling, and the spiritual formation of clients.

- *Blurred personal–professional boundaries:* It is important to maintain clear boundaries and self-reflection. Counsellors need to evaluate their personal prayer practice.

- *Expanding definitions of training:* Taking courses on spiritual formation, getting away for times of prolonged solitude and prayer are useful ways of aiding reflexivity on prayer issues.

- *Confronting dominant views of mental health:* Issues of religiosity and spirituality give a different understanding of mental health well-being that needs to be considered, e.g. reliance on self-determination versus reliance on God.

- *Establishing a scientific base:* More research needs to be carried out by practitioners to establish the effectiveness and use of spiritual interventions such as prayer.

- *Defining relevant ethical standards:* Precautions must be taken to avoid misusing prayer and hurting people as a result. Counsellors need to be more aware of the potential harm and benefits of using prayer. The place of supervision (peer and individual) is important in maintaining ethical practice. Written, informed consent is recommended. It is also recommended that at the contracting stage, clients should be informed that spiritual interventions might be used in treatment. It may also be necessary to inform insurance companies that spiritual interventions are utilised, but some insurance companies may not recognise spiritual interventions, like prayer, as a legitimate counselling strategy. Finally, McMinn argues that counsellors need to consider carefully if it is ethical to charge a fee for counselling that includes spiritual techniques, such as prayer, as prayer is more than a counselling technique.

McMinn's work demonstrates careful professional concern for the client and is especially important as it comes from a Christian counselling perspective which is often criticised for putting scriptural and faith needs before client needs (Gubi 1995).

Tan (1996) states that there are potential abuses or misuses of prayer in psychological treatment. Although prayer can be used as a defence or escape from exploring painful issues more deeply, it can also be used in a meaningful and therapeutically helpful way. Prayer is not always appropriate in counselling with non-religious clients unless they are open to, or request, prayer. Prayer may not be appropriate when clients are struggling with bitterness or resentment towards God, or having a crisis of faith. Rose (1996) argues that there can be a danger of omnipotence among practitioners who employ prayer: 'I don't need a supervisor because I pray'. Prayer can be a matter of invoking God to bring about what we are convinced should happen, leaving us closed to the possibility of change within ourselves. It is important that the counsellor does not get caught up in countertransference issues that result in praying for particular outcomes.

Richards and Bergin (1997) state that therapists who use a theistic, spiritual strategy face potential difficulties with dual relationships, displacing religious authority, imposing religious values on clients, violating work-setting boundaries, and practising outside the boundaries of professional competence. Richards and Bergin have some serious reservations about therapists praying with clients during sessions. Praying in sessions increases the risk of role boundaries becoming confused. The danger of unhealthy transference issues arising is greater. They suspect that clients who have unresolved issues of anger towards, or dependency on, God and religious authorities are more likely to project these issues on to the therapist. Although they can be used to therapeutic advantage, Richards and Bergin believe that the risk outweighs the potential benefits, although they give no justification for their conclusion. Praying may be more appropriate in certain settings and with certain clients, e.g. church settings, or in private practice with devoutly religious clients. However, therapists in such situations should be alert to the dangers of using prayer. Therapists who pray with, or encourage their clients to pray, need to make sure that they work within their client's religious framework so that they do not impose their own beliefs about, and practices of, prayer on the client. In general, it is not a good idea for the therapist to teach a client how to pray because there is a risk that the therapist will impose their own beliefs about prayer.

Magaletta and Brawer (1998) argue that because prayer has immense variance, it is necessary for the counselling profession to consider the relevant ethical issues carefully, so that clients can be better protected, and better use can be made of prayer as a healing agent. In considering the ethical implications of prayer, they draw upon the six general ethical principles, or aspirational goals, that are espoused by the American Psychological Association (1992). Under principle B (integrity), they argue that therapists should be aware of their own beliefs, values and needs in order to avoid imposing their prayer beliefs on their clients. As prayer is susceptible to the slightest bias that a therapist might have, it is essential to be aware of one's beliefs preceding engagement in prayer at a combined level so that prayer is not led in a manner that is unfamiliar or uncomfortable to the client. It may not be true to one's integrity to pray with someone from another religion, or of no religious faith, because it might compromise the therapist's beliefs as well as the client's beliefs. Praying with a client in the context of a secular organisation may also compromise the integrity of the organisation. Under principle A (competence) and principle D (respect for people's rights and dignity), they argue that although many therapists use prayer competently, based on their own experience of prayer, it may be limited because of the diversity in prayer. Therapists need to be aware of different prayer practice and be sensitive to the way that prayer is practised by their clients. Under principle E (concern for others' welfare), therapists need to be aware of issues of power and intimacy in the relationship, and the part that prayer plays in them. In some cases, the client may use prayer to gain spiritual one-upmanship towards the therapist. At other times prayer may help to eradicate issues of power as both therapist and client come before God as equals in prayer.

Rose (1999) asks that, if prayer is to be used in counselling, then by whom, and when, is it to be implemented? If the counsellor prays then they may reveal a concept of God that is alien to the client; the agenda may become that of the counsellor, and reveal her hopes and dreams for the client, which do not resonate with her agenda. If the client prays then there may be pressure to perform and to please, or the prayer may contain an indirect communication for the counsellor rather than a direct communication with God. If prayer is offered at the beginning of the session it may detract from the immediacy of the client. If offered in the middle, it may detract from the context and the moment of where the client is in their process. If offered at the end, prayer may be a place to dump issues without time for exploration.

In my previous research (Gubi 1999, 2001), a number of ethical implications emerged from the data. One interviewee felt that it was not appropriate to pray with her clients. She was happy to explore issues of spirituality but not to have those issues acted out in the session. Another interviewee felt that prayer could be part of the session as long as the client was able to reflect on their process in the act of praying. Another interviewee questioned if this was possible as it was difficult to maintain an act of reverence and mystery around something you then go on to explore in terms of its psychological process. These are quite different ways of thinking. To use prayer in this way would require a client to be sufficiently psychologically minded to be able to step back and reflect on the process. Prayer at the end of a session might be a place to dump and run from difficult issues, rather than face them and work through them. Prayer could be regarded as indirect communication with the counsellor rather than as direct communication with God. This might question the honesty and congruence in the relationship. Other ethical issues encompassed 'who do I become to my client if I initiate prayer? What impact might praying have on the relationship?' Prayer may affect the level of mutuality and power, and raise issues of transference, countertransference, spiritual inadequacy and compliance. However, this is true of other therapeutic strategies and interventions, e.g. the 'empty-chair' technique in gestalt and directed 'acting out' in psychodrama. As long as boundaries are clear and the potential transference issues are explicitly acknowledged and worked through, then prayer need not be precluded.

It is important that the counsellor gives careful attention to the words that she uses, to the client's values and level of spiritual development, and to their understanding of prayer, if she is not to impose her belief system on the client. Prayer can be a way of the counsellor expressing her hopes, desires and aspirations for the client. Care needs to be taken because it is very difficult for a client to distance themselves from the 'here and now' experiencing of prayer to think about it. Prayer can carry connotations of magic, victimhood and helplessness, and is a risky intervention to introduce into the counselling agenda. Prayer can make the counselling process less focused and set up all kinds of unhelpful dynamics in terms of how the client sees himself and how the counsellor sees herself.

In other published work (Gubi 2002), I state that prayer is a contentious intervention that can be used quite abusively, but that is the same for all interventions in counselling. In some forms of helping in which prayer is used (e.g. prayer counselling or Christian counselling), so-called evil spirits are sometimes exorcised (cf. Collins 1988, p.570), abuse issues are sometimes re-enacted to bring about closure (cf. Bennett 1984, p.82), and prayer is sometimes used ritualistically as a 'formula' for healing with little respect for the client's needs (cf. McMinn 1996, p.79). Prayer can be viewed as a 'quick fix' to emotional problems. These are quite inappropriate because they can leave a client unable to understand why they still continue to feel damaged. The message is that they should now be whole, or that completion or resolution of issues should have been made, and they may be unable to bring their sense of continuing pain back to the counselling. Prayer can be used to manipulate a client to comply with what the counsellor thinks is best for the client, e.g. 'Almighty God, we come to you confident that it is your will that X should go to Y and say "…".". So we pray for your spirit to come upon him so that he will do your will' (Gubi 2002, pp.101–102). Prayer may feel intrusive and create an oedipal triangle (mother/counsellor, father/God, child/client) which may prevent the natural emerging of, and trust in, the counsellor–client relationship.

Rose (2002, pp.1–49) states that in all situations, where there is intimate involvement with another person, there are dangers of power being abused, of unresolved dependency and exploitation. Boundaries are important – yet prayer is about breaking down barriers between people, and in prayer, boundaries of time and space become less important. Even if the client is prayed for in private, there is the possibility that prayer can be a form of subconscious influence on the other. It is important that prayer is not used to exhort the client to forgive too quickly, or to pass over their grief, without confronting the feelings. Prayer can be used to avoid or dilute the counselling process, so it is important that the counsellor does not draw too quickly on religious resources, like prayer, to bypass the complexities of the counselling relationship. God can be seen as fixer, judge, scapegoat or alternative companion in ways that create barriers to self-discovery, relationship and personal responsibility. Prayer must not be seen as a magical formula to bring about predetermined results. The client must not imagine that the counsellor has a special hotline to God. Although the counselling session may be confessional at times, the counsellor's role is not that of spiritual guide. Prayer can cross boundaries in a way that is not always appropriate in the counselling situation. Prayer can too easily be used to side-step difficult psychological work. A client who asks to pray may be saying that the sessions are too uncomfortable and that they would rather God put it right so that the pain can be avoided. Or a client who asks God to enable the counsellor to help her may put pressure on the counsellor to act in a way that the client perceives is helpful, but which may not be the best way forward. Prayer needs to be treated sparingly and with a keen sense of timing. Clients who engage in prayer regularly may be reluctant to receive psychological help. They may feel that counselling is self-indulgent, or that they are resisting God's help. Therefore, to be prayed for by the counsellor may be terrifying. If the client's upbringing is religiously strict and abusive, the idea of prayer may be frightening or repellent.

In a survey that I conducted into attitudes towards prayer in counselling (Gubi 2004) 66 respondents had a reserved attitude towards the use of prayer in counselling, or were extremely opposed to its use. Those who were extremely opposed to its use, and who gave a reason, felt that it was unethical and inappropriate to bring a third dimension into the work, that it was defensive practice, or that it 'perverted' counselling into a different type of relationship. Others made the following comments:

> About as relevant as examining the entrails of a dead chicken in the session.

> I don't believe in magic…

These two comments are dismissive, and seem to link prayer with voodoo practices and belief. They pay little attention to the importance that the spiritual belief of their clients might have on their therapeutic process, thus raising the question of whose agenda is more important in the therapeutic relationship – the counsellor's or the client's? This issue of the 'counsellor's agenda and integrity' versus 'client need and agenda' was also demonstrated in other ways. Four respondents felt that prayer did not form a part of their counselling orientation, so prayer was inappropriate in their practice. Five of the respondents stated that prayer could not form an honest part of their practice because they were atheists or non-believers. One respondent claimed that her training taught her that her faith should not intrude on her work. Another respondent stated that religion was a private matter that had no place in a scientifically informed process. It could be argued that whilst all of these attitudes demonstrate a high degree of professional integrity, with the counsellors being firmly grounded in themselves, their beliefs and their approach, these comments could also represent an unwillingness, or an inability, to move beyond a particular frame of reference in order to embrace their client's world and all that might be therapeutically beneficial for them. This could arguably be 'prejudice' – a notion that has no place in ethical counselling practice as it hinders client autonomy and compromises the principle of beneficence in that the counsellor is unable to act in the best interest of the client because of the views, attitudes and beliefs that they hold.

Other respondents (33) were against the use of prayer in counselling for reasons that are related to the effect that prayer might have on the counselling process and on maintaining unhelpful dynamics within the clients' process. These were that:

- Prayer can lead to collusion between counsellor and client, leaving remaining fundamental assumptions unexplored.

- Prayer could be directive, or an imposition, if it is a product of the counsellor's own views and beliefs.

- Prayer can be manipulative and disempowering, by taking away decision and responsibility for empowerment from the client.

- Prayer can take responsibility away from 'self'. Some clients can take refuge in a God without, who is always forgiving. This can distract the client from taking responsibility for themselves.

- Prayer can be an avoidance of having to do the 'dirty' work (facing difficult personal issues).

- Prayer, if simple and formalistic, can be defensive and dangerous because it can prevent counsellors addressing interpersonal issues which they find difficult.

- Prayer can be used as a way of avoiding staying with the 'here and now' of the session.
- Prayer can enable the client to adopt a limiting and self-deceptive stance.
- The use of prayer can raise issues about control and boundaries. It can cause confusion about roles: 'I am a counsellor, not a priest. I believe it is important that clients know where you are coming from...'
- The use of prayer can be caused by the counsellor's sense of inadequacy and insecurity more than by the client's needs.
- Prayer can be used unhelpfully as a way of 'tidying up' uncomfortable feelings or unfinished business – a process that reduces the client's ability to explore uncomfortable areas further by preventing the expression of emotions needed to be worked with and fully experienced.
- Prayer by the counsellor can put pressure on the client.
- A counsellor who prays overtly might be seen as being judgemental or proselytising.
- Prayer can be a way of the client controlling the counsellor.
- Prayer can be a way of preventing the counsellor staying with feelings of stuckness and their own inadequacy.
- Prayer can be a form of 'delusional thinking' with incompetent practitioners.
- Prayer can be invasive in the counselling relationship and make it less equal.
- Prayer can change the dynamic of the therapeutic relationship.

Other respondents felt that there was a danger of losing sight of the client if prayer was introduced: that turning to God within myself would result in the withdrawal of attention away from the client, that prayer would introduce the counsellor's agenda rather than following the client's lead, that overt prayer was an imposition – a 'doing' rather than a being. One respondent felt that s/he would question the nature of the relationship between him/her and the client, if the client was needing to go outside of that whilst being in the room with him/her.

Five respondents felt that there was a philosophical difference between prayer and counselling which meant that they were diametrically opposed. This was described as:

God will take care of everything versus client self-responsibility.

Counselling is a process where one suspends one's own value judgements and belief systems in line with the client's. It is therefore inappropriate to bring prayer into the counselling process, even if dealing with a Christian client.

Counselling is about finding power within oneself and taking personal responsibility for my own life. Prayer is asking an outside power to somehow intervene on my behalf and magically make life better.

One respondent stated that if a counsellor is praying during the session, then s/he was not being with the client. It was equivalent to falling asleep in the session. Any counsellor who prayed in front of the client should consider refunding a portion of the client's fee and entering further therapy. One respondent felt that all counselling should be based on the theory: 'You should know what you are doing and *why* at any given time'. At present there is no theory that underpins the use of prayer. Another respondent had experienced cases of overt prayer being used by another counsellor and considerable damage and misunderstanding had arisen as a result.

A way forward

When faced with these potential problems and dilemmas, it is difficult to consider that prayer may be appropriate in counselling. But most, if not all, of these dimensions exist in all counselling interventions. It is evident that prayer is not risk-free, but neither is the process of counselling and psychotherapy. Counselling and psychotherapy contain a creative tension between risk-taking and accountability, between a psychological sensing of the process and the experiencing of not-knowing and mystery. Good practice does not require the avoidance of risky interventions, but that all interventions are contributed with sensitivity, reflexiveness and care. Prayer requires the same sensitivity, awareness and professionalism on the part of the counsellor, rather than a denial of its value. How this might be achieved is explored in the next chapter.

CHAPTER 4

The Ethical Use of Prayer

Considering that prayer exists right at the centre of spirituality (Ulanov and Ulanov 1992, p.24), and that pastoral counselling is acknowledged to have a history which predates the modern psychological era (Clebsch and Jaekle 1964; Rose 1999), it is surprising that more is not written about the use of prayer in pastoral counselling. When it is written about it is largely to state the benefits of prayer (e.g. Collins 1988; Hurding 1985) or it is written about in popular terms to aid self-help (e.g. Bennett 1984; Lawrence 1993) but little was researched or written before 1990 about the practice of using prayer therapeutically or ethically to aid professional reflection and practice. The assumption could be that religious practitioners should know how to use prayer instinctively with no requirement for research or guidelines for ethical practice. Prayer may be thought to be so fundamental to healing in religious contexts that its use has been taken for granted. Prayer may be conceived as being so fraught with difficulties that it has not been considered worthy of research and comment. Perhaps it is because ethical issues in relation to prayer and counselling have only recently begun to be considered with the emergence of accepted professional norms and the regulation of counselling. However, since 1990 there has been a growing amount of research and in-depth writing on the subject.

The place of prayer in counselling and psychotherapy

Canda (1990) provides a holistic approach to the use of prayer in the social work context. There are commonalities in the issues to be considered when determining ethical practice in a social work context and those in a counselling context. Canda defines the range of options for the use of prayer as follows:

- *Option 1:* The working relationship is viewed as prayer and the worker relates to the client in a spiritually sensitive manner. Explicit acts of prayer are not used with the client.

- *Option 2:* Prayer is not used with the client but instead the client is referred to a religious specialist for spiritual direction.

- *Option 3:* Collaboration is made with the religious specialist on the client's behalf.

- *Option 4:* In-session prayer activities are cautiously engaged in only at the client's request. This approach must be protective of the client's self-determination and the worker must feel comfortable and competent in sharing prayer.

- *Option 5:* In-session prayer activities are encouraged at the worker's invitation. The client must indicate readiness and interest. Manipulation, coercion and proselytisation are not acceptable.

Canda stipulates that a number of conditions have to be present if prayer is to be used. The worker needs to assess the client's interest in prayer. Through an evaluation of the client's spiritual beliefs and practice the client may imply an openness to prayer. The worker needs to adopt an empathic attitude that fosters mutual trust and respect towards religion and spirituality. Such an attitude needs to respect any difference that there may be in the spiritual orientation of the worker and the client. An open exploration of agreement and difference can empower the client to make an informed, self-reflective and self-determined choice and avoid any manipulation of the client. The worker needs to have a highly developed awareness of her own spirituality and be actively involved in dealing with personal and professional issues of spiritual growth. The worker needs to be informed about, and open to, spiritual practices and prayer activity other than the ones that she regularly uses. Canda states that the spiritually sensitive relationship needs to be well established so that mutual respect and trust are present. The invitation to pray needs to be tentative and exploratory rather than directive. The client must determine whether to use any prayer activity, and to give what is used their own meaning and not that of the worker.

Webster's (1992) research considers the issues around the use of prayer in pastoral counselling from an object-relations perspective. His research provides a model for the use of verbal prayer in pastoral counselling that is also applicable in a mainstream counselling context. It is an empirical and reflexive study based on a systematic analysis of Webster's own counselling experience of using prayer with clients. Data are drawn from case studies that involve process evaluation, outcome study and effectiveness evaluation based on verbal reports by clients and Webster's own observations and conclusions. Although it is limited because it does not draw from a wide range of practitioner experience, its strength is in the insights gained through the depth of reflexiveness that Webster is able to engage in and by the clarity with which he is able to communicate them. Webster states that when a client asks to pray, many levels to the question need to be considered.

> What does this question mean to the client? How is the client relating to the therapist with this question? What relationship to God does it suggest? Why does she ask the therapist to relate to God now? What will happen to the client–therapist relationship if attention is given to God? To remain sensitive to this woman's meaning, a multitude of possibilities deserve consideration. (Webster 1992, p.1)

However, these uncertainties do not rule out the use of prayer. Webster argues that prayer is a way of reuniting the creature with its creative ground. Prayer pursues the inward journey towards the realisation of self, not as a form of being that is isolated from others, but as an organism that is ultimately dependent on God and others for existence. Prayer engages one in a process of communication, attending to, and listening to, a transcending other and affirming whom one is. Prayer realises the possibility of communication with the source of Being. Prayer puts one back in touch with a capacity for being and with personal meaning for life. Prayer can transcend limits imposed upon the individual or society. Prayer can contribute to the rhythmic process of human movement between dependency and autonomy that leads to a maturing capacity to depend on a trustworthy environment without losing one's sense of autonomy and one's ability to be authentic in relation to an other. Prayer can contribute to the hope of transcending one's worst fears. Rather than blind ourselves to the world, prayer can transform our vision and make us see our world in a different light (reframing experience).

There are three forms of prayer that can be integrated into the therapeutic context. Webster identifies these as centring prayer, imagistic prayer and verbal prayer. *Centring prayer* is defined as solitary prayer in which attention is given to the rhythm of breathing, a simple phrase, or a combination of the two. This kind of meditation opens awareness to the presence of the transcendent and brings into focus the 'false self'. Webster states that the therapist may use centring prayer as a means of preparation before meeting each client. This enables the counsellor to encounter the client without an agenda that obstructs the counsellor's ability to be present to the client's immediate reality. Likewise, the client may benefit from centring prayer, either at the beginning or end of the session as a way of focusing or integrating the therapy. *Imagistic prayer* is a way of constructing mental pictures in order to re-experience and dwell on a situation from the past, present or future. It is also a way of reliving dreams. A prayerful attitude trusts the process of attending to what comes from within the client and is in essence non-directive. *Verbal prayer* is used to express what has been discovered within. Clarifying meaning and stating experience comes from words. Verbal prayer articulates the connection between inner and outer reality.

> Verbal prayer realises the self as an organism that is ultimately dependent upon God and others for existence. When the conscious mind relaxes its firm, independent hold to give room for the truth about oneself, God can recreate and transform the person from the ineffable centre within. (Webster 1992, p.71)

Verbalising prayer opens the mind and heart to transcend existing limits of perspective and will. Verbal prayer is not restricted to petition. Webster gives an example of such prayer at the beginning of a therapy session.

> Lord, here I am in my spirit still fluttering about. I want to turn all my attention to you, turn all that over to you as I turn to you. I give you my heart, my God, in this special time with (my therapist). I ask for your touch and your kindness; I give thanks to you for these times and for your presence in everything, always leading and nudging and encouraging and feeding and nurturing. I look forward in anticipation to all you do in my life, in the lives of those that I love and those whose lives are connected to mine. (Webster 1992, p.72)

Verbal prayer discloses one's relationship with God to oneself and to others. Verbal prayer leads on to the frontiers of one's notions of God that require growth and an enlargement of heart and mind. Words elicit and enable the client and therapist to attend more deeply to experience; they become instruments for expression of the client's true self; and link the client to the therapist, who can offer acceptance and validation of the client's true self (p.75). Webster states that verbal prayer serves purposes that are consistent with the purposes of psychotherapy. He suggests that the therapist may have an opportunity to pray when circumstances in the session result in five general scenarios:

- when a client expresses a desire to turn attention to God
- when a client is developing a sense of autonomy
- when a client is ready to accept the need for dependence
- when a client is ready to welcome the possibility of transcending self-imposed limitations
- when a therapist is able to mirror the client's relationship with God.

When a client requests prayer, Webster discusses what the client has in mind and what this means in the therapeutic relationship, e.g.

Joyce: Can we pray during therapy?

Jim: If you would like to. But what prompts you to ask?… What have you in mind in terms of praying here?… When we enter into prayer, I want you to feel free to pray in words or be silent, to do whatever is comfortable for you… How does that seem to you?… Do you have any idea of when you would like to pray in therapy? (Webster 1992, pp.91–92)

This is done in a respectful way, allowing for the unfolding of the meaning to the client's request. He communicates the notions of freedom, client control and autonomy that are necessary in authentic prayer, and does not impose what prayer should be for the client. Webster argues that a therapist should not introduce a client to verbal prayer if the client has not requested it. Therapists should reflect on their impatience with a client's progress that can often motivate their need to pray when the client has not suggested it. This can be attended to more appropriately by praying for the client outside of the session. If prayer is suggested, it should be in the context of the client expressing a need to be in touch with a transcendent reality, e.g. in the AA 12 step programme, making contact with the Higher Power (Alcoholics Anonymous 1981, p.8), but this should only be after the client has discovered a personally owned power. Any suggestion of prayer should be presented in such a way that the client feels free to accept or decline the suggestion. Care should be taken to ensure that the client has not accepted out of compliance.

Webster recommends that in determining what language is suitable for prayer it is important that both therapist and client are authentic, but this must be tempered by the use of language and imagery that will be meaningful for the client so that the experience will be one of connection rather than contradiction. An important ingredient of verbal prayer is the acknowledgement of, and affirmation of, the client. However, such affirmation must be sincere. This can help a client to put negative experiences into a more positive perspective. The therapist must use non-threatening words and determine when the relationship is strong enough for the client's limitations to be mentioned without losing the supportive dimension of the relationship.

Prayer in the session should be a co-operative venture. When a client does not want to pray at all, but wants the therapist to pray, one must question what the client values in the prayer. This requires a balance between the client's need for sufficient trust and safety to tolerate the truth, and the client's need for help in exploring what is difficult but true. Webster gives an example (not stated in detail here) of a client who requests prayer from her therapist but who is reluctant to pray herself. Through gentle exploration of her reticence it becomes clear that the therapist's prayer provides her with a framework in which she feels sufficient psychological space to attend to her true self. As the therapist enacts the part of her that she feels should pray, the client has room simply to be.

Webster states that he has rarely spent more than ten minutes in verbal prayer with a client. He recommends no more than five minutes, being careful in sensing whether the client would rather continue in conversation than pray. Prayer should not be forced by either therapist or client. He stipulates that the therapy hour must not be extended to include prayer. If prayer is missed, and the client is disappointed, he recommends considering what this means to the client. Although prayer is sacred, it is not exempt from boundaries. Verbal prayer is addressed directly to God, but it is also an indirect communication to the other participant. When the therapist prays audibly, the client will be influenced by what is spoken and vice versa. Prayer at the end of a session is oriented to helping the client stay with her feelings, not to pray them away. Prayer can deepen awareness of feelings. Prayer can be a way of enabling a client to stay with feelings so that she can begin to appreciate what such feelings mean to her. Prayer can serve both as a way of accepting feelings and as means whereby the therapist can articulate unknown feelings or thoughts that the client has denied or repressed. However, the therapist must be careful to assess the client's readiness and ability to assimilate new awareness into consciousness. An example Webster gives of this is: 'God, sometimes it feels like you're a pain and an irritation. We can't make you do what we want and it feels like you don't care' (Webster 1992, p.116). In conclusion, Webster states that the client's request to pray can be accommodated in the interest of building rapport. However, it must not alter the structure of therapy and can ultimately serve the client's discovery of truth after sufficient tolerance has developed in a client to receive its meaning. He presents the following guidelines for praying verbally with clients:

- The clinical encounter presents the therapist with the task of discerning motives for prayer and of choosing a course of action that will lead the client toward greater capacity for truth.

- The therapist attends to the client's manner of relating to others, particularly those ways in which the client distorts 'the other' in relationship.

- The therapist's reluctance to pray may be assessed in terms of: the therapist's transference upon God; the client's transference upon God; the therapist's countertransference response to the client; the therapist's assessment of the client's transference.

- The therapist attends to the psychological and spiritual development of the client, to whether and how the true self is expressed by the client in relation to God. The therapist attends to what images are most meaningful to the client.

- The client determines readiness for prayer; the therapist participates in a way that communicates respect for and understanding of the client.

- The therapist accepts a client's request to pray in a respectful way and allows for an unfolding of the meaning of the client's request. The therapist communicates what freedom and autonomy are necessary to both client and therapist in authentic prayer.

- The therapist's familiarity with various styles of prayer creates balance and flexibility in relating to God in psychotherapy.

- If the therapist prays aloud, the therapist must use language and images that will be meaningful for the client.

- The therapist can minimise the effect of cross-cultural differences by acknowledging in the introductory comments that they exist. If the difference is too great, then silent prayer is best.

- Because prayer is a co-operative venture, both therapist and client are given freedom to pray aloud or in silence when prayer is introduced into therapy.

- Prayer properly occurs within the time limits of the therapy. The clinical hour should not be extended to accommodate desire to pray.

- Prayer can be used at the beginning of the session to become conscious of the therapeutic activity in relationship with God, during or ending the session to assimilate or integrate an awareness that is emerging into the client's consciousness in relationship with God.

- Prayer can serve both to mirror acceptance of a known feeling and to articulate an unknown feeling or thought that the client has reason to deny or repress. Prayer can serve as an avenue to lead the client gently toward awareness of something new.

- Verbal prayer demands a high degree of sensitivity and extended supervision of clinical experience.

- Evaluation of a therapist's response to a request to pray with a client aloud should consider: what feelings are associated with a client's request for prayer with the therapist? How does attention to and communication with God affect the client's relationship with the therapist? Does prayer serve as a symbol of safety for the client? Is prayer needed to establish rapport? Is the client able to reflect upon what motivates the request to pray? Does prayer enhance a client's transparency or create distance in relation to the therapist? How does the client need the therapist in prayer – as a boundary for transitional space or as a participant within the transitional space? Does verbal prayer contribute to a client's ability to tolerate the truth?

Rose (1993) conducted semi-structured interviews with 11 counsellors who had had a minimum of three years' counselling experience and who had indicated that they had prayed for clients. The interview data were analysed using grounded theory (Strauss and Corbin 1990). The aim of the research was to explore something about the relationship between prayer and therapy from the point of view of the therapist. It is not clear from the research how the interviewees were selected in respect to how they initially came to be approached, whether they were all cultured in a particular Christian agency, whether they practised in a mainstream or pastoral context, what level of training each had, or whether this sample would be representative of counsellors in general. However, the research is useful because it provides an indicator as to how prayer is used by some practitioners in Britain and demonstrates different levels at which prayer influences counselling. Rose states that the two most frequently mentioned behaviours are orientated to the therapist's work rather than to the client, specifically in terms of the counsellor wanting greater insight, sensitivity, wisdom, higher consciousness and groundedness for the work. There is also a desire for wanting the session to 'work', and for handing it over to God for him to do something. 'I don't want to control but obviously I have a vested interest…' (cited in Rose 1993, p.27).

Rose states that some of the prayer activity is known to the client and some is not. There was a general consensus among the interviewees that even though prayer may be routine to the therapists, it should not be imposed on the client, although most interviewees would discuss prayer with the client if the client brought the subject up. Some interviewees did use prayer, and talking about prayer, actively in the session, in a cognitive sense, with the aim of helping the client to pray themselves while leaving it open for them to reject the idea of praying should they wish to. Rose concludes that prayer has many different meanings for those who practise it and the interaction with therapy is inevitably a complicated one. Several cluster around the idea of prayer as a resource for therapists. Others indicate an awareness of conflictual aspects. There also appears to be a profound interaction, as experienced by some therapists, between the two practices whereby both involve a way of being with the client that allows change to happen (p.34).

Ten Eyck (1993) conducted research into how mental health professionals understand and use inner healing prayer in the context of psychotherapy. Using a modified Delphi technique (cf. Stewart and Shamdasani 1990), graduate participants (doctorate or masters degree level) who used inner healing prayer were selected from three prominent Christian counselling associations and sent a questionnaire of closed questions (n=150). Those who returned their questionnaires (n=120) (80% return rate) were then sent a second questionnaire of open questions in order to collect qualitative data. Finally, from the returned second questionnaire, eight people were selected for structured telephone interviews because they displayed a comprehensive knowledge of inner healing prayer and appeared to be representative of the overall sample. The telephone interviews were transcribed to maximise utilisation of the data given. No specific method of analysis is stated. In summary, inner healing prayer (IHP) is defined as the direct inclusion of God in the psychological healing process that adds a positive, but ethereal, element into the relationship. This is regarded as essential to the integration of the spiritual and psychological, providing a holistic approach to therapy. Inner healing prayer shortens therapy whilst addressing deeper issues, or core problems, and produces more permanent results (from the therapist's perspective). It is seen as a positive way of addressing therapeutic issues that empowers the client to change. This conclusion is corroborated by Garzon (2005). IHP involves a direct invitation for God/Jesus to enter the healing process. It is particularly potent in dealing with past traumas. It is a process in which God becomes more intimate and personal and is experienced in the person's deepest pain.

In terms of how IHP was introduced and practised in the session in Ten Eyck's study, the only comments stated were the importance of being sensitive to the needs of the client and to their spiritual development. Some therapists had no concerns over introducing it to clients yet were hesitant and cautious in addressing the subject with peers. Others only introduced it if the client was a Christian, or if they specifically asked for prayer. IHP was felt to address diverse cultural needs providing that the client was open to the possibility that God might work in his/her life. During IHP, it was important that the client was in control and was not drawn into a process that they did not want. All telephone interviewees agreed that IHP shortens therapy because the process infuses the client with forgiveness and love. If imagery was introduced, it had to be done carefully and the counsellor had to be sensitive to those clients who were not visual. Sensitivity to the client was a main theme. This was articulated through the need to follow the client's lead using their images, words, or whatever they presented, thus allowing imagery to unfold through client participation. Inviting God into the image empowers the imagery in a manner that is conducive to healing. Ten Eyck's research seems to indicate that prayer is a panacea for healing that is tempered only by sensitivity to the client's needs and wishes. It is interesting that Ten Eyck found only a few limitations, raising suspicion about the depth of reflexiveness that participants engaged in. However, Ten Eyck does encourage accountability through supervision and adequate training for practitioners.

McMinn (1996) writing from a Christian counselling perspective states that some counsellors insist that prayer should always be part of the therapeutic process with Christian clients because they believe that prayer is an essential part of all Christian experience. This is disputed by Johnson and Ridley (1992) who suggest that it is dangerous to assume that all Christian clients respond similarly to the variety of Christian interventions because, like other clients, Christians represent a wide range of individual differences. Other counsellors believe that counselling should remain distinct from spiritual or pastoral interventions. Whilst praying with a client may encourage denial, refusing to pray may hurt the therapeutic rapport and prayer may be an avenue through which feelings are explored. Praying with the client may lead to a sense of comfort and hope in the midst of feelings of despair. However, it could also contribute to feelings of dependency and subsequent abandonment at a time when the termination of the relationship is imminent. Rather than adopting an 'all or nothing' approach to prayer, McMinn argues that we should ask the question, 'Which forms of prayer should we use with which clients and under which circumstances?' (p.65). McMinn argues that prayer can enhance clients' spiritual lives and help clarify their perspectives. He cites Craigie and Tan (1989, p.98) who state: 'Praying with clients that they may be liberated from resistant misbeliefs, that they may be empowered to do the truth, and that they may come into a deeper relationship with the truth can sometimes be a most powerful experience'.

McMinn states that some counsellors choose to pray in marital therapy because it models effective communication. Others choose to pray with their clients because their clients desire prayer to be a part of the counselling relationship, and prayer enhances therapeutic rapport. Others advocate using meditation, contemplation or imagery in the sessions as a form of prayer. Others pray during sessions without disclosing their prayers to their clients. Others pray during pauses in the conversation as a way of maintaining a spiritual focus in the counselling and as a way of staying with periods of silence. However, it must not compromise the counsellor's listening acuity. Silent prayer can sustain the counsellor through difficult and stressful work. Prayers of petition for clients can be an essential part of the discipline of a spiritually vibrant counsellor.

McMinn argues that if Christian counsellors are committed to the welfare of their clients then they have an obligation to pray for those in their care and that no case could be made against a counsellor praying for clients outside of the counselling session. Praying for clients can also help to restore the focus of humbly seeking God's direction. Devotional-meditation assignments may be helpful for some clients, especially for those suffering from anxiety-related problems and depression. However, McMinn warns that clients may be concerned about being 'spiritual enough' to please the counsellor. Closing eyes in prayer may be threatening to a socially tense client. Clients may wonder what the counsellor is doing or thinking during prayer times when eyes are closed. McMinn argues that it is probably better to make a tape recording for the client that will enable them to meditate in a place where social demands can be avoided or lessened. Some counsellors believe in offering their clients training in the use of prayer to enhance the client's spiritual coping. However, McMinn warns against prayer training because: (a) it detracts from the overall therapeutic process; (b) it may pose ethical problems for counsellors representing their techniques to insurance companies; and (c) there is no evidence for the effectiveness of prayer training, which calls into question the credibility of prayer training methodology.

McMinn believes that although routine in-session praying can model commitment to spirituality, it introduces significant risks to the counselling relationship with minimal benefits to the client. Praying routinely with most or all clients risks praying words of meaningless repetition that lose the essence of prayer. He concludes that prayer is more than a counselling technique. Counsellors should consider the potential effects before using prayer in counselling. He advocates that praying for clients privately is always useful, but other forms of prayer, such as routinely praying aloud in counselling sessions, introduce both potential benefits and risks to the client. Counsellors need to define clear ethical guidelines for the use of prayer in counselling. It is rare that Christian counselling literature gives the quality of attention to ethical matters that McMinn's writing does. His advice is considered and appropriate, even for mainstream counselling. He does not presume the historical adequacy of prayer as a licence for its use in counselling, but gives a carefully balanced reflection of the issues.

Tan (1996) states that prayer can be used by the therapist before, during or after the therapy session, at the beginning or end of the therapy sessions, or at any time during the session. Different forms of prayer can be used, e.g. quiet meditative prayer, general prayer aloud with the client, specific prayer aloud with the client, inner healing prayer or prayer for healing memories. Citing Finney and Malony (1985a, 1985b, 1985c), Tan suggests that prayer should only be used in psychotherapy if the goal of therapy is spiritual development. It should not be used simply as a technique for anxiety reduction or desensitisation. Tan particularly emphasises the use of prayer in the healing of traumatic memories that are unresolved or remain emotionally painful. Citing Seamands (1985) and Propst (1988), Tan writes that in such prayer, the counsellor uses guided imagery of Jesus walking back into the past with the client, healing and comforting the client in the midst of the traumatic event, which is re-experienced in imagery. However, Tan warns that the use of prayer in this way is not a panacea that ignores the depth and complexity of human problems and emotions. As some clients are not good at visualising guided imagery, Tan suggests an alternative, seven-step approach to inner healing prayer from a Christian perspective:

- Start with prayer for God's healing and protection for the client.
- Help the client to relax as deeply as possible using breathing and relaxation techniques.

- Ask the client to go back to the traumatic event and relive it (visually) if possible. The counsellor should be gentle and supportive, periodically asking about what is happening and what the client is experiencing.

- After enough time has elapsed, the counsellor prays, asking for God to come and minister his healing grace and love to the client.

- There is a period of waiting in quiet contemplation and meditative prayer. The counsellor again gently checks out with the client what they are experiencing. This is a time of letting go of the need to control, and building trust in God who truly cares. It is not result-centred or experience-seeking *per se.*

- After enough time has passed, the session of inner healing prayer is then closed with prayer, usually by both counsellor and client, unless the client is too shy to pray. It is usually a prayer of thanksgiving.

- This final step involves debriefing and exploration of the experience. It will often involve forgiveness by the client of those who have hurt him/her, and a letting go of the bitterness and resentment. This is, however, a process that takes time and it is unreasonable to expect instantaneous results.

(Summarised from Tan 1996, pp.372–374).

This approach is dependent on a more creative counselling orientation. There is a danger of such a technique leading to the client feeling that bitterness and resentment should be resolved if the therapist has indicated it will. However, Tan is keen to stress the importance of not expecting instantaneous results, and of proceeding carefully, according to client need.

Rose (1996) states that prayer is used by counsellors between sessions as a way of changing the counsellor's conviction through trying to see the client in a way that God would see them. Some counsellors pray for insight and sensitivity so that the counsellor will know how to pitch responses. Prayer is a way of waiting on God. Some pray in intractable situations. Others pray that the client will experience the love of God. Prayer is a way of handing the client over to God in the hope that God will do something in his time and way. Prayer is a response to powerlessness. When everyone has done all that they can in a situation, God can somehow help where others cannot. Prayer is a way of maintaining connection. Prayer can be a way of maintaining communication with clients on an unseen level. Prayer is evident in the session as a way of being with the client. Prayer can be a process of self-emptying and attending to nothingness, suspending the desire for contact or resolution. Prayer can be a way of seeking help in the session at times of counsellor 'stuckness', anxiety, or loss at how to proceed. Prayer can be a place where, in between sessions, clients can process some of the deep psychological pain that they are going through. Prayer can be a resource that is essential to being able to work as a counsellor, a nourishment (a 'getting fed' process, and a recharging process), a process of containment for very difficult feelings, and a channelling of power and healing. Prayer can be a way of both counsellor and client attending to the transcendent dimension that enables trust in sustaining and healing power. Citing Weil (1963), Rose argues that prayer is reflected in the quality of attention (allowing in the presence of) that is present in the counselling relationship. Prayer can also be evident in intercession and in the capacity to relate. Rose's writing is useful because it provides an insight into the hidden influences of prayer on the counselling process, through its impact on practitioners. This is a dimension that, although alluded to, much of the other research on the subject does not explore. Rather than explore strategy, Rose's writing examines process.

Richards and Bergin (1997) state that psychotherapists sometimes pray silently for clients during or outside of therapy sessions, pray vocally with clients during sessions, and encourage clients to pray by themselves outside of therapy sessions. They argue that prayer should not be viewed as a substitute for professional competency but prayer can be used as an added resource to assist their clients. It may be appropriate for therapists to encourage religious clients to turn to God through prayer for assistance, strength and wisdom. Even therapists who do not believe in prayer, or pray themselves, need to remember that clients' perceived relationships with God can be a great source of strength and comfort to them. With respect to contemplative or meditative prayer, they believe that the research demonstrates that the trusting, passive attitude to release and surrender of control, isolation from distracting environmental noise, active focusing or repetition of thoughts, task awareness, and muscle relaxation (cf. Martin and Carlson 1988; Payne, Bergin and Loftus 1992) can have such significant healing effects on the mind and body (cf. Benson 1996; Borysenko and Borysenko 1994) that it is surprising it is not used more in therapy. However, the use of such imagery needs to be consistent with the client's religious or spiritual beliefs. In-session time that is devoted to such practice can be great, so clients should be encouraged to engage in contemplative practices outside the session once the client knows how to do so. It is not clear whether Richards and Bergin offer their views through personal experience, or through careful study of the literature. However, their approach to the use of prayer in counselling is one of caution rather than advancement.

Koenig and Pritchett (1998) draw conclusions about prayer from anecdotal evidence that they present as guidelines for using prayer with clients. They do not disclose how the anecdotal evidence is collected and evaluated, nor from whom it is obtained, although Sperry (2001) draws heavily on their comments in advocating how prayer should be used as a therapeutic intervention. Koenig and Pritchett (1998) suggest that prayer is more of a delicate issue with psychiatric patients than it is with medical patients because of the boundary issues involved. They state that prayer is used relatively rarely with patients and that guidelines for using prayer are problematic. However, they conclude 'with some trepidation' (p.332) that there are four ways in which prayer is used by counsellors. The first is the counsellor praying directly with the client. This, they claim, is the most controversial. The second involves praying for healing for the client away from the face-to-face context. The third involves praying for guidance on diagnostic and treatment matters. The fourth involves encouraging the client to pray within the session whilst the counsellor remains silent. Koenig and Pritchett comment that spiritually attuned clients may expect their counsellor to pray with them in the sessions, but argue that this is a controversial intervention, particularly for clients with severe emotional issues. They warn that incorporating prayer may have unpredictable consequences for the therapeutic relationship that can affect boundary issues and be detrimental to the therapeutic alliance. Prayer can also produce a level of intimacy that may be threatening to both patient and counsellor. It can also disturb a counsellor's neutrality and objectivity.

They argue that praying routinely with all clients is unwise. However, they identify four benefits: prayer can effect comfort and hope that can extend beyond the session; prayer can convey a sense of the counsellor's caring and commitment for the client; prayer can combat the client's sense of loneliness and isolation; prayer can enhance trust in the client–counsellor relationship.

Some indications for when prayer might be useful are: (a) when a client discloses to the counsellor that religion is important in the way that they cope with problems; (b) when the client and counsellor are from the same religious background; (c) when the client either asks for prayer in the session or shows no hesitation when the counsellor asks for permission to pray; (d) when the client has sufficient ego strength and general psychological stability that disturbance of boundaries is not an issue; (e) when the situation decides that prayer would contribute to the advancement of therapeutic outcomes.

Prayer is often appropriate when the client is working through some kind of acute situational stressor such as the death or serious injury of a spouse or loved one, deep personal disappointment, severe or life-threatening illness that is out of the client's control, or some other kind of discrete stressor. Prayer can also be helpful to clients who are struggling with chronic behavioural problems such as addiction to alcohol or gambling. In these cases, prayer can counteract the sense of hopelessness that would otherwise paralyse further efforts to overcome the problem.

In approaching clients about the use of prayer, Koenig and Pritchett suggest that counsellors should find a way of introducing the topic that is non-offensive, non-intrusive and which reduces the risk of adverse consequences. They state that the counsellor should first assess if prayer is congruent with the patient's worldview. If so, then they suggest the following words as a way of introducing the topic. 'Some of my patients find comfort in prayer, others do not. Would my praying with you over this situation be helpful to you, or do you feel that it would not be particularly helpful?' (Koenig and Pritchett 1998, p.333). The client must be given clear and specific permission to reject the offer for prayer without feeling uneasy or feeling that they have disappointed the therapist. They also recommend that if the counsellor has prayed with the client before, the same cautious approach should be taken every time a new occasion for prayer arises. If the client shows sincere interest, then they suggest that prayer be conducted in the following manner:

- First, the prayer should be brief – typically less than a minute, especially if the counsellor does the praying.

- Second, they suggest that the client does the praying, rather than the counsellor. The counsellor should listen attentively and offer support at the end of the prayer by saying 'Amen'. They believe that the client is the best person to determine the content and form of the prayer, and that personal and spontaneous prayer should be encouraged rather than memorised prayers. By listening attentively to the client's prayer, the counsellor may learn things about a client's motivation and priorities that may otherwise not be revealed.

- Third, if the client asks the counsellor to pray, then the prayer should be general, supportive, affirming and hopeful. They suggest either a prayer for strength and support, or a prayer for a sense of being loved and cared for, or a prayer for the successful resolution of a specific problem that the client wishes to be resolved.

- Fourth, they recommend that during the next session the counsellor explores with the client how they felt about the prayer, allowing the client to report both negative and positive experiences for it to be truly 'present' within the therapeutic encounter.

Magaletta and Brawer (1998) propose a tripartite model which they claim describes the localisation of prayer within the therapeutic relationship, delineates the amount of intimacy that is potentially generated within the relationship, and specifies the degree of therapist knowledge that is required at each level. The tripartite model comprises three levels: the client level, the therapist level, and the combined level. At the *client level*, prayer is used by the client away from the therapeutic relationship as part of their ongoing process of seeking healing from emotional distress. This may have been suggested by the counsellor in order to help clients to cope with ongoing distress away from the session, or it could be independently implemented by the client as part of her coping strategy. This level involves the least degree of intimacy within the therapy hour and requires little involvement on behalf of the therapist. This process enables counsellors who are uncomfortable with prayer still to use prayer as a therapeutic tool if the client requests it.

The *therapist level* finds the counsellor praying for the client away from the therapeutic relationship. Counsellors may offer a specific prayer for the client or employ prayer in general preparation for a day's work with clients. Some counsellors may consider their work as prayer, with prayer being considered to be a dispositional state, a way of living, or an approach to life. Magaletta and Brawer claim that this level can be employed by counsellors who practise in an organisation that does not favour the direct use of prayer in therapeutic work, or when a counsellor would like to include prayer but is uncomfortable with, or not knowledgeable about, the client's prayer orientation. They claim that the intimacy level that is generated in the counselling relationship ranges from minimal to substantial depending on the intimacy naturally experienced by the counsellor in their prayer life or, if the client has been told that the counsellor is praying for them, the degree of valence that prayer holds in the client's life. Some therapists report that the healing generated in prayer comes from transmission of empathy that occurs when clients know that they are being prayed for by the therapist. However, there is no evidence or referencing to research that indicates this claim is produced.

At the *combined level*, the counsellor and client are praying together. This can occur at the beginning, during, or at the end of a therapy session. The content of prayer will depend on the mode of communication (e.g. the counsellor praying audibly for the client as the client listens, the client praying audibly as the counsellor listens, counsellor and client praying together either audibly or silently) and whether the counsellor's and client's religious and spiritual beliefs are similar. Magaletta and Brawer claim that this level contains the most mutuality and can therefore generate the most intimacy. It is also susceptible to ethical problems. To negate these problems this level requires a moderate to high degree of therapist knowledge of, and experience of, prayer. They conclude that prayer will vary in its purpose, form and content at any level, and will lead to many different ends. It thus behoves the counselling profession to pause and consider the relevant ethical issues in order to protect clients and make better use of this potentially healing agent with clients who have active prayer lives. Counsellors must monitor themselves through self-understanding, education, training and research so that they can avoid both denial of, and/or utter fascination with, prayer. Thus they might better understand, properly implement, and safely employ prayer as a potentially healing agent. To conclude, Magaletta and Brawer offer a set of guidelines that are summarised below:

- *Guideline 1: Conducting an informal assessment.* Therapists should self-assess their prayer beliefs, practices and biases regularly. Therapists should ask: why they want to pray for or with a client (purpose); examine how they intend praying for or with that person (process); and determine what petitions, if any, they will make (content). Such reflection will lessen the therapist's own conscious or unconscious push toward value conversion in therapy and will help to determine the degree to which prayer might restrict a client's freedom. It will also help the therapist to identify with the process that the client goes through. A thorough assessment of the client's religious and prayer beliefs and practices should be obtained. This allows the therapist to glimpse the valence of prayer for a particular client and suggests that this dimension of their life is not off-limits in therapy.

- *Guideline 2: Decisional balance.* After initial assessment, these data are used in the context of other therapeutic variables to inform a decision about the appropriateness and degree of the use of prayer. This can lead to three possible outcomes:

  - *Guideline 2a: Decisional balance outcome: prayer is contraindicated.* Prayer may not be appropriate. It is not appropriate to use prayer if it is not an authentic part of the therapist's lifestyle. Prayer may be harmful when working with delusional or psychotic clients. Prayer may foster unhealthy transference.

  - *Guideline 2b: Decisional balance outcome: making a referral.* It may be more appropriate for a client to be referred to a spiritual director, chaplain or pastoral care professional, as a helpful adjunct to therapy. Such referral is appropriate when issues involving prayer continually retard the therapeutic process, or when prayer is considered to be the sole agent of therapy while ignoring other therapeutic agents, or if the client's prayer-life is associated with guilt and shameful feelings.

- *Guideline 2c: Decisional balance outcome: localising prayer in the therapeutic relationship.* If, after careful assessment, prayer is established as a natural and appropriate aspect of therapy, the therapist and client can determine where and how it can be incorporated. Time must be given for the relationship to form, i.e. for trust, empathy, respect and mutual understanding of prayer to develop, before prayer at any level may be considered, and then, only after consent (written or verbal) has been gained to allow the client to be aware of the purpose and content. Prayer must also be reflected upon to monitor its effect on the therapeutic relationship.

- *Guideline 3: Educating for competence.* Magaletta and Brawer argue that therapists should receive training in prayer in order to broaden their personal experience of prayer in a way that will enable greater openness to the prayer practice of others. Training will also enable greater competence to develop. Training should include knowing how prayer can be of use in the therapy hour, and how and when to refer clients to more appropriate spiritual resources. Supervision should create a recursive loop in which values and competence should be readdressed within the context of the supervisor–supervisee relationship. Magaletta and Brawer state that as long as therapists monitor themselves through self-understanding, education, training and research, they can avoid both denial of and/or utter fascination with prayer. Thus they might better understand, properly implement, and safely employ prayer as a healing agent.

Magaletta and Brawer provide useful guidelines that come from their own considered experience as therapists who are working out how to be ethical and competent in their practice. Although useful, the guidelines presuppose that there is sufficient training and supervision available and easily accessible to enable Guideline 3 to be met.

McCullough and Larson (1999, pp.99–103) state that the literature on prayer suggests five ways that prayer can be used productively in mental health care. Although written in the context of mental health care, the guidelines can be summarised for counselling in the following way:

- First, counsellors can assess the types of prayer used by clients to understand their overall style of religious coping. Clients' preference for certain types of prayer may reveal something about their style of religious coping, or reveal information about the client's psychosocial functioning, e.g. petitionary prayer is a call for divine help. People tend to call on God or a higher power for help when they do not know how to solve their own problems. This may provide useful information about the client's resources to solve their own problems.

- Second, counsellors can encourage clients who pray, or who express a desire to pray, to use various types of prayer outside of the therapeutic session as an adjunct to the work done in the session. Although there is little merit in suggesting to clients simply to pray more, various forms of prayer such as contemplative or meditative prayer may help to ease distress. Prayer can boost clients' morale; their hope for recovery from, and resolution of, their problem; their comfort with the process of counselling; and their openness to the work of counselling and psychotherapy. Encouraging clients to pray for guidance, wisdom and strength might help them to obtain short-range outcomes and to become more effective participants in counselling and psychotherapy.

- Third, counsellors can use prayer to facilitate cognitive-behavioural change with highly religious clients. Encouraging clients to use prayer for coping, or encouraging them, if appropriate, to pray, can help them to incorporate therapy into their worldview. Prayer might also be productively viewed as an important source of material about clients' schemas and beliefs about themselves and others, and the world. Redirecting clients into more hopeful styles of prayer might be an important vehicle for facilitating changes in clients' self-talk and beliefs.

- Fourth, counsellors might, in some circumstances, find it productive to pray with clients. McCullough and Larson argue that clients and counsellors should only pray together when three circumstances converge: (a) the client requests in-session prayer; (b) the therapist is convinced after careful reflection that the therapeutic boundaries will not become confused with a particular client; (c) competent psychological care is being practised. With these cautions, there are times when in-session prayer is appropriate and helpful but such interventions will have the potential to be ethically problematic.

- Fifth, counsellors can pray about, or for, their clients. McCullough and Larson argue that it is not unethical, inappropriate or therapeutically counterproductive for practitioners to pray for their clients out of session. This is true even if counsellors do not let their clients know that they are praying for them. If one believes in the power of intercessory prayer to effect positive outcomes for clients at a distance, then it is all to the good. Short periods of intense prayer focused on a particular client may open the counsellor's mind and yield insights about the client's life that they may not otherwise have gained. It is difficult to feel dislike for someone for whom one is praying. Such prayers may not necessarily change the client or the counsellor, but they may give the counsellor a transcendent, transformed, empathic perception of the client and their needs.

McCullough and Larson conclude that prayer can be a resource for helping clients and counsellors to reach for a relationship, reconnecting them to themselves, each other, their worlds and the transcendent.

Dobbins (2000) states that with pentecostal protestant Christians, he has found the process of 'praying through' issues to be helpful. 'Praying through' is a process whereby a traumatic experience is cognitively restructured and reframed. It is a method of gaining new and less painful insights into past experiences or relationships by the reinforcement of new thoughts and feelings by repetitious reflection. It is a process of four steps:

- First, the client is encouraged to talk honestly with God about what is hurting him. This involves pouring out feelings, however they are experienced. It is also helpful for the client to write an extended therapeutic letter to the person whom the client perceives is responsible for the pain. The letter is not posted.
- The second step is to relate emotionally to the content of the letter. The client is encouraged to cry and express himself through prayer so that underlying emotions will be discharged

in readiness for a less painful way of interpreting the events and relationships referred to in the letter.

- The third step is to meditate, asking God's help in finding alternative and less painful ways of interpreting the events and relationships referred to in the letter. The client should be encouraged to believe that God will provide such a view.

- The fourth step is to spend time thanking God for the new way of looking at the hurt and mentally rehearsing the new interpretation. Dobbins claims that this is important in consolidating therapeutic gain. The fourth step is to be repeated until there is nothing more to write, after which closure should be encouraged by destroying the letters through burning or burying. This lessens the likelihood of further rumination and increases the possibility of permanent closure on the issues that have been 'prayed through'.

Dobbins does not provide any evidence into the effectiveness of this approach which borrows techniques from cognitive analytic therapy (i.e. the letter writing) and gestalt psychotherapy. The cathartic nature of this approach is evident, but the potential for client abuse is great. The approach requires a high level of competency and the ability to stay with intense emotions. It would be easy for the counsellor to impose or suggest alternative ways of interpreting events and claim that they are from God. It would be important to de-mystify this process and to validate any new interpretation as coming from the client, thereby empowering them with the responsibility for the way that they view life.

Rossiter-Thornton (2000) has developed a useful adjunct to psycho-therapy entitled 'the prayer wheel'. He claims that it is easy to use, puts the client in charge, does not require any particular belief, is flexible, is psycho-logically sound, and it can be used by anyone. The prayer wheel involves a handout that enables the client to focus on a number of tasks. A summary of these is:

- *Count your blessings.* This theme enables the client to focus on all that is going well in their life.

- *Sing songs of love.* This theme enables the client to focus on singing love songs (hymns, poetry, secular love songs) to the Maker of Life (collective unconscious, one's higher self, God).

- *Request protection and guidance.* This theme enables the client to focus on asking protection from negative thoughts and deeds of self and others.

- *Forgive self and others.* This theme enables the client to focus on issues that need forgiveness and can highlight areas in which the client is stuck.

- *Ask for needs – yours and others.* This theme enables the client to focus on what they need. Writing it down enables the client to see how many needs are answered over a course of time.

- *Fill me with love and inspiration.* This theme enables the client to focus on positive emotions, positive influences in her life, or something that has inspired her.

- *Listen with pen in hand.* This theme enables the client to focus on sitting quietly, writing down any thoughts, images, impressions, words or feelings that come to mind.

- *Your Will is my Will.* This theme enables the client to focus on acceptance of what is. 'Send me what I want, but if it is not what I need, then send me what I need.' This acknowledges limitations and fosters a healthy interaction and interdependency with others, the Maker of Life, and the environment.

Rossiter-Thornton suggests that the prayer wheel is used daily for 40 minutes, with the client spending five minutes reflecting on each theme. Issues that the technique raises for the client can be explored in the therapy session. The goal is not to achieve dramatic outcomes but for the client to take some control of her life and develop a technique that can guide her. Rossiter-Thornton provides qualitative evidence of the prayer wheel's use and benefits via case studies but invites further research to evaluate its effectiveness.

Earlier research that I conducted (Gubi 1999, 2001) revealed ways in which prayer already influences mainstream counselling in Britain. Prayer can be seen to influence counselling at two levels – the 'covert level' and the 'overt level'. The *covert level* is when prayer is not directly verbalised in the session by either counsellor or client, but nevertheless influences the session in some way. At this level prayer was used by counsellors for 'grounding' themselves in preparation for the therapeutic process when issues seemed insurmountable for the client. In such cases the counsellor would pray for the client away from their presence. Such prayer was an expression of hope as well as a recognition of the limitation of the counsellor's responsibilities. It could also be understood as a process of handing the client over 'in trust' between sessions in the desire for something else to reach the client that was over and above what other relationships could provide. This engendered a sense of the client being upheld and brought a feeling of 'lightening the load' and feelings of relief for the counsellor. Those counsellors who prayed for their clients away from the sessions did not pray for magical intervention or cure. Instead their prayers reflected the hope that clients would move towards a place where they could access the resources that lay within. Silence in the sessions was also considered to be prayer (particularly those moments when 'being' was more productive than 'doing'), or as a prayerful and spiritual space. Two of the interviewees talked about being surrounded in counselling by the presence of God and they believed that the quality of attention that was present in the counselling relationship mirrored a prayerful attitude.

The *overt level* is when prayer is used explicitly in the session, either through the verbalisation of prayer by counsellor or client, or through contracted 'prayer space' in the session for silent prayer. All of the interviewees felt that prayer at this level was contentious and could have ethical implications. There were two counselling approaches where interviewees felt that prayer could have a more natural home. These were identified as psychodrama and gestalt – two approaches that involve the acting out of emotion to aid completion of unmet needs. In these approaches the cathartic expression of anger could be made through prayer so as to liberate the feelings – especially if the anger is with God. An example of this is the client saying: 'Oh God! Why? Why have you left me to suffer like this on my own? Oh I feel so alone...so isolated...so scared. It seems so unfair that you have put me through this...that I have to experience this. Oh...I don't know what to do. I really don't know what to do!' (Gubi 2001, p.430). This is similar to using the 'empty-chair technique' and enables a better understanding of introjects, defences and transference issues which are projected at God and which could affect relationships that the client has with others and with which she maintains a sense of victimhood in her life. An example of this is: 'God, why are you always punishing me? Why can I never get it right for you? You always seem to favour other people and never put any breaks my way! Why? I know that I am not a good person, that others are better than me. Perhaps that's why. I know that I can be difficult to love because of the things I've done in the past...' (Gubi 2001, p.430). One interviewee felt that prayer could be used as a reformulation of that which is expressed in the session in order to enable the client to have a greater awareness of her process as well as feel supported. An example given was: 'Dear Lord, Sam has expressed his fear of becoming a father. He is scared of taking responsibility for his life, and it feels that this is an area he will need to work on. Help him to realise the inner resources he has to deal with these fears and to come to acknowledge a way forward that is growthful for him. Amen.' (Gubi 2001, p.431).

In prayer, communication is indirect, using the intermediary of God. In verbal prayer, it might also be difficult for the client to disagree with what is being expressed, which could endanger the counselling relationship. However, such danger does not prevent the gestalt practitioner from inviting his client to partake in an experiment or cause the psychodramatist to withhold an effective activity. Prayer, like all therapeutic interventions, needs to be used with caution, sensitivity and awareness. There are potential issues of abuse and power in all therapeutic interventions that need to be monitored carefully without precluding engagement in the process. Prayer need be no different, nor more dangerous. The research concludes that prayer can have a place in mainstream counselling with clients who are able to step back from the act of praying and reflect on their process. Prayer needs to be used with mature reflection on, and developed awareness of, the possible ethical implications, transference issues, and effects on mutuality. It must have regard for the client's spiritual development and be supported by good supervision (Gubi 2001, p.433).

Rose's (2002) book brings together much of what she has written in her previous research (Rose 1993, 1996, 1999). Rose highlights the dilemmas and the justification of those who use, and who reflect on using, prayer in their counselling work. The strength of this book is in its ability to capture practitioner experience and thinking using anecdotal material, and in the way that complexity is woven into clarity without loss of creative tension. Rose presents a unique view by examining the issues that inform the internal reflexiveness that underpins good practice. Rose concludes that prayer can benefit counselling as a means of containing panic, as 'arrow prayers' (very brief prayers offered quickly in the moment, e.g.

'Lord, help me') in requesting help, as a form of internal supervisor, as a way of maintaining contact with the client between sessions in the sense of thinking about the client, as a way of easing tension and staying with a situation, as a way of trusting God's healing power, as a place for wrestling with emerging consciousness, and as a way of coping with issues between sessions. The anecdotal evidence brings the issues to life and gives insight into the conflict that prayer causes some practitioners.

Finally, in my research (Gubi 2004) prayer was felt by some of the respondents to bring an extra dimension to the work, to be a useful bonding catalyst between counsellor and client, to be a precursor to relaxation or to exploring frightening issues, to be very effective as a visualisation type experience, to be a good form of healing and comfort at times of distress and can be part of the transpersonal experience in the counselling relationship, to be positive if the client and counsellor have a shared understanding of what is happening, to be a way of surrendering to 'something other', particularly when experiencing strong countertransference or unknowing. Some of the respondents felt that it was important to be led by the client. Prayer was appropriate if the client wanted to pray or requested prayer, or prayer was integral to their personal construct, or it was clearly therapeutic for the client to express herself in prayer, or prayer was from a place of good intent, or prayer was centred on the client's values and inner world. At such times it was important for the counsellor to be respectful of the client, be congruent with this process without identification, to be empathic with the client, and truly to listen and relate, trying not to judge, be biased or make assumptions about the client.

However, its use was rare and never routine. Ten respondents stated that it was important to reflect on the client's religious and/or spiritual awareness as part of a holistic approach to counselling (including exploration of spiritual self and inner light). Overt prayer would only be used if it was felt to have a beneficial effect on the emotional and mental state of the client, or if it furthered the client's own development, awareness and self-nurturing. Otherwise it might detract from what was going on between counsellor and client. Two respondents felt that it was important to explore how the client perceived the way that prayer affected the dilemma. If prayer offered insight, then it was likely to be helpful. If prayer meant 'external help', then it was not likely to be helpful. For 28 respondents, the use of overt prayer could be appropriate, but its use had to be tempered by a number of constraints:

- Prayer has to be culturally appropriate. The client's construct clearly has to include prayer.

- It needs to be used with discretion, care and sensitivity. It must never be forced or its use abused.

- The client has to feel that it is appropriate and has to want to use prayer – preferably at their initiation or request.

- The counsellor must not impose her beliefs on the client, or use the space as an opportunity to express her beliefs, however subtly.

- The client needs to feel free to express their faith.

- The counsellor should be able to give a coherent account of their practice, in relation to the client and his/her difficulties, as with any other intervention.

- Prayer needs to be used with as much consciousness and awareness as possible, be concerned for the truth, and not manipulative in any way.

- The counsellor must not take on any additional power.

- The counsellor and client must have a shared understanding of what is happening.

- The words of prayer must be carefully chosen and coherent with the client's imagery and language. There has to be an awareness of value-connected associations and historical/social connotations.

- It is wise to explore carefully and sensitively the client's motives and reasons for using prayer 'now' – what is it in 'this moment' and in the context of what is happening that prompts the client to desire prayer?

- Ideally, the use of prayer should grow out of the counselling relationship, rather than being the reason for the choice of a particular counsellor.

One respondent felt that prayer only had a place in purely Christian counselling. Two respondents felt that the use of prayer should be contracted, with some sense of mutual understanding, definition and agreement established. One respondent felt that it was important not to act on behalf of the client as this would undermine autonomy. Prayer should never be imposed. One respondent felt that the content of the prayer should be as neutral as possible. Four respondents only used prayer at the end of a session, or after a number of sessions (benedictory prayer or holding prayer). One respondent preferred to use a 'spiritual phrase' because of the fear that the word 'prayer' might cut him/her off from the connection with the client.

This chapter gives some insight into how prayer is used in practice, as it is expressed in research and in the literature. However, most of the research is small-scale and is based largely on the experience of pastoral and Christian counsellors with the exception of my previous research (Gubi 1999, 2001, 2000, 2004). It is evident that practitioners are becoming more aware of the need to consider all interventions within an ethical framework, and what is considered to be 'good practice' in the counselling profession is reflected in suggested strategies and methodology for implementing prayer. If prayer is to become accepted as a legitimate therapeutic intervention it cannot be regarded as being exempt from the demands of good ethical practice. So how is prayer used by those whose work includes prayer?

CHAPTER 5

How Prayer Influences Practice

Many counsellors I have met, who integrate prayer into their practice, philosophically and epistemologically regard all counselling as prayer. They conform to the view that psychotherapy is already a spiritual exercise in that both psychotherapy and spirituality dare to open up to what is inside and both go further into a deeper level (Canda 1990; Rowan 1993). This way of thinking can impact on a counsellor's motivation for counselling, provide a frame of reference from which he makes meaning of the counselling process, and can influence the attitudes and beliefs that underpin his 'way of being'. This chapter explores what some practitioners mean by, and how they understand, 'prayer'. It seeks to understand how prayer provides a philosophical and existential framework for understanding their work in an apparently more meaningful way than standard counselling theory provides.

Prayer as communication with higher self

Mary described prayer as 'being in touch with your higher self, inner self or other self'. She believed that this process involved listening to the wisdom that is at the core of each person. The experience was described as a:

> very affirming communication…when you are in touch with this other self you become greater…it is part of something creative…to do with love, wisdom, compassion. (Mary)

Although seeing parallels with the Christian concept of God, she felt that the label of 'God' was limiting God to 'very much being outside of me and outside of life as we know it'. Although she described prayer as being the 'key of my life, never mind my work', she never used the word 'prayer' in her client work because:

> it sounds to me like me here, asking God there to do something for me or somebody else, or me here thanking God there, or saying how sorry I am, or crawling about in abnegation. (Mary)

Mary provides insight into the difficulty of using language in describing the process of prayer and spirituality. Mary describes prayer as being in touch with 'Higher Self', 'Inner Self' or 'Other Self'. Whilst this concept of prayer may cause problems for some who regard the denial of self to be central to their spirituality, nevertheless the concept of 'self as divine' is central to some spirituality (e.g. Buddhism, Judaism, Christianity). 'He is under the duty to express his individuality. For bearing the divine image, he bears it uniquely... Therefore he is obliged to discover and develop his uniqueness. Otherwise, to all eternity some aspect of the divine nature shall have been left latent and unfulfilled.' (Steinberg 1975, p.70). From this perspective, it is a spiritual task to find oneself, to strengthen and actualise oneself (Pargament 1997, p.51). For Mary, prayer is a profound connection with 'self' that involves both transcendence and immanence (Still 2001). This is a complex concept, not dissimilar to the concept of polarity in gestalt philosophy (in this case prayer involves connection with both inner [inferring depth] and higher [inferring height] parts of self), which some writers have tried to grapple with in relation to the spiritual dimension of counselling (e.g. Thorne 1991).

> There is a sense of the therapist being responsive to the intuitive rather than to the powerful rational part of his or her being and, as a result, being endowed with new and often complex understanding...there is a powerful experience of relating at a new and deeper level...there is the experience of the transcendent, that is to say, of two people being linked into something greater than themselves...in this transcendent state there is an overpowering sense of energy, well-being and healing...' (Thorne 1991, p.183).

Whatever word or metaphor is used to describe the spiritual experience, and however important prayer may be for the counsellor ('key to my life, never mind my work'), it is important that language is not used that will inhibit the client (or the counsellor) or impose an alien sense of the transcendent other (or God) on the relationship. Prayer also involves listening to 'self' – developing a trust in one's awareness and insight (internal supervisor) – listening to the wisdom that is at the core of each person.

Prayer is communicating with God

Other interviewees described prayer as some form of communication with God. Lorna defined prayer as 'the raising up of the mind and heart to God...focusing directly on God'. For her, the process of prayer involved 'a conscious reaching out to commune with God...to be really present to God' in which one's awareness about 'God in everything' is heightened. Emma defined prayer as 'speaking with, being available to, hearing from, God'. Like Mary, she felt that the label of 'God' was beyond definition, but she still felt that it was important to keep the label, recognising that God was much bigger than any definition that she could offer. Fran defined prayer as 'communication with God'. For her, prayer was also the spiritual awareness that 'God is between me and the client'. Communication with God encompassed the process of asking for help, asking for wisdom, saying thank you, and giving voice to 'all that's going on within me which is unspoken most of the time'. Joyce and Joanne described prayer as 'conversation with God', although not necessarily verbal conversation. Joyce felt that prayer could involve a sense of 'being with' or 'in the presence of' another without communication or connection – a process akin to sitting in the same room as another. Joanne felt that although prayer was not necessarily verbal, the sense of 'presence' left her feeling loved and accepted. At other times, prayer involved qualities of prompting, crying, demanding, listening and hearing God speak back through different ways:

> ...whether it's through my dogs, or through something I read, or something I see on television, or work I do with clients – there's a sense of God being able to speak through every layer of my life. (Joanne)

Rebecca described prayer as 'talking' with God. For her, prayer involved praising and glorifying God, and expressing appreciation for all that He does for her. Gemma and Vivienne felt that prayer involved both talking and listening to God, and was characterised by communication and relationship, whereas Donna described prayer as simply 'talking to God'.

Although not explicitly using the label 'God', Michael described prayer as 'conversation…conducted in the presence of some awareness of things as they are in life'. Prayer involved a 'leap of faith' and an act of conversation, whether out aloud or in one's mind. Prayer was suggested to be a 'space into which meaning comes' – space that is characterised by a quality of generosity about the emerging meaning that evokes a tear to the eye, or a lump in the throat. Rachel felt that prayer was 'being consciously aware of God'. By God, she meant 'the presence of that other without which there would be no relationship between people'. For Amanda, prayer was '…opening myself up to God, and to the direction of the Holy Spirit, in words and in attitude…'

From these definitions it is clear that prayer involves some sense of relational experiencing of otherness (termed as God). Interviewees describe this experiencing in different ways: focusing, speaking, reaching out, hearing, being available to, being with, being in the presence of, being in a space into which meaning comes, giving a voice to all that is going on within me. This sense of 'relational connectedness with otherness' can also be found in how prayer is defined by the participants in my previous research (Gubi 1999) and also from the work of many Christian writers (e.g. James 1902; Yungblut 1991). The gain of such relational connection is described by the participants as: having a sense of God in everything, gaining help and wisdom, feeling loved and accepted, appreciation, an awareness of the quality of generosity, direction.

The concept of how God is understood is also interesting. Rachel stated that God was 'the presence of that other without which there would be no relationship between people'. It is clear from this statement how God is central to the relational element of her counselling work. Without God there would be no relationship and no 'becoming'. 'If dialogue is at the heart of our becoming persons, then dialogue with God will facilitate our becoming most fully who we were created to be. It is in conversation with God, with that which is other than ourselves, that we become' (Payne 1991, p.42). Michael described God as 'the presence of some awareness of things as they are in life'. From this statement the concept of 'acceptance' can be seen as connection with God. This creates a meaningful sense of the therapeutic process for Michael, by grounding the therapeutic process in the spiritual, transcendent dimension – what Thorne (1991) describes as a 'shared belongingness to a transcendent order'. This reveals a sense of how the interviewees' counselling work is underpinned conceptually by prayer, and that the counselling work is part of something bigger than self. This helps to place the work in some sort of wider sense of reality.

The sensation of praying

Lorna suggested that the sensation of prayer was like a feeling of 'being carried, being protected or having an ally'. There was a sense of companionship and presence, but 'it mightn't be a feeling of great joy, or tremendous sorrow, but more a feeling of being touched.' Emma experienced 'a sort of resonance within' in which she felt warmth and reassurance. She questioned how much prayer was about self-assurance (reassuring self-resonance) rather than conveying or receiving messages from a higher spiritual being. Emma was clear that prayer was not about talking to a different level of 'self'. Prayer was talking to a 'God' found 'within' and 'without of' self – something 'apart from' and 'different to' self. Prayer was a process of drawing comfort, similar to how a child draws comfort, love and support from the close contact of a hugging parent. But as God is a non-visible, non-tactile being, she felt that prayer involved 'working from the inside, out'. Emma felt that it was the 'process of praying' from which the comfort was had, not in the knowing that the pray-er had heard or been sent anything from the process. She acknowledged that, for her, there was a juxtaposition (and struggle) between God as friend (where closeness and approachability was experienced), and God as Creator (something abstract and unapproachable). For her, faith was about finding ways of building relationship with, and gaining accessibility to, God; but it was also about acknowledging both aspects of God, and not ignoring either. Joyce related an occasion when she had experienced what she described as 'being in the presence of God'.

> Some years ago I had an extraordinary experience. I was ill, and I heard this voice – I'd been reading a book about healing, and it was talking about you know, that when people ask for healing, God will listen to them, and give them healing, and I got very angry about that, and I was saying you know, 'Why does God only heal those that ask to be healed?', you know, 'Why can't a loving God heal people who need healing?', and I was kind of railing against it internally. I mean I wasn't saying any of this

out loud, but I can remember sort of sitting up in bed, and it was fairly early in the morning, and I heard this – it's not a voice, I can't say I heard a voice, in a sense that you would hear me speaking, or you speaking. But it was like hearing something else, and it just said 'Accept your healing', and that was really profound, you know, it was like 'If you'd just stop shouting about it and just got on and took it, you know, then maybe something would…', and it was very strange because…I had a very close friend who lived in the same village, and she used to come in and out quite a lot…and on her way back she called in to see me, and I was downstairs by this time, and she came into the sitting-room where I was, and she was sitting there, and she was chattering away about this tutorial, and suddenly she stopped and she looked at me and she said, 'What's happened?', and I said, 'What do you mean, what's happened?', and she kind of became tearful and kind of choked up, and she said, 'I feel as if I'm sitting in the presence of a saint', and it was a very extraordinary feeling. It was almost like something, whatever this thing was that had happened to me, was in some way visible to her, and so I suppose, I don't know what you asked me now, now I got onto that, but – you said something about sensations, did I have sensations when I was praying – I suppose I would say I was praying then, you know, I was having a conversation with God, but I was having a kind of an angry conversation, and it wasn't like I had a sensation in my body, but it was like I was *in* a sensation, I was *in* something, rather than it was in me – you know, I was in – I was in some sort of presence. (Joyce)

Although her experience had been an internal process, it had had an unconscious effect on her externally which her friend was sensing. Joyce did not really have an awareness of physical sensation in her body. She felt encompassed in something that she felt was profound. She rejected the feeling of being 'connected' with something or 'communicating' with something, but described the sensation of prayer as more a sense of 'being with' or 'in' something, rather than a process within her.

When you're in a relationship with somebody, it's more than just thinking with them, it's being with them, yes, being with…it's like, you know, sitting in silence with my husband is being together, without any kind of overt connection. It's that kind of being with. Somebody looking at us sitting on the sofa together, reading our separate books or papers, or something, might think 'look at those two', you know, 'not even communicating', but there's a sense of being together. (Joyce)

Ben described the sensation of prayer as a 'knowing' that was experienced in his body as a 'tingling sensation' down his spine, neck and brain. That sense of 'knowing' was described as:

> ...it's a knowing that you are just being directed. It's like a sort of a taking over, or a moving power, so there's an awareness there's a greater power than you that's moving you into certain areas, or helping you to discern, or choosing the right words to say. So it's very much a presence, and a sense of being in a fast-flowing stream on a raft, I suppose. You know, the raft is us, as a person, but the stream is the Holy Spirit. You're just aware that you're going in that direction. (Ben)

This sensation of a warm, comfortable, gentle tingling in the neck was also experienced by Anne, accompanied by a sense of openness. For Vivienne, the 'knowingness' was accompanied with a dulling of her hearing, coupled with the sensation of being bathed in 'light'.

> I feel as though I'm encased in warmth, and comfort, like somebody described it to me as warm oil being poured all over you, and it does feel like it starts at your head and gradually drifts down. (Vivienne)

Ben stated that to be without prayer in his work was to experience a sense of dryness. At the times when he has not prepared, through prayer, to work with clients, and he has to rely on his own strength, he has a feeling of something missing that is unquantifiable. When he has prepared to work with clients through prayer, he experiences working at a different level, where there is a sense of spiritual power and enlightenment.

> I have those intuitive moments, and those flashes of inspiration. The difference is it's on another level, I think. It's on a higher level, in a sense, so you – it's both/and in a sense, so you get a real sense of spiritual power, and spiritual enlightenment, rather than just you know, those sort of 'a-has', or 'it reminds me of', or 'I can see this logically from what this person's said'. (Ben)

Amanda had a powerful intuitive sense of being 'prompted' or 'urged' – 'this is right, this is the thing to do', accompanied by a 'quickening' or 'fluttering' sensation in her body – 'some sense of knowing in your body that feels right but it's difficult to quantify'. Gemma felt that sometimes when she was talking to God, she did not experience any sense of presence, but she knew that he was hearing her. At other times she described herself as feeling 'filled with the spirit'. This was when she experienced feeling a real sense of closeness and presence. Gemma also stated that she spoke 'in tongues' – an experience that began with a sense of the 'spirit touching my lips', and a sensation that sometimes made her tremble, but only on rare occasions in church – but not with clients. Donna did not always feel any sensation in her body, but her faith was that God was there nonetheless. In her prayer, she generally had a visual concept of Jesus, but at times of desperation, she had the sensation of crying out to God – an experience that is characterised by a sense of speaking to a 'more powerful, older, wiser type of higher power'. Michael described the sensation of prayer as being something 'beyond you' that is carrying you and that is peace-inducing.

> When I'm very distressed, frightened or anxious, got a big challenge ahead…I suppose it (prayer) sort of takes me, by some mysterious process, beyond the narrow compass of my anxiety, and often sort of shifts a dark mood…and replaces it with a sense of knowing where I am, and what I have to do, and the limitations of my person, and some more, sort of, friendly acceptance of who I am… I don't always know when I'm praying, and perhaps to talk about a sort of, a calming and peace-inducing prayer activity that sort of centres down and focuses, and the breathing gets deeper, and well, that is to say, there's less of it and it sort of, deeper down in my lungs, and there's more room to think, more room to you know, sort of feel myself going into it now, to sort of pause and consider – it's a sort of quietest, sort of, prayer. (Michael)

Joanne described the sensation of prayer as having a 'sense of God's presence in her heart and chest'. This was accompanied by a feeling of 'glowing' – of taking a breath, and feeling warm, loved and totally accepted. Like Gemma, Rowena stated that for a lot of the time, there was an absence of God in her prayer. At other times, there was a strong sense of God's presence.

> …a lot of the time in prayer, in contemplative prayer, there's a sense of an absence of God, the absence and presence of God, and my experience is, and in talking with other Christians, that a lot of the time, there is a sense of 'nothing's happening'…not a void, no, just an absence. But knowing in my heart that God is there. He knows my intentions. He knows I am there, loving him, yearning, longing for him, you know, and in my life as a Christian there have been times when yes, there have been – not great

flashes of light, but a very strong sense of God's presence with me for a time. (Rowena)

Shelagh defined prayer in terms of sensation. Prayer, for her, is the quietening of the mind that enables connection with whatever is higher than her. Quietening the mind enables the unconscious to speak, and this is the 'entrance' into the divine and the spiritual.

Schreurs (2002, p.203) states that involvement in a spiritual relationship involves becoming totally engrossed. This means withholding your own preoccupations and interests in order to pay full attention to the other. In this form of prayer (contemplation) you forget yourself because you are paying full attention to God as he manifests himself at the actual moment to such an extent that you are totally absorbed by it. This quality of attention or 'presence' in counselling is prayer. It is a state of 'letting be' (allowing-in-the-presence-of) which also lets be (in the sense of bringing to fulfilment) (Rose 1996, p.19). 'Attention taken to its highest degree is the same as prayer...' (Weil 1963, p.105). Yet, in the midst of this quality of presence, whilst being fully engrossed in the other (e.g. the client), the counsellor becomes more fully aware of his or her own body – listening to self in relation to other. Therefore, it is not surprising from the data that the sensation of prayer is present in the counsellors' awareness of experiencing. The sensation of prayer is described by the interviewees in various ways: feeling carried, protected, having an ally, companionship, presence, being touched, a resonance within, warmth, reassurance, comfort, being 'in' something, feeling encompassed in something profound, knowing, tingling sensation, openness, bathed in light, fluttering, loved, quickening of the mind. Again, the words and metaphors make it a difficult thing to conceptualise. One interviewee, Ben, used the analogy of pain, in which the results are observable and known yet it is difficult to describe the feeling of pain to someone who has never experienced pain.

Prayer as trust of the process

Joyce stated that the notion of 'trusting the process', which is common in counselling, was akin to prayer. For her, the process is God. This concept of 'God being the process' was also expressed by Donna. For Donna, there was no difference between saying 'trust the process' and 'trust God'. Joyce described the most difficult, but loving and cathartic, moments of counselling, where the client takes huge risks but feels held, loved and accepted, as true prayer.

> I should think that there are times when I'm sitting with a client and they're telling me really difficult things that they've done. Last week I was with a young woman who was struggling to tell me about having dealt in drugs. She's now a psychologist, and she was obviously deeply ashamed of this, and I felt very – I imagined it must be a bit like being God, when people confess to God, and let God know them in their darkest places. And it's very humbling, and it's very moving and there's something about being able to truly accept that kind of offering without any sense of judgement, or recognise, and understand, with compassion, the kind of, the reasons why people do things, and particularly when they're owning something, you know, when they're actually really understanding what they've done wasn't OK. And sometimes I think that's a bit like – I think it's what going to Confession should be… It's almost like experiencing both sides, because when people talk to me like that, I'm very reminded of my own distress and pain, owning my own darker parts, and it's very beautiful, you know, seems quite tender and exquisite when people can share that level. And it seems to me like that's what God is like, at best. That you can actually be known fully, in every dark corner, and totally know that you are OK with God. I'm hoping that's what God's like…that I can be accepted and loved for who I am. (Joyce)

Joyce felt that her work as a counsellor was prayer. 'I do think that there is something of God in the process. Maybe God is the process.' Joyce gave an example of a client where 'so much of our work seemed like a prayer'.

> So we got into a very deep communication with each other, on a very spiritual and deep level, where she would talk about feeling like 'the tabernacle was within her', you know, that God was housed within her, and I don't think she'd ever really found anybody to say those things to before, and I really understood what she was meaning, and so there was a real sense of – I don't know what it was really – but I think it was love. I really did love her, and she used to say to me 'I don't want you to go', and it was hard for me to go, because you know, I knew how much it meant to her, and she'd just give me a hug, and she'd say, 'Oh, I really love you,' and it was – it did feel – kind of, like a sort of spiritual love, and so yes, the work was like praying, a lot of the time. It was like, you know, God was in the room with us… It's like there was that kind of empathic resonance,

yes, and that somehow in that, it was – God was there, in the touching of those two parts, you know? And the love was there, in those two meeting places. (Joyce)

So those moments of love between counsellor and client, where the empathic resonance is greatest, can be experienced as prayer. God's presence was felt in the quality of the I–Thou relationship. Rachel experienced prayer as being infused in all aspects of life, and believed that no therapeutic encounter could take place without the presence of God, or without some sort of unexpressed prayer. Rachel found parallels between the Eucharist and the counselling environment in that both counsellor and priest were responsible for creating a space in which God could be present. Something happens in that space which is both known and mysterious.

> You set it up, and you withdraw right to the edge, and you leave that space for the person you've set it up for, and then something enters the space… I think in the Eucharist, it's much more powerful, because you're explicitly there with God in mind. Whereas in the therapeutic thing, it's like implicit. But it's the same thing, because what you're looking for, or what they're looking for, is healing, change, release; and it seems to me so similar… You know, it comes from somewhere else, or it comes from within them, however you describe it, but it certainly doesn't come from the counsellor… It's almost that process – that unquantifiable thing that we trust in – without actually quite knowing what it is…it's so paradoxical, if that's the right word. Not contradictory, I don't think…because you know what you're doing, but you also haven't got a clue what you're doing. (Rachel)

Hannah defined prayer as 'aligning herself' with the process of life. For her, prayer was about taking herself to the quietest place inside herself.

> I go to what I think of as the quietest place inside me. I trust that what I come to think or feel or believe or sense from that place is more likely to be right, in a sense of the right direction, than would be choices, feelings, thoughts that I might have when I'm in a more scattered place. (Hannah)

Sometimes it is an experience of nothing, rather than of something, but Hannah often felt blessed, grateful and sometimes awe-struck. Anne felt that both counselling and the Christian journey were a process, and that prayer was part of both. Rowena expressed the process of counselling as prayer, because in counselling she is listening to the client, to God, and to herself. This process of 'listening to God' is prayer and is inseparable from listening to herself and to her client. When asked how that process differed from listening to her 'internal supervisor', she replied: 'I think my internal supervisor might be God...'

It is evident how the counsellor's faith can create a frame of reference for making the counselling process more meaningful. Rather than deny the mystery and unknowingness of the therapeutic process, this existential perspective grounds these profound therapeutic moments in a greater sense of reality through the language of spirituality. This makes the process feel more 'whole' for the counsellor. So widely used concepts in counselling, like 'trust the process', the 'internal supervisor', the therapeutic process itself, the empathic resonance and connection, the 'unknowingness' of counselling, all have the quality of prayer about them and can be regarded as being akin to prayer. For the counsellor, nothing is denied or avoided in the process. Instead, the process takes on a more profound and meaningful significance because it is grounded in a deeper source of being than just 'the psyche'.

The motivation for counselling

Mary viewed prayer, as she defined it, as being her motivation for counselling.

> We're both two human beings in the service of their inner self, their view of God, or the divine... I do feel that it is very much about the link with the sacred, whatever that may be...the link with the divine. The whole thing is the service of something higher and deeper...service of joy, compassion, wisdom. (Mary)

Emma felt that although she did not need her clients to know about her Christianity, it was integral to her work as a counsellor.

> It doesn't say on my business cards 'Christian counsellor'. In a sense, I don't have a need for them to know that or not to know that. It informs me as to about who I am, and the way I see people, and the way I see that therapy is a positive development – that there's hope in that, and that there's value about a person. I think it is about valuing people, acknowledging their needs, their integrity, my integrity, I think it informs

me more than just a specific slice of traditional how people have experienced prayer in a prescribed way. (Emma)

Gemma believed that God had called her to be a counsellor and that God supplies her clients. She could not separate her counselling from her faith. Her vocation was her counselling work. Joanne believed that prayer was at the centre of her work as a counsellor. She believed that it was God who sent her the clients that she works with and she had a sense of working with God in her client work, which gave her a great feeling of security. Rowena felt that it was important that she saw Christ in everyone, as did Lorna, and she prayed on their behalf as a way of 'holding them' before God. For her, counselling was a way of responding to God's unconditional love for her.

> I do it because, as God loves me unconditionally, I endeavour to love the clients unconditionally. As a Christian, it's also for me about seeing Christ in everyone, so that includes clients. Obviously I know a great deal about them all, and when I pray, it is merely holding them before God, and not asking him to do anything. In a way, I haven't got a shopping list out, I'm not hoping for anything, I'm just saying, 'today, Lord, you know, I hold before you, like, the client I've just seen, who is a Christian'. Not all my clients are... Prayer isn't about doing; it isn't like, sort of, I don't see prayer as ringing up God and saying, 'Well, will you do this and make life better for this client?' – I don't see prayer in that way at all. I merely just lift them before God, and in his graciousness I believe that he will do what he wants to do for that client... It's not about me manipulating God or me manipulating the client, it's just offering them – holding them before God. (Rowena)

Whilst there is not much research into what motivates people to become counsellors, it is clear that for some counsellors, their religious faith sustains and motivates them in their work (Gubi 1995). For many of them counselling is a vocation. Prayer acts as an intrinsic dimension that underpins the sense of service to something higher and deeper. For Mary, Emma, Gemma, Joanne and Rowena, prayer and faith are central to their work and to how they view their work and their clients. It is a perspective that requires a response from them. That desire to respond motivates them in their work and is prayer because the response deepens the connectedness with, and service to, something bigger than self.

Prayer enables counsellors to frame their work philosophically in a way that is spiritually meaningful for them. This, in turn, provides a perspective on their counselling work, an attitude to their work, and a way of understanding the process of their work. Although all interviewees have trained as secular counsellors, their faith has provided them with a deeper sense of what they do, of who they are, as counsellors, and of their clients. Counselling is 'prayer in action' (Canda 1990).

Prayer underpins practice

It is evident so far that prayer encompasses a 'way of living' (Magaletta and Brawer 1998) that underpins the counsellor's life and the counselling process. From this perspective, existing practices and concepts, that are already acceptable to the mainstream counselling profession, can be understood as prayer. Regarding such concepts and practice as prayer creates a more meaningful sense of their reality for the practitioner. This section will explore the data that relate to how prayer is used by some practitioners to underpin the therapeutic process. At this level – that Magaletta and Brawer (1998) call the 'therapist level' and that elsewhere I refer to as the 'covert level' (Gubi 2001) – prayer is not part of the explicit therapeutic frame. However, prayer may be part of the implicit therapeutic frame in that prayer practices become integrated into the counsellor's way of being, so that what is offered to the client is intrinsically 'contaminated' by prayer. Although this is unlikely to interfere with the immediacy of the dynamics of the therapeutic alliance, or directly influence the client's agenda during the session, this aspect of prayer can still have an ethical dimension to it. The analysis of a survey that I conducted (Gubi 2004) indicates that counsellors integrate prayer into this dimension of their work more than into any other dimension, with 59 per cent of British Association for Counselling and Psychotherapy (BACP) Accredited Counsellors and 88 per cent of Churches Ministerial Counselling Service (CMCS) Approved Counsellors using prayer covertly in, or to support, their work.

Placing the work in the care of God

Mary stated that if a client is in a really desperate state, then she often lights a candle for them after the session.

> I put the candle in another room and sort of hand them over to whatever it is to look after them because you can't – they are gone – to know that somehow they are being looked after in a way you can't yourself, handing them over to the universe or whatever. (Mary)

Mary acknowledged that this practice was more for her benefit than for the client's.

> It's a symbol – it helps me to think there's something looking after them...I don't honestly believe that it would have the slightest effect on them...not when the chips are down. (Mary)

She therefore does not feel that such practice is unethical because she is not acting on behalf of her client, but on behalf of herself, although 'it would be nice to feel that something of warmth and comfort might creep into them'. Fran described this process of handing the work over to God in the trust that he would take care of the process and the client. This was done in the form of arrow prayers, of which the client was unaware. Gemma prayed for intervention – for God to heal, or give peace to, or reveal something important to, the client. Vivienne spent two or three minutes 'lifting the client up to God' after a session. She hoped that by doing that, God would bless, comfort and reassure the client.

> I can't put my arm round a client. I can't wipe away their sadness, or whatever, but I'm sure the Lord can and does do that. (Vivienne)

It is clear that some counsellors feel the need to offer prayer as a process of 'handing over' the client to a higher power in order to place the work (or the client) in some kind of caring trust. This practice is also evident in the literature (Gubi 1999, 2000, 2001; Rose 1993, 1996, 1999, 2002). Some counsellors prayed for intervention (healing, peace or revelation). Others simply prayed for comfort and reassurance. One counsellor used the ritual of lighting a candle after the client had left. Others simply handed the work over to God in the moments that followed the ending of the session. These practices help to clear the counsellor's mind in readiness to receive the next client or to move on to the next task of the day. The practice is therefore beneficial to the counsellor and helps to put her mind at ease in that, although she is not there for the client during the rest of the week, the belief is that the client is still being upheld by something greater (Gubi

2001). This is a practice that Rose (1996) refers to as 'containment' and 'maintaining connection'.

Praying for clients away from the session

All of the counsellors who were interviewed prayed for their clients away from the session. This raised the question as to whether it was ethical to pray for a client without his/her permission or approval. This was answered in a variety of ways.

> Well, I would respond by saying that, you know, my faith life is important to me. I actually believe I'm only doing this work because of that. That's the bottom line, really, I suppose. If it weren't for that I wouldn't be doing this anyway, and at some level I think that clients are probably attracted to me because at some unconscious or spiritual level they actually know that they will get something extra than they might get with someone who doesn't see the world like that – and life beyond the world like that. So you know, it's one of those things, you know, that it's part of the deal but it's a very unspoken part of the contract… But I'm conscious it might be an unwanted extra, and certainly the man, the client, about whom I used to pray in the sessions, and who, the work with whom I very badly felt I needed help, was not a believer at all. The thing was, there was such a positive transference through most of the work that he would have seen it as being well-intended, even though he wouldn't have, I think, cared much for it in some ways. (Rosie)

Rosie argued that prayer sustained her so much at times when the work felt heavy-laden or oppressive that she felt energised, and her sense of vocation was so re-invoked that she could not carry on without it. Therefore she felt that clients would gain more from her prayer, through her benefits from it, than they would be 'hurt' or disempowered by it. Rosie felt that it would only be ethically unsound if there were some maleficent intent. For her, prayer was about promoting her clients' well-being through sustaining her own well-being. Ben hoped that his intercession would bring about change in some way.

> My hope would be that there would be a power for change, or a power to help them in that situation, or help that particular difficulty, and it's not necessarily just Christian clients. They can be secular clients. I suppose I see it in terms of it's part of God's healing ministry that he's bestowed on

me – that's part of what I do, you know, that's – it's like another aspect of the package. That's how it feels, anyway. (Ben)

Ben acknowledged honestly that, at some level, it was part of his need to be a perfect counsellor who gets good results. He also acknowledged that praying in this way was acting on behalf of the client in that covertly and subtly he was influencing the client's life in some way. However, he cited a colleague who had said:

> 'Some people say this particular way of working is manipulative.' She says, 'It is. I admit it. But if it's manipulating people from unhealthy states and dis-ease to living fulfilled lives and happiness and not looking back, and they'd rather have B than A, then that's ethical, and that's OK'. And I think the same is true here, I'd say, you know. The fact that they don't know I'm praying for them, yet they get better, you know, is OK. So it's fine with me. (Ben, speaking about a colleague)

Donna sometimes found herself praying for clients as they popped into her mind. They often tended to be the more desperate clients who might struggle to get through the week. Donna likened prayer to just thinking about them sometimes and wondering how they were getting on, especially if she knew that the client had limited, or no, support through the week. At other times, in praying for them, she hoped that the situation might be made better supernaturally.

> You can be part of that supernatural magicness… I know he (God) can use me… I mean, I know from clients that that can happen. (Donna)

Donna described this prayer as bringing an extra dimension to her work. When challenged on the notion that God might already know the needs of the client, and thus prayer might be pointless, Donna stated that prayer was important to maintain relationship with God. She likened it to the analogy of a married couple who, after living with each other for a long time, would know each other's needs. However, if they never expressed those needs to each other, relationship and connectedness would be diminished or be lost. So it was with prayer. Although God may know the needs of the client and the counsellor, it was still important to bring those needs consciously before God in order to maintain and nurture relationship with God. Michael stated that if he had a client about whom he had concerns, he would, on occasion, contact a group of nuns who were in a closed contemplative order and ask them to pray for the client. In doing so, the client's name would be withheld in order to protect confidentiality, but Michael would hold the client's name in his mind. Michael regarded this type of acting on behalf of his client as perfectly ethical, and argued:

> What I do for my clients by way of clinical supervision and reflection and prayer is my business, not theirs. (Michael)

Rebecca was explicit to practising Christian clients about the fact that she prayed for them. Something might come up in discussion with a client where she might say to the client, 'I'll pray about that for you'. She had never experienced any concern or opposition to that and felt that most people were quite accepting of that and would never question her motivation. If faced with opposition, Rebecca thought that she would respond by simply owning the way she worked and if that was problematic for the client, then they might have to discuss ending the relationship. Rebecca's sense of integrity as a counsellor was paramount, and that included her beliefs.

> I would probably say, 'Well, you know, for me I pray about everybody that I'm going to work with every day, and that would not be a possibility for me. And if you really find that that's going to impinge or impact, then we'd probably have to discuss not working together'. (Rebecca)

Rebecca felt that her accountability as a counsellor was first to God, and if faced with a complaints committee, she felt that she would have no problem in saying, 'This is how I am as a therapist, this is my rationale – I do ask the Lord to protect people who are often very vulnerable. This is what I do…' Rachel hoped that clients would find meaning and have a sense of feeling 'held' from her prayer for them. In explaining her rationale, she related a time when she felt desperate, and knowing that others were praying for her enabled something within her psyche to shift, and a certainty to emerge which pervades every cell in her body.

> People would pray for me and the thing would shift… In my own experience, there were two times when I seriously contemplated suicide, and there was something about what I discovered at that point about the nature of God, or whoever, or the other. It was something about being held at that point, which I think has given me now some sort of unshakable belief about a meaning, even though it's very difficult to

substantiate rationally...but I think it springs from that, because when those moments were past, somehow something in my own spiritual or psychic makeup had shifted, and I knew it had shifted in an irrevocable kind of way, and I knew that there were some things after that, that I couldn't lose, and one of them was that idea about the meaning behind things... The way I explained it or felt it to myself was – it was like there was something about God that had made its way into every cell in my body, and that because it had happened in that way I could never lose it. It was no longer something cerebral. And then following that, there came the sort of conviction on the same level, not on an intellectual level, that's just the verbalisation of it, that love and life were stronger than any death or destruction that there was... I suppose the thing is that they will be held, whatever that means, but that's what it will mean for them, because of course when you yourself are at that moment, you don't feel anything like that, but it's afterwards you may come to recognise that there was something holding you, and I suppose it's that – that they'll be held, really. (Rachel)

Anne sometimes prayed that her clients would gain insight to stop doing the silly things that messed their lives up, and realised that such a prayer was an expression of her hope for the client. Vivienne prayed 'for' those clients that she didn't pray 'with'. She did wonder how those clients would feel if they knew that she prayed for them. However, she suspected that they would be quite pleased to think that she cared enough to do that.

I sometimes wonder whether people would be upset to know that I prayed for them, but actually even real non-Christians, people who are quite agnostic, or quite atheist, have at times rung me and said something terrible that's happened to them, or some awful story, or some crisis, and I'll always say, you know how there's a kind of a thing that you say, 'I'll think of you', I usually say 'I'll pray for you'. And I've never – I don't think anyone's ever said, 'Oh no, please don't do that'. They tend to say, 'Oh, if you like'. But I get the feeling they're quite pleased. (Vivienne)

Vivienne did not feel that it was either unethical or an intrusion to pray for her clients and she felt that the benefits outweighed the potential difficulties. She also felt that it was a dereliction of duty not to pray for a client if she felt it might help them in some way.

Much of the literature on the use of prayer in counselling indicates that many counsellors who use prayer pray for their clients (Koenig and

Pritchett 1998; Lange 1983b; McMinn 1996; Rose 2002; Sperry 2001). Certainly research into intercessory and distant prayer seems to indicate a positive effect (Astin *et al.* 2000; Leibovici 2001; Roberts *et al.* 2001). Although Bullis (2001) indicates that 83.5 per cent of mainstream counsellors feel that praying for their clients is ethically appropriate, Magaletta and Brawer (1998) raise the issue of whether it is better to gain the client's consent for the counsellor to pray on the client's behalf as part of their 'treatment'. Magaletta and Brawer state that some clients may not want their counsellor to pray for them. Dossey (1993, pp.74–79) demonstrates that prayer can have an influence on the unconscious mind of others. This raises questions about whether it is ethical to use 'techniques' if the recipient is unaware that they are being employed. Dossey (1993) suggests that the measure of 'intent' is ultimately what governs the ethical correctness of the use of prayer.

> We may not always know when or whether prayer is desired. I would maintain that as long as our efforts are filled with compassion, caring and love, there is little reason to fear that our prayers for others without their consent are somehow unethical. (Dossey 1993, p.80)

This measure of intent is evident in what the counsellors share. Ben states that it is ethical to use prayer as an unconscious influence in the client's life if it is for the betterment of the client. Rosie states that it is only ethically unsound if prayer is used with maleficent intent. It is interesting to see how other counsellors justified the ethical use of prayer. Michael compared the use of prayer with reflecting on, or thinking about, his client. He felt that he did not need his client's permission to reflect on, or to think about, his client – yet both activities sustain and improve his work. So it is also with prayer. Rosie's prayer was promoting her client's well-being through sustaining her own well-being. Vivienne felt that the benefits of prayer would outweigh the potential difficulties, and that it would be a dereliction of duty if she didn't pray for a client when she felt that it might be helpful. Several of the counsellors felt that clients would feel 'cared for' and 'held' if they knew that they were being prayed for. This might enhance the relationship. Magaletta and Brawer (1998, p.323) state that gain can be had from the transmission of empathy that occurs when clients know that they are being prayed for by their counsellor. If prayer can enhance the relationship in this way, then it could be argued that clients should be told, and if they are told, then why not gain consent? Certainly, none of the counsellors who were interviewed, who told their clients that they were 'prayed for', experienced any opposition or problems. It could therefore be argued that gaining consent is unlikely to be problematic. Magaletta and Brawer (1998) conclude that the decision to gain consent in this matter is a personal one. They state that perhaps the most ethically conservative stance is to pray, 'Thy will be done'. This removes expressions of the counsellor's hopes and intentions that may be considered to be inappropriate or unethical. But if the counsellor prays 'Thy will be done', then what is the purpose of prayer? Donna states that the purpose of prayer is to maintain connection and relationship with God. Praying for the client keeps the focus on the spiritual dimension of the work so that it is not taken for granted or lost. This gives the work a meaningful perspective and reminds the counsellor that the work (and the process) is bigger than what takes place in the therapeutic alliance, and is largely undetermined, full of 'unknowing', and out of the counsellor's control ('Thy will be done'). For some counsellors (e.g. Rebecca) prayer also reminds them of their accountability to something greater – a focus that prevents them from being complacent or too sure of themselves.

Attunement

Mary stated that prayer could be used as a form of attunement – 'to note how you feel when you know that a particular person is coming, does your heart sink or rise, do you feel warm, or chilly, or bored, or whatever, and just to note that…' She argued that this sense of attunement or 'centring of self' enabled congruence. Ben also used prayer as a way of getting 'in tune' before his client arrived. He described his process as:

> So I bring prayer into my work by – with clients, whether they're Christian or secular, I would pray beforehand, before I meet the person initially. I would pray that all things come together in the right way so that when I meet that person, the relationship's built up fairly quickly, and pray that the Holy Spirit is in there somewhere, pulling it together, making that happen. And then the traditional way, or the customary way that I prepare a session is to go through my notes, and then about ten minutes before the client is about to arrive, I would then just open myself up to God, to the Holy Spirit, and just calling, just getting in tune such that I'm able to be a

vessel, so it's not me doing the counselling. I mean obviously I'm doing the counselling in terms of my skills, knowledge and experience, but it's the Holy Spirit moving through me, and showing me areas to work on. So that's how – that's regardless of the client, and sometimes even though it's a secular client been referred, they could be quite spiritual, and even though it's maybe a Churches Ministerial Counselling Service client referred, they may not be believing at that point they are referred, so their faith may have gone very dry, so it makes no difference there. (Ben)

It is interesting that Ben's purpose of his attunement is so that he can allow the Holy Spirit to flow through him. For him, this means being intuitively open to his client on a spiritual level – not just relying on his own sense of being, but feeling inspired and guided in some way at a spiritual level. Michael described his process of using prayer for attunement as a way of recognising his needs and shelving them to enable him to have a quality of listening attention that: 'hovers and is flexible, and doesn't have its own needs too much to the fore'. Prayer was a way of 'taking him out of the picture' and sustaining him for his day's work as a counsellor. Rachel shared this concept of prayer as aiding attunement, but offered a different view on it. Rather than prayer removing something of herself, she felt that prayer enabled her to be more of herself.

Really, the prayer is not so much for them, as a reminder for me, in a sense. You know, the prayer before they come, it's setting the thing up, it's helping me, so that when they're there, I can be myself. (Rachel)

Prayer gave her a confidence that meant that she did not have to get 'hung up' about her importance in the counselling relationship. This enabled her to become less anxious because there was a realisation that not everything depended on her.

I am praying for them, but I think, on another level, it serves as a reminder that it's – because I'm aware that it doesn't all depend on me, then I can just let go, and be myself, and go with the session, somehow. I mean, it's that feeling that nothing is irretrievable, and that every mistake is an opportunity to learn more, and for me, it's part of getting out of a very pessimistic mind-set, and into one of, sort of, hope and opportunity. (Rachel)

Hannah spoke about 'holding' her client 'in the light' – a way of aligning (attuning) herself to the client she was going to be working with, and removing herself from her head, enabling her to stay more fully with 'not knowing'.

> If I've got somebody I'm finding it really difficult with, I will hold them in the light. I often take a couple of minutes before sessions to be silent with whoever's going to come before they get there... I go to my 'yes place' and open my heart as much as I can towards this person whom I may be having difficulty with, or may be having difficulty seeing how to work with them, or they may be somebody I know is in a lot of pain. I will just, kind of, hold them in my consciousness. Surrounding them with light... Consciously, I think, I do it for their benefit, but also I am assuming when I do that, particularly if it's somebody that I'm not sure about how I'm working with them, or whether what I'm doing is being useful, or effective, it's also for my benefit, because I am assuming that when I do that, I'm aligning myself in some way with the process, and allowing it, that I'm getting out of the way, and not blocking things. It does benefit me, because the more times I return to my quiet place, the more I'm able to be consciously in touch with my belief that, you know, life is a process and a journey, and I can get out of my head...asking questions again. (Hannah)

Amanda stated that before the client arrived, she often sat in the client's chair and prayed for them, and for herself, as a way of preparing for the work. Rowena regarded praying before the client's arrival as a way of reminding herself that she was not omnipotent, that she actually had a need to rely on God and not on herself. In so doing, she was filled with peace from deep within her soul and a sense that God was all around her. This helped her to put aside any anxiety in readiness to receive the client.

Prayer is used to quell anxiety, to heighten the senses, and to raise awareness. This enables the counsellor to become as 'present' as she can be, which frees her 'quality of presence' or 'quality of listening attention' to gain a deeper psychological contact and relational connection with the client. Prayer, at this level, enables the counsellor to be more 'fully-present' and congruent by enabling aspects of the counsellor that may be inappropriate or inhibiting (e.g. anxiety or a lack of confidence) to be put aside so that the work will not be inappropriately affected by them. Prayer also reminds the counsellor that the work does not solely rely on him/her, and that s/he is not omnipotent and has to have all the answers. Prayer enables the counsellor to feel more comfortable with the unknowing. Thorne (1991, p.16) writes:

> If I can let go of anxiety and simply relax, I experience what I can only describe as a new resource which becomes available to my client and to me…the process is akin to resting in the presence of God.

Prayer increases the capacity to relate (Rose 1996, p.17). Using prayer in this way is not ethically problematic, and because it seemingly carries no sense of risk, more counsellors feel able to integrate prayer into their practice in this way.

The stilling of the mind

Lorna stated that prayer enabled her to become a more reflective person. It stilled her and gave her a sense of peace and calm within. Prayer enabled her to regain her sense of vocation for her client work, giving her meaning, purpose and direction. 'It helps me to make sense of things, or to live with the "not being able to" make sense of things.' This is especially important in the middle of a session when she is stuck. This helps her to put aside her sense of panic and just to be there for her client.

> Sometimes when one person gets transference, and I am tempted with countertransference and I begin to recognise it, you know, it can be quite difficult to save my feelings now. I recognise them, but I'm not going to throw them back at the client, you know? So where I think I might have difficulties within myself, I say 'you just lead the way, God, and I'll do my best. (Lorna)

Fran argued that sending up 'arrow prayers' at times of difficulty in the session did not take her away from her client but instead it actually enhanced the work. Prayer helped her to stay in touch with her own sense of not having, or needing to have, the answers; to stay in touch with the not knowing. She believed that it was the client who had the answers, and God who had oversight of the process.

> It helps me with my sense of inadequacy, that actually I'm not on my own in this, and that God does care very much about the person I'm with, and about how I am, what will I say, and the way I am, so it keeps me grounded in that… I think it feels a very safe basis to be working in… (Fran)

Fran described prayer as being a vital underpinning for her work and felt that if she did not have this dimension to her work it would be unlikely that she would have trained as a counsellor because of the risks in being so closely and intimately involved in people's lives. Fran felt that it would be presumptuous to think that she could rely solely on her own skills without her work being underpinned by prayer. Yet she recognised the need not to be complacent, by trusting solely on God to make things right.

> I wouldn't go around just doing what I thought and trusting God to make it OK... I still need to keep my skills honed and to be very aware of what I'm doing and...aware of all my empathic reactions and transference and countertransference and all that sort of thing... (Fran)

Fran argued strongly that prayer was not a way of avoiding difficulty, but a way of staying with difficulty by drawing on an extra dimension (the spiritual dimension). She identified that extra dimension as feeling a sense of safety.

> It makes all the difference between being on your own and having to rely on yourself, which could be a good thing. However, it could be a bad thing also, and makes the difference between...luck and well, safety is the word that comes. It's something to do with safety, you know, putting myself and my clients in God's hands brings an extra dimension of safety, really to the work. It doesn't mean that I won't fail. I do make mistakes and I do fail. However, those failures are in God's hands too, and that's a tremendous help, really. (Fran)

Fran recognised that this could be challenged as her reaction to feeling a sense of inadequacy, and she recognised that this was the way that she coped with all aspects of her life in which she faced difficulty and anxiety. When challenged on how ethical it was to pray during a session without her client's knowledge, Fran said, 'It's who I am. I can't be different from who I am'. Fran stated that she did not necessarily receive divine inspiration from her arrow prayers, but that they enabled her to put her anxiety aside and to go on trusting and accepting that things would be OK with the session in God's hands. Donna believed that prayer prevented her from feeling 'alone' in the counselling work. When challenged on whether prayer might prevent her from fully experiencing the 'aloneness of the client' by taking her away from that experience, she replied that prayer removes the anxiety about having to experience the client's aloneness, enabling her to experience it more fully. Donna also took comfort in her belief that Christ knew what it felt like to be alone.

> That would make me think, if the prayer takes me away from their aloneness, then can I really understand how alone they are? I think I can. I think part of me praying is because I know he knows about aloneness. (Donna)

Hannah felt that prayer enabled her to see people in terms of being on a journey that had purpose and that was unfolding. Prayer did not help her to deny, or escape from, the dreadful things that her client was experiencing. Prayer helped her to stay more fully in the difficulty and pain, without the need to know and understand.

> …but some kind of 'the floor that I'm standing on is about, no matter how awful it is, if we stay with this, something else will happen'. I mean, that enormously supports me, and it does make it possible to stay with dreadful things, I think. I don't feel I need to understand. I've stopped wasting time now, asking why. And I pray in sessions, I mean, there are, you know, moments when I think I just don't know what to do here, I will pray. I will ask myself or God, if I'm talking to God at that moment, to help me. (Hannah)

Vivienne sometimes prayed for the gift of knowledge, wisdom and discernment during a session. She did not feel that praying in the session took her away from the client. She likened it to developing 'helicopter skills' – being able to 'hover' and be aware of what was going on inside her, what might be going on with her client, what would her supervisor say, what does her internal voice say, and what does God say? She felt that that 'extra dimension' gave her reassurance, peace, calmness and active help.

As well as attunement before a counselling session, prayer is sometimes used in the session to help the counsellor stay with the client. At times of panic, stuckness and anxiety in the session, prayer enables the counsellor to return to a place of stillness and calm. These feelings of anxiety can come from issues of countertransference that need to be reflected on. Prayer can be a means of putting the countertransference aside in order to stay fully in the moment. Prayer also helps counsellors to stay with 'not knowing' and 'aloneness' because the counsellor has an awareness that something greater than him/her has oversight of the process. This trust in something greater (or God) gives the counsellor the ability to concentrate on staying with difficult feelings whilst being grounded in something safe. None of the interviewees felt that the process of prayer took them away from the client, as suggested by a respondent in Gubi (2004) who stated that 'If a counsellor is praying during the session, then s/he was not being with the client. It was equivalent to falling asleep in the session. Any counsellor who prayed in front of the client should consider refunding a portion of the client's fee and entering further therapy.' Instead, all stated emphatically that prayer helps the counsellor to stay with the client because the spiritual dimension of their work gave them a sense of meaning, purpose, reassurance, calmness and peace. Whilst prayer can be used to avoid or dilute the intensity of the counselling process (Rose 2002), it is clear from the counsellors that prayer seems to enable them to stay more fully with the intensity of feelings. Prayer becomes a vehicle for greater focus (McMinn 1996), enabling the counsellor to stay with feelings that evoke risk or anxiety within them.

Praying in the session at times of helplessness

Joyce described times when she used prayer as a response to feeling helpless, or when a client's situation felt hopeless. Praying enabled her to reach a level of acceptance of her limitation of what she could do to help the client by handing the problem, or the person, over to God and trusting in the overall purpose. This helped her to have trust in something more ultimate and purposeful at times of hopelessness.

> There are moments in sessions when I just find myself saying – not exactly 'help', but you know, 'watch over', really, 'this person, or us here', and really it's when things feel desperate – it's the sort of 'dei profundus', you know. And the other times I pray are generally when I feel they're kind of hopeless – not that they are hopeless, but you know, I'm thinking about a young woman who is so sad because she has a history of abuse, and she's now 42, and has up to now been incapable of making close relationships, and yet longs to have an intimate relationship and children, and I feel so sad that I think she's just beginning to be able to do that, and it's almost like it's too late for one part of her, her longing to be fulfilled, ever. And I suppose I just – it's those situations when I find myself just saying, you know, 'do something – I can't do something'. It is also feeling like, that's also possible, you know, that actually something could happen, that you could do something that I can't do. So I suppose that is when I think of

> God being outside myself, and that is like beyond me, and my capacity...
> It's more like a trust, it's not even a hope, or a desire, or an expectation, it's
> more like 'I know you can if you choose to, and if it's your will, really' –
> and it may not be, but there must be, there may be, there probably is a
> purpose in this, and that I won't understand that. So there is a sense of –
> also a kind of an acceptance in that, but I kind of have to believe there's a
> purpose in it, because otherwise, you know, probably too hard. And I
> think I do believe that. (Joyce)

This was also part of Rosie's coping, especially when faced with listening
to very damaged clients expressing things that she has felt, 'I don't know
what I would do with it', in which situations are hopeless or rock-bottom.

> It consists of me, in my head, saying something, making a connection to
> what I believe to be beyond me and this life, and it reminds me that there
> are other powers and forces than we can see and touch, and I do believe
> that through all of us, some of that power, energy, force, can be connected.
> I think any of us can be touched by it, can be empowered by it, and on
> those occasions that I do that, usually in the counselling session and just
> before, I'm usually feeling pretty much in need of it! So that's what I'm
> doing, and that's what I'm hoping for by doing that. (Rosie)

Rosie acknowledged that it could be seen as an inability to stay with the
helplessness, but argued that she would probably have felt helpless many
times with the client before praying in this way. So it was not that she
would use prayer to avoid experiencing the client's (and her) feelings of
helplessness, but that her ability to cope with such feelings had a limit, and
at that limit, only God could help through the sense of hope gained from
the process of seeking help and guidance.

Ben prayed inwardly at times of 'stuckness'. As his solution-focused
approach demanded that he generate possibilities to help clients move on,
he prayed for direction – to be shown which way to go, or how to get
around the stuckness. His experience was that ideas came easily, or a clue to
a possible direction was offered through prayer. He stated that situations of
stuckness tended to occur when he had not prepared for the session
through prayer. When challenged as to whether it could be argued that the
Holy Spirit actually took him away from experiencing his client's
stuckness, he replied: 'That's interesting, yes. Not thought of it that way
before. Have to go away and think about that one!' However, he felt that

his approach to counselling did not necessarily involve having to experience his client's world, and stay with that experience. Although there was a level of empathy with the client, the focus of the work was on validating the client's experience, normalising the feelings, and then moving on through exploring the possibilities of a solution.

Gemma prayed for more insight into the client's process, and for protection at the times when she discerned evil spirits, or the devil, in the client. She believed that God was with her in the counselling sessions, and that through prayer, God would guide her in whatever way he wanted, or that 'he might leave me helpless to be helpless with the client'. So prayer did not guarantee that the counsellor would be rescued. Sometimes it enabled better empathy. Donna stated that prayer at these times of helplessness was as much for herself as for her client.

> Sometimes when a client's telling something that's traumatic, that's almost – knocks the wind out of me when I hear it – I find myself saying, you know, 'Be with me as well, when I'm hearing it', it's for me too. I'll say, 'God, help me, that I can hear something so dreadful', or I sometimes can be the opposite and say, 'Help her, or help him, speak the words' – I'm amazed that they can even say it. So it's in that sort of despairing, story-telling, the deepest part of the client's story that sometimes I find myself doing it. But not only for them, sometimes I think it's for me too. (Donna)

In doing so, she hoped for some form of protection or armour for herself to assist her in hearing the difficult material. For her client, she hoped that the client would gain greater ease in telling their story, and that the experience would not be too tortuous for either client or counsellor. At times when Donna prayed like that, she described feeling 'held' and feeling more able to cope with what she was being told. Donna stated that it helped prevent her from running out of the room – something that the client might expect to happen. Prayer did not take away the rawness of what was being shared, but enabled Donna to have a sense that she was not hearing the material on her own. That sense of 'another's presence' made it easier for her to hear and absorb what the client was saying, and to feel supported in what she was hearing. It also enabled her to stay within the client's frame of reference, and able to remain focused on the client whilst being surrounded by the 'mists of despair'. When challenged on whether the act of praying took her away from the client at times of helplessness, and might actually be a defence that could get in the way of fully experiencing the client's helplessness or difficulty, Donna likened it to the ability of a counsellor to reflect on the process internally and still be fully present with her client. Although she stated that she would like to pray covertly more during her sessions, she did acknowledge a fear of not being able to stay within the client's frame of reference. But she also acknowledged that the fear was more about her need to be cautious than about the reality of prayer interfering with the client's process. She reserved covert prayer for times when there was no sense of hope or for times when things were difficult to hear – times that she did not encounter very often in her work. Joanne often covertly sent prayers *to* her client during the session.

> …this unceasing quality of prayer, I'm not consciously aware of praying, but I know I am, even if I'm talking with you… I would say whenever I think about my work, or particular bits of my work, it's like I send good thoughts, and vibes, and prayers to that person, so it's a kind of a – there's a kind of like, I feel like clients who are, who I'm working with, are in some way united to my system, I suppose, in some way. (Joanne)

This gave Joanne a sense that she was being protective of her client and that she was an intermediary towards her client's reparation of their wounded self. Her hope was that such prayer helped her client to create something good within themselves. Hannah regarded prayer at times of helplessness as being a recognition of how limited she was. It was also a recognition of that which is beyond 'my own helplessness or the client's own helplessness'.

> If I get really frightened by the session…then that's sort of like what I think of as 'emergency prayers', sort of the idea of 'help', really, or you know. Then another kind is if we get into something really distressing for them, or very difficult, and in that kind of time, sometimes if they're crying or very distressed, that kind of thing, when I'm just sitting with them in that, then sometimes in my head I'll use tongues as a way of praying for them. (Hannah)

Prayer served as a reminder that very little of what happens in counselling is down to the counsellor. Instead, whatever happens is due to the client or to 'something else' (the process/God). Anne prayed for wisdom and insight into the client's process, and recognised that her prayer was partly a response to feeling helpless. Anne also prayed at times of 'stuckness' which enabled her to find a way of staying with, and experiencing, the stuckness rather than praying for a way of escaping it. Anne was also aware that through unconscious communication, a client may sense that the counsellor had 'broken off' and was having a 'chat' with God, so prayer had to be short, quick and cautiously done.

Rose (1993) identifies the two most frequently mentioned behaviours by counsellors who integrate prayer into their practice as 'pray when feeling anxious' and 'ask for help for self as counsellor'. Both of these behaviours are likely to occur at times of feeling helpless. The analysis of the data from my survey (Gubi 2004) demonstrates that 37 per cent of BACP Accredited Counsellors, and 65 per cent of CMCS Approved Counsellors, have prayed for guidance during a counselling session without their client's knowledge of what they are doing, whilst 25 per cent of BACP Accredited Counsellors, and 54 per cent of CMCS Approved Counsellors, have prayed for a client during a counselling session without the client's knowledge. Is this behaviour ethical? From what the counsellors are saying, prayer enables fuller attention, not less; and indicates a commitment to promoting the client's well-being (beneficence). This point is emphasised by Donna who likens it to the ability of the counsellor to reflect internally on what is going on, whilst still being fully present with the client. There is a sense of being able to stay more fully with difficulty when it is underpinned by a trust in something ultimate and purposeful through prayer. This is especially so at times of helplessness. Prayer can enable the counsellor to cope with the intensity of the helplessness, by helping her to remain grounded in hope even when things (or the client) feel hopeless. Prayer helps the maintenance of the 'as if' quality of empathy by preventing the counsellor from becoming overwhelmed by the despair and hopelessness that can sometimes prevail in counselling. Prayer also enables the counsellor to feel 'accompanied' in hearing difficult material. Some counsellors send prayer *to* their clients during the session in the hope that such prayer will support the client in creating something good and reparative within the client. Prayer contributes to the sense of 'being with' and 'connection' with the client, enabling a greater empathic communication. Rather than detract from the client, prayer used in this way promotes the client's well-being and enhances the quality of the service being provided.

Prayer as a spiritual discipline

Many of the counsellors began the day with prayer and other spiritual preparation (e.g. Bible reading). Ben stated that sometimes during this time, he would receive a strong call to pray for a particular client or situation. Gemma also started each day with prayer in which she brought the clients whom she was going to work with that day to God. Michael began the day by meeting with a group of people and praying the 'office' of the day. He found this act to be very supportive in his counselling work and, on occasion, he brought any client about whom he had concern to the liturgy of the office. Rebecca consciously went through her diary at the beginning of each day and prayed for each individual person she was going to be working with that day. She also had a time of prayer at the end of each day in which she 'cut herself free' from all the people she had worked with. Anne also began her day with a regular quiet time in prayer that usually lasted about an hour. She believed that she was called as a Christian to intercede on behalf of the world and this included her counselling work. Rowena spent an hour and a half 'with God' in prayer each morning. This included saying the morning office, interceding for world, national, local and family affairs. This was a time when she would remember her clients in prayer. In the evening, she would also spend 20 minutes in prayer, gathering up the day and giving it back to God, and after self-examination, asking for forgiveness for any areas of her life in which she felt that she had failed.

West (2000, 2002) and Canda (1990) argue that in order for counsellors to be open to their clients' spirituality, they need to acknowledge and develop their own spirituality. Gubi (2001), Sperry (2001) and Thorne (1994, 1998) demonstrate that spiritual practice, like prayer, is used to enable counsellors to cope with the demands of their work. Simon (1989) states that all counsellors should practise a programme of authentic spirituality if they choose to work with the spiritual dimension of counselling. This is a way of preventing burnout and maintaining balance in the counsellor's life (Shelly 1983). It is clear that many of the counsellors who integrate prayer into their mainstream counselling work have a regular spiritual discipline in which clients are brought to God and reflected on. This is a way of giving the work over to something greater and a useful forum for reflection, self-examination and development. Some counsellors use prayer in this way to focus on the demands of the day or to 'cut free' from the demands of the day. Such practice can be regarded as fostering self-respect in that it creates an opportunity for the development of self-care and self-knowledge.

Client prayer as support for the counsellor

Michael had experienced a client who disclosed that she prayed regularly for him (her counsellor). He felt that it was important to accept the act in its intention, and to acknowledge with humility that the counsellor has as much need of prayer as the client, without the session becoming focused on the needs of the counsellor.

> Sometimes she will say, 'I've been praying for you'. Now, that's quite a challenging thing to say to a psychodynamic counsellor, and I feel it's extremely important to accept the statement uncontroversially, not to resist it, say, 'Oh no, you're not allowed to do that', you know, 'I'm the one with the hotline to God round here', and it can take you into some very interesting experiences of reciprocity, in which there is the risk that the counsellor's personal agenda becomes much too much the topic of the conversation. That's undesirable, but the other side that is worth exploring is again, a sort of matter of empowerment, and of sharing, because if you're known as a counsellor who is part of a church, then it's, as it were, implicit in that you receive as well as give. You're caught up in that rhythm, and that you're, you know, entitled to your difficulties and weaknesses, just like everybody else is. (Michael)

There seems to be a fine line between the client caring for the counsellor, and the client taking responsibility for the counsellor. It is clear that Michael is aware of that boundary and is careful to monitor it. Although it seems to be unusual (in that only one participant talked about this phenomenon and there is nothing written about it in the literature), there is a sense of reciprocity and mutuality in this process. If the client chooses to pray for the counsellor, this could be an indication of a recognition of the counsellor's need and humanness which can make the counsellor seem to be more approachable and lead to greater equality in the therapeutic alliance. This is different from the counsellor asking the client to pray for him, which would be inappropriate and focus on the needs of the counsellor rather than those of the client. But a client who makes the choice to pray for his counsellor could be recognising the existence of others in the world if they have been blind to the needs of others. As such, prayer could be a sign of empowerment and growth. The client with faith may also feel that he has an investment in maintaining and sustaining the counsellor through intercessory prayer. This may be open to exploration and be indicative of underlying insecurity, or it could be accepted as being the gift that it is intended to be. It is for the counsellor to discern which side of the boundary the client's need lies. Lynch (1999, p.88) argues:

> If the essence of what is therapeutic about counselling is a human encounter in which the counsellor offers acceptance and engages empathically with the client, then an over-scrupulous preoccupation with boundaries could arguably be seen as detracting from these human qualities.

Maybe sometimes just accepting what is given, with the spirit in which it is given, is enough. Thorne (2002) argues that not to accept the client's love, however flawed, may be to send a judgemental message that condemns them 'to continuing alienation and to a sense of their unworthiness to be a part of the human family' (p.17). Refusing a client's prayer for the counsellor that is given out of love and concern may also send the same message.

Summary

This chapter has demonstrated how prayer influences counselling at a philosophical and a covert level. Although the practice of prayer at this level does not directly influence the counsellor/client dynamic, but acts as a support for the counsellor, there are ethical implications to consider. Prayer is used to sustain the work of some counsellors through regular spiritual discipline, preventing burnout and aiding reflection. Prayer is used as a way of attunement and centring in preparation for work with clients. Prayer is used as a way of assisting the counsellor to stay in the moment, especially at times of anxiety, helplessness and hopelessness. Prayer is used to place the work 'in trust' between sessions, enabling the work and the client to feel upheld by something greater. Prayer is used in intercession on the client's behalf. Prayer is a way of sustaining the counsellor through intercession. These practices largely have the interest of the client at heart and are mostly ethical, although an awareness of the centrality of the client's autonomy, and the boundary between the counsellor's needs and the client's needs, have to be continually reflected on and kept in focus in order to maintain ethical practice. So what of the more contentious practice of integrating prayer overtly in practice?

CHAPTER 6

How Prayer Is Integrated in Counselling

The content of previous chapters seems to suggest that using prayer explicitly with clients is fraught with ethical complexity. Many counsellors even consider it wrong to introduce prayer into counselling (Gubi 2004; Rose 2002; Sperry 2001). Yet prayer is clearly part of the work of some practitioners. It is therefore important to discover how counsellors who use overt prayer in their work integrate it into their therapeutic practice and how they justify its use ethically. This chapter enables their voices to be heard.

Client referral

Many of the counsellors who were interviewed (Gubi 2003b) stated that many clients chose a particular counsellor, or were referred to a particular counsellor, because the counsellor was known to be a Christian who is a counsellor. This was so for 13 of the 19 counsellors. The assumption in such referrals is that there will be common ground between counsellor and client and that the counsellor will be more respecting, understanding and enabling of the client's values and beliefs. The client may also feel more understood and 'safer' with a counsellor who is a Christian. Some of the counsellors had worked, or currently work, in contexts where clients would expect them to be a Christian, e.g. one counsellor worked in a GP practice and a Christian counselling agency where all the staff were known to be Christian, one counsellor worked as a prison chaplain, one counsellor was involved in a diocesan counselling service, several of the counsellors worked with clients referred by the Churches Ministerial Counselling Service (CMCS), and one counsellor worked at a Christian institute for counselling. All of the counsellors worked with non-Christian clients in secular or Christian settings.

Three of the counsellors worked with the transpersonal and/or with the psychosynthesis approach. Their clients knew before they came that working with the 'spiritual' dimension was an important aspect of these counsellors' work. Many of the counsellors expressed an awareness of the assumptions that clients might carry about them. Some accepted them and worked with them, but others expressed a discomfort about them. In spite of these assumptions, most of the counsellors stated that they prayed very rarely with clients (Christian or otherwise). One counsellor, Ben, stated that he had probably prayed with only 2 per cent of his clients over 20 years. Another counsellor, Amanda, recalled using prayer only with nine clients out of more than 240 clients in nine years of practice. None of the other counsellors was able to quantify their experience in this way, but all counsellors stated that they rarely used overt prayer with clients. Most of the counsellors did not reveal their faith to their clients unless the client asked, or unless it felt appropriate to self-disclose to increase the sense of empathic connectedness and understanding. One exception to that was Rebecca who informed all her clients that she was a Christian. Many of the counsellors commented on how some clients 'just knew' that they were spiritual or Christian. Rachel described this 'just knowing' as some form of unconscious communication.

> Some people come as Christians, and they know that I am, and then that's all open. But a lot of people aren't, and it's not something I talk about, but it's amazing how often we get on to the spiritual, or their idea of God, or – I mean, it's not amazing really. But what I mean is, I think people with the idea of the unconscious communication that goes on between people, that's why I don't think it's necessary for me to introduce these things because people know anyway, on some level, a lot of the time, that there is something spiritual going on, and that there's a door open, and they can explore that if they want to. (Rachel)

Others worked in environments where there was evidence of their belief system, e.g. Michael stated that there was a crucifix and an icon in the room in which he worked, so his belief system was unspoken but on display.

> By no means everyone I work with is a Christian, but they all know I am, and I never, ever raise it – it's just, as it were, part of me. (Michael)

Others (e.g. Anne) deliberately removed any signs, such as wearing a crucifix around her neck, in case it acted as a barrier to the expression of emotion, such as foul language or anger.

Choosing a counsellor is a problematic experience for many clients. It is especially so for clients who want to explore 'spiritual issues' in counselling (West 2000, 2002). It is not surprising that a client may want to choose a counsellor whom they perceive as sharing similar values to their own. Counselling is not a value-free environment (Lyall 1995; Lynch 2002). The extent to which these values are made explicit (either through unconscious communication, the signs and symbols that are on display in the counselling room, or through candid verbal revelation), especially in the context of a counsellor who has a religious faith, is personal and can be influenced by the level of authenticity that the counsellor's approach demands of her. Whilst it may be personal, Davies and Ackroyd (2002, p.225) argue that a client may spend a lot of time trying to ascertain the counsellor's real frame of reference, and look for signals of genuineness or of incongruence, and so it is important for a counsellor to be open to a discussion about their identity. Whilst the context of Davies and Ackroyd's argument is about the disclosure of sexual identity, their argument is also relevant to the context of disclosing spiritual identity. Davies (1998) argues that even before the client has arrived at the consulting room, many will have already 'checked out' the counsellor to discover their reputation and their counselling orientation, to ensure their safety, and in preparation for them to be in psychological contact with the counsellor. Explicit affirmation of spiritual values in 'pre-contact' information (Davies and Ackroyd 2002) may assist in developing a greater readiness in establishing psychological contact and lead to a deeper relatedness with some clients, where the sacredness of cherished beliefs will feel respected and understood, and where the client will not feel threatened by therapeutic activity that may feel contrary to her beliefs and values (Gubi 1995), or the explicit affirmation of values may inappropriately influence the counselling agenda, and lead to unhelpful transference phenomena (Hinksman 1999). This dilemma is evident in what the counsellors share but, in spite of the assumptions that clients may have about those counsellors who make their faith explicit, prayer is still not often used in the counselling relationship. Even though the client may be aware of the counsellor's faith, and of her willingness to bring that faith into the counselling relationship through the discretionary use of prayer, the minimal use of prayer indicates that the autonomy of the client is respected.

Contracting

Lorna stated that in the introductory session she checks out what her client's coping mechanisms are. In so doing, she is looking to gain a sense of the whole person, including the spiritual. One of the coping mechanisms utilised by those who have a spiritual dimension to their lives might be prayer. Although not consciously seeking to ascertain if a client uses prayer in the initial assessment, Lorna might ask a client, 'How are you about prayer?' if she intuitively felt that it was something that might be useful or acceptable to the client. If the client does not want it, then she does not pray with her client. 'I would be sensitive to the fact that I wouldn't pray or even suggest it with the majority of my clients.' Rebecca stated that she always informed all her clients that she was a Christian.

> There are people who've come to me who have no idea that I'm a practising Christian... I will always say, 'One of the things you need to know about me is that I am a practising Christian. Apart from telling you, I will not be bringing my faith overtly into the room and attempting to convert you, or something, but you may decide that you don't want to work with me', and I always ask the people I work with, be they supervisees or clients, whether they have a religion or a faith. (Rebecca)

With 'practising Christian' clients, Rebecca has an agreed contract to pray in the session – usually at the beginning of the session. She felt that it was important to ask about her clients' belief systems at the contracting stage because she was clear about the fact that she could not work with clients who were practising Muslims, practising Jehovah Witnesses, those who were involved in spiritualism or the occult, or making a decision about abortion. Rebecca did not feel that she was prejudiced, judgemental or discriminatory, but that she was being honest with herself and with her client.

> I don't have the conflict about it, and I think it's a load of nonsense in the counselling world to say that, if there is something that a person owns, that we actually push it aside, and then work with what's underneath, because of being human beings. That bit will always be there. I think what

I am doing, for me, is being honest about saying, 'This is not about the person of you, but because of what would come with you, in this particular area, I would not be doing you a service, and I'm not prepared to offer you a service'... Because, you know, always there would be a bit like the person who would want to come and say, talk about having an abortion – I would always be wanting to do something else with that... I don't feel like I'm discriminating. I feel like I'm being open and honest and clear, and making decisions, because I really think many clients are done a disservice to by people appearing as if anything they say or do is acceptable, and reality is, it's not. And I think, you know, having been a client, I know that from when I've sat in the client's seat. (Rebecca)

Rebecca recognised that her views might preclude her from getting a job as a counsellor because she would have to be clear to any employer that there were certain clients whom she could not work with, but her belief system was a priority in all aspects of her life, including her counselling work. She did work with people of no faith, or of non-practising faith (expressed more as a cultural allegiance rather than as a conscious influence). She did not bring her faith overtly into the sessions with them, except to inform them about herself at the contracting stage.

Emma did not initiate prayer, but only prayed if and when clients asked for it as part of her philosophy that counselling is a creative space. She did not feel able to introduce it into the contract because she was cautious about influencing the agenda.

...if I say it is OK to talk about spiritual things here, then I could be accused of introducing something into the client's agenda that they may not have considered, or wanted to bring, and if I withhold from including it in the contract, there may be a message here saying that it's not OK to talk about these things. (Emma)

By stating that counselling was a creative space, her assumption was that clients might feel able to bring anything to that space, but she acknowledged that clients rarely brought issues of spirituality and prayer to her. In her contracting, she asks the client to identify the areas that he wants to look at. If that identifies areas of spirituality, or taps into the fact that she is a counsellor who is a Christian, then Emma feels more able to work holistically with the client. Vivienne expressed that if a client informs her right at the beginning of the counselling relationship that he is a

Christian, she always asks sensitively if he would like to use prayer in the sessions. Some clients have said 'yes', and some have said 'no'.

The British Association for Counselling and Psychotherapy (BACP) Ethical Framework for Good Practice (2002) requires counsellors to provide clients with adequate information about the terms of the services that they offer. It also requires counsellors to minimise conflicts of interest in order to protect the interests of the client and maintain the trust in the practitioner (p.9). If a counsellor is able to offer prayer in her work, it could be argued that under the pretext of providing adequate information about the terms of the service, she could make her client aware of her use of prayer. To fail to make her client aware of this information might be unethical if she later used prayer in the therapeutic relationship. However, it is unclear what constitutes 'adequate information'. It would seem unreasonable to expect a counsellor to list every intervention that is available for her use, so why should the use of prayer be seen as different from any other intervention and be singled out for explicit mention? Prayer can be a contentious intervention, but it is no more dangerous or abusive than other interventions that are commonly used in counselling as long as it is used with the same sensitivity, reflexiveness and care that is expected of all intervention in good ethical practice (Gubi 2001, 2002), at the 'right moment' (i.e. one determined by a sensitive awareness of the client's needs and an intuitive sensing of the situation in which prayer might be therapeutically helpful), and with the 'right' client (i.e. one who is open to prayer, and who is able to step back from the act of praying and explore their process) (Gubi 2002). Working with 'the right client' at the 'right moment' requires prior knowledge of the client which can be gained from the information that is disclosed by the client.

The literature argues that it is better to contract with the client overtly to use prayer when appropriate, after carrying out an 'assessment' of the client's spiritual beliefs. West (1998) argues that counselling is an implicitly spiritual space in which clients can be spiritually present, and that it is important to communicate a clear acceptance of spirituality in order for clients to overcome the taboo of bringing spiritual issues to counselling. This can most appropriately be done at the contracting stage. Richards and Bergin (1997) state that therapists should carry out a religious–spiritual assessment of their clients to enable them to have a better sense of their client's world, to assess how 'healthy' the client's religious–spiritual orientation is and how it impacts on the presenting problems, to determine whether the client's spiritual beliefs can be a source for healing, to determine if any spiritual interventions (like prayer) can be helpful, and to ascertain if the client has any unresolved spiritual doubts that need to be addressed in their therapy. Magaletta and Brawer (1998) also strongly recommend conducting a formal assessment that includes knowledge of the client's spiritual beliefs, globally, and of their prayer beliefs and practice. They recommend asking questions like, 'Have you ever used religion/prayer to cope with your life's problems? Do you have any religious practices that seem to influence your problem?' The depth of the enquiry can range from asking the client's 'feeling state' preceding, during and subsequent to prayer, seeking information about what it means to the client if a prayer is not answered, and how their current prayer beliefs and practices have developed (Magaletta and Brawer 1998, p.326).

It is evident that some counsellors (e.g. Lorna) tentatively attempt to discover their clients' coping mechanisms at the contracting stage and to introduce the notion of praying in the counselling space if prayer is one of the ways the client copes. Other counsellors (e.g. Emma) prefer to leave the use of prayer within the context of regarding the counselling environment as a 'creative space' where the client is free to express herself in any way that she wishes (including prayer), which is akin to West's 'spiritual space' in which the client is free to explore spiritual issues when they arise. That way a client does not feel 'obliged' to pray or to explore spiritual matters because it has been explicitly raised during the contracting. Some counsellors (e.g. Rebecca and Vivienne) prefer to be more expressive of their Christian faith, whether or not their client is a Christian. In so doing, they are able to give their clients a choice of continuing to work with them, whilst knowing that, or of leaving. This enables the counsellor to make some choices about the viability of the work that she is able to do with the client, along with her client making a similar choice about his counsellor. This minimises a possible conflict within the counsellor's sense of integrity and ensures that she is true to herself, and thus to her client. The recurring theme that is evident is that each counsellor is required to make choices that are not detrimental to her integrity – an integrity that is formulated by values and beliefs (counselling or otherwise). However, in contexts where choice may be limited by practical matters (e.g. in a small primary care practice where there may be only one counsellor and where the client cannot financially afford to go to another counsellor but is in desperate need of support) such choice may not always be possible so the counsellor's integrity may have to be compromised.

Using prayer non-contractually

Most of the counsellors did not include the use of prayer in their contracts with clients. Fran listened out during the sessions for certain criteria that would indicate to her that prayer might be acceptable to her client. She defined the criteria as:

> What they've said and told me, the fact that they are a Christian – someone who believes and lives by the Bible (or tries to) and is a regular church-goer. (Fran)

However, Fran acknowledged that this criterion involved making certain assumptions about her client that might not be accurate, and that potentially precluded others because of the narrow definition she used of what it means to be 'Christian'. Indeed, Rosie stated that, in her experience, very few Christians with whom she had worked wanted to pray. 'I've worked with a lot of clergy ministers of various denominations, and very few have wanted to do it.' Joyce also did not specifically contract the use of prayer with clients. She just worked with the clients' needs as they arose. If the client wanted to pray then she would integrate prayer into the work.

> He said to me one day, would I pray with him to die, and so at the end of the session we would just sit and pray together for him to die... (Joyce)

The ability to pray in this way, although difficult for the counsellor, was part of her empathic communication, and acceptance of her client, which gave her client comfort. Rosie also only prayed at the client's request. Prayer was not built into the contract. Rosie related one experience where the client had 'sussed out' her religious connection and had asked Rosie to pray with her.

> I was quite touched, really, that she would open up another aspect of our relating to that, so I was, I suppose you could say I was a bit seduced by it, but I, you know, therapeutically, but I was quite touched by the idea and was very happy to do that together. (Rosie)

From this quotation it is possible to gain a flavour of the internal conflict within the counsellor, between being instinctively happy with the request to pray (with its sense of seduction for the counsellor), which is marginally held back by a sense of reservation in questioning whether it was therapeutically 'right' to be seduced, and to pray. Within the context and moment of that particular relationship, Rosie felt that it was acceptable to pray with the client, but she stated that she would not pray with every client who requested prayer.

> It would be so much in the context of that relationship... With this Salvation Army person, I felt very safe and very confident that what they were wanting to say would be something I could go along with. I suppose there could be a situation in which I might not feel comfortable, but that hasn't arisen... I suppose there could be a situation in which I might be asked to do something that I wouldn't be comfortable with – I mean, I don't know what that would be, but I suppose there could be, but it hasn't happened. (Rosie)

Ben also did not contract to use prayer with clients, but simply used prayer when he felt 'inspired' to do so, although he very rarely felt inspired to use prayer overtly in his counselling work.

> Sometimes it just seems appropriate with someone to say, 'Can we just stop and pray about this area, or pray for direction here for you', or at the end of the session I'd say something like, 'I just feel it's appropriate to end in prayer – is that OK?', and usually I've picked up that that's fine – I mean no-one's ever said no, and they've always looked comfortable with that, so sometimes it just seems right, before we finish. (Ben)

None of his clients had ever refused his prayer. When challenged on whether his clients would feel able, or feel sufficiently empowered in the relationship to refuse, his reply was: 'I'd not thought of that before'. Ben stated that the times he had stopped in the session to pray were 'Holy Spirit directed'.

> I would say it tends to be again, Holy Spirit directed in terms of, it's as if that's my instruction at that point in time, and the client never looks uncomfortable about it, or feels uncomfortable about it, because the Holy Spirit's in charge, and a decision's been made, like this has got to happen now, so I do it in obedience, really. That's the way, I suppose. Yes, it's not something I would contrive. It's not something I would prepare for beforehand, far from it... I am being directed at that point, so it's not a personal decision of mine, or a particular reason, as such – it just seems to

be the right thing to do, and it always is, which gives me confirmation that it is from the Holy Spirit, from God. (Ben)

The language that Ben is using here to make sense of the process raises concerns about whether he is abnegating his responsibilities as a counsellor through reliance on being directed by something outside of himself. Indeed, it almost feels as if Ben is allowing another agenda to take precedence over the client's agenda. However, further exploration indicated that Ben was doing nothing more than all inspired counsellors do. He was responding in a very intuitive way to his client, by having a sense of where they were, and having a feel for what was right for them. The difference was in his belief about where that intuitive sense came from, and how he made sense of that. He believed that he operated in obedience to the Holy Spirit. Another counsellor might have described the process of intervention as a response to their client from their congruent or intuitive self, in the context of the moment. For Ben, praying in this way is a response to spiritual congruence. Ben stated that he had a sense of the spiritual level of the client, and he found that he only prayed with clients who were at a certain spiritual level.

> One gets a sense of where they are spiritually, a sort of continuum, I suppose, and anyone who's sort of – I mean I had that sort of discernment, I guess, and I think anyone who's sort of 7 or less wouldn't get prayed for in a session. So it's those in the sort of, 8, 9 and 10 that it's more likely to happen, and we're more likely to have discussions on a spiritual plane, as part of their overall counselling package. (Ben)

Although Ben gave a lot of the responsibility over to the direction of the Holy Spirit, he did acknowledge that he had some sense of whether the client was 'right' to pray with.

> …if there's any spirituality there at all, and I think it just seems to be the way it would flow; I would get a sort of – maybe the sort of warning signs would be up, that maybe this is an appropriate person, so I'd be sensitive to the guiding of the Holy Spirit to pray with a particular person during that session, and so it would be a sort of, if you like, an unfolding of steps, but it may or may not come to anything, so I would just know if and when it's appropriate. (Ben)

When pressed on what might prevent the use of prayer in the session, Ben responded:

> Thinking of some examples, perhaps, have got in the way – yes, someone who says that they used to pray, but they feel that they've done something or whatever, or they feel that their relationship with God has become distant and it's very hard to pray now, and that he's sort of 'over there' instead of here – that would get in the way. Obviously outright disbelief would get in the way. Anything where someone is sort of, wanting to get very close, restore that relationship, or move to a closer relationship, that would be the other side of the coin. I guess, that would be the signal that maybe that's an opportunity that's about to crop up. (Ben)

Although Ben strongly believed that the process was 'Holy-Spirit directed', he did acknowledge that there were certain indicators that increased the likelihood of prayer being used in the session. These he identified as: someone wanting to restore their relationship with God or gain a closer relationship with God. Indicators that prevented the use of prayer were: someone who had no relationship with, or belief in, God, someone whose relationship with God was strained in some way, or someone who would find prayer difficult. Ben did recognise that his process of discernment could be broken down into unconscious levels of awareness in bringing the use of prayer into the session, and that it was not just when he felt inspired to. Nevertheless he still felt that ultimately it relied on a 'signal' from the Holy Spirit to go ahead.

> I guess when it happens, you just know that it's right to happen. I suppose it's a bit like thinking of a church service, or perhaps an open Christian meeting, where the minister or the person who's leading the particular part of the service says, 'If God's speaking to you here, in this point, I'd like you to declare it, or say it', and sometimes you get a sort of a definite shout, 'Speak it out', and you go in obedience. It's a bit like that, I think, so the decision not to would be, 'No, I'm not getting that signal to do that', rather than, 'I'm hearing that strong message and no I daren't stand up and say it!', which would be a human thing. That's probably the best way to describe it, for me, anyway. (Ben)

For Ben to go against what he describes as 'obedience to the Holy Spirit' would be incongruent to his sense of self. For him, prayer has to be part of his 'in-tuneness' with the client, has to feel 'absolutely right', and 'happens naturally' as a result of that in-tuneness. It is not liberally applied, and indeed he was critical of those who prayed routinely with clients. Such prayer, he argued, was incongruent and unethical. Joanne described similar processes to Ben. However Joanne, who used more creative approaches such as gestalt and psychodrama in her work, talked of:

> ...trusting the flashes, it's trusting the insights, so when I'm working with someone, I'm fully present with them. (Joanne)

Like Ben, Joanne sometimes felt moved to introduce prayer into the work, but she felt it came more from a sense of intuitive attunement with the client than from some spiritual force. Joanne always made sure that it would feel appropriate to pray with the client, as she would with any other intervention. Joanne had experience of clients being able to say 'no' to her. Joanne also stated that she had felt moved to bring prayer into the work on a number of occasions, but that an appropriate opportunity had not arisen, so she had withheld it.

> I think when I hear something coming, I hold it, and if there seems an opportunity to say anything, I will, but no, I just feel excited sometimes. I just feel God. (Joanne)

This sense of intuitive 'rightness' also informed Hannah about when to use prayer. Hannah felt that if prayer was a part of the client's world (culture) and concepts like 'God' and 'prayer' were a 'currency' that made sense to the client, then she would use it if it felt like the 'right' thing to do. Gemma also did not contract the use of prayer with clients, but always asked the client before she prayed with him/her. Gemma stated that she never refused her clients prayer if they asked for it. She always encouraged her clients to do the praying if they asked her to pray, as part of taking responsibility for themselves, but if they found it difficult, she would not withhold prayer from them.

> I'm trying to get them to take responsibility in all the aspects of whatever we're counselling, I would ask them to do it for them, too. But as it usually comes at the end of the session, I don't want to refuse the prayer, either. So if they find that too difficult to do, which they do sometimes, then I will pray. (Gemma)

Amanda felt that there were times when prayer should be withheld even if the client wanted to pray. She gave three reasons and examples of times when prayer felt inappropriate for her, and where she withheld its use. First, Amanda felt that prayer could inhibit the expression of anger:

> I think it can put things within a very Churchy, Christian, sort of context, and, where you're very nice, and you don't swear, and you don't get angry, this sort of thing… I mean, this was a client who did get very angry sometimes, and ended up throwing a book across the room. I doubt whether she'd have felt free to do that if we'd sort of, brought God in at the beginning. I'm not saying God isn't here, but brought in… (Amanda)

Second, Amanda felt that prayer could be used by a client to control the counsellor:

> He was a very, very powerful man, and he came in, and he was going to start the session with prayer, and so on – a very, very controlling man – and it was a fight with him not to pray, because there was a different sort of setting altogether, and he wanted to keep the counselling with his own, within his own Christian parameters. He would say, it was all very black and white with him, you know, and he was talking about his brother – a lot of the work was about his brother – and he'd say things like, 'There comes a time when I have to tell him that I'm right and he's wrong', and I found it very difficult working with him, really, and to avoid praying, which I did… The need to avoid prayer was a number of things, then – it was, I felt that he was using it to control the session, and to control me; it was also to keep it within the right levels, so as it didn't stray outside his particular view of Christianity, which was fairly narrow. Well, I perceived it as fairly narrow, so yes, that was a different one, really, it was fighting it and not using it. But I did use it, at the end. (Amanda)

Third, Amanda felt that sometimes it was important to challenge sensitively a client's expectations of counselling, or their avoidance of facing up to the issues that they needed to confront. One of the ways of challenging a client who seeks solace continually in prayer is to withhold prayer in the session:

> I have a lady who worked for a local Christian organisation, and I felt that, well, this particular organisation I see as fairly structured, and I want to say biblical, but I don't want to give the wrong impression – but everything seems to be referred to verses of scripture, and I experienced this lady as quite narrow, and so I avoided – I think she would have expected me to use prayer. She came actually via a GP referral, but that

was her setting, and this was about a divorce, and difficult relationships within the family subsequent to the divorce, with her children, and the only time I used prayer was in the final session, just to commit the work we'd done to God, which I didn't feel, particularly, was complete, but that was the end of the eight sessions that were being paid for, you know, by the surgery, so – and she didn't feel she could afford any more, so I just committed that to God, and asked that the healing would be ongoing... She didn't openly say, 'I want to pray about this', or 'I want to pray in the session', and I didn't offer her the opportunity because I wanted her to experience a different sort of counselling from what she would have been, you know, she would have been used to, or she was seeing in the organisation for which she worked. I wanted it to be broader... (Amanda)

Although arguably influenced by the counsellor's agenda, Amanda felt that she was being trusting of her intuitive 'hunches' in relation to this client, by enabling her to have a different experience from that which she was used to, or expected. In discerning whether prayer was appropriate to use with a client, Amanda stated that she looked for clues as to how 'acceptable' prayer might be to the client. This did not mean that they had to have a specifically Christian belief system, but the client needed to be looking for some sense of meaning in their life and have a sense of another dimension to life (the spiritual).

I think one point would be how well I felt – how much engagement there was between myself and the client. I think it would need to be fairly firmly established, but I would see that it could be firmly established after a few sessions rather than a long time – it just depends on the clients. So that's one part, and I think I would have picked up clues probably, maybe over a period of sessions, about the sort of client this is, and if it's likely to be acceptable... It would have to be a client who had some sense that there might be a God out there somewhere, otherwise to whom would we be praying? It would be just some sort of psychological trick, even... Sometimes I'd pick it up from the client's sort of, philosophy of life, really – 'There must be some meaning to this' – I'm trying to think of other things clients say – or maybe in a questioning. You know, 'What is the point of life?', or 'What is it all about?' – that type of thing, and we'd perhaps explore that, but I think I'd pick up a sense if there was definite hostility, where it wouldn't be appropriate... I'd introduce it. But by the time I'd got to that, I would know a lot about the client, I think, because working from a psychodynamic perspective, I would start with a history, and with early life, and have picked up quite a lot about what life was like at home, you know, that would have been told to me, so all those things would help me to decide…a higher power, or whatever, another dimension. (Amanda)

Amanda also felt that close attention needed to be paid to the language of the client. Using the word 'prayer' might not always be appropriate and could actually be off-putting with some clients.

Well, I think with the lady that had lost all the children – 'Is there a way in which you would like to offer these children back to God, or release them to God?' It was a letting-go of these things which were hurting her so much after all these years. I suppose the word 'prayer' was implicit, but it wasn't explicit… I think the word prayer, actually, could be off-putting, couldn't it, with some clients… I think it could be off-putting because their only experience of prayer may be what they've had at school assemblies, or they don't understand it, or it might be frightening, because it's unknown. Or it may be very child-like – there may have been children's prayers and then nothing, so maybe prayer belongs to that part of their life but not to the whole. (Amanda)

During the interview, Amanda realised that when she prayed with clients, she closed her eyes. Having thought about it, she felt that it might be better to keep her eyes open to observe what was happening for the client during the prayer. By closing her eyes, she felt that she entered her own frame of reference rather than 'being with' the client in their frame of reference. The sense of 'being with' (empathy) was 'closed out'.

Donna also did not contract with clients to use prayer, but she 'felt her way with it because it often doesn't happen'. Donna only prayed with a minority of her clients and she very often did not pray with Christian clients even if the spiritual dimension of the client was explored and the client talked a lot about her relationship with God.

I wouldn't put it in my contract. I wouldn't say. I would just leave it to the client. If the client wants to bring it up, then I'd be very open… (Donna)

Donna stated that if God is openly talked about in the session, then there often wasn't a need to 'tag him on at the end' through prayer. She cited an occasion when she was working with a client who was exploring her relationship with God and her relationship with her husband. Donna decided not to introduce prayer into the session because to do so would have felt like 'we have to ask God's permission to feel angry and do all the things that most people would do after being treated so badly'. Donna acknowledged that her agenda had determined whether prayer should be used in this case, even though all the signs were that prayer would be quite acceptable to this client.

> This client didn't ask for it, but told me it was OK, but we somehow still didn't do it. (Donna)

Michael stated that he would not introduce the concept of 'prayer' into the relationship, in the sense that he would not use the word 'prayer' with clients because that might lead to an intellectualisation of what could otherwise be simply and powerfully experienced.

> I don't like the idea of…modelling a God who has to, sort of, muscle in on the act, and say, you know, 'What about me?' – a sort of jealous, insecure God. Not at all an attractive thought to me. So I probably wouldn't bother to use the word prayer, or specify it in that way. I'd just get on and do it… That's true of the way I try and do counselling or therapy – it's with less sort of, interpretation, which sort of intellectualises the thing, and puts it 'out there', and makes a little God of it… It's about having the theory sort of drop away, or not drop away – having it internalised, so you think, OK, so what's going on here? Right, let's do it, let's do something about it. Let's live it together. So I think it's probably true of my approach to the whole enterprise, really. (Michael)

Rachel related an experience that she had had when a client had been referred to her by a local church. Due to the client's nervousness and reluctance to engage with the session, the client asked if he could pray. Rather than stay with his anxiety, Rachel colluded in the hope that the client would feel safer – something she later regretted.

> I felt that it was because he really was very anxious about getting into the therapeutic side of things, and I think that he hoped in some way it would make it safer…that I would somehow be less powerful because we'd done this. It was like an equalising thing. And in fact, he found therapy extremely difficult – we did some work, but in the end I think it got too close, and he wanted to stop, and then, in the last session, when he wanted to stop, he wanted to pray again, and instead of just letting him do it, I joined in and I felt it was – I shouldn't have done it – one, because it was

terminating prematurely and there were things that were unresolved, and things unresolved in our relationship; and two, because I wasn't really sure what was going on, so I felt that was another thing; and three, that I somehow put – I did what he wanted, somehow – he wanted something of me there to make it more on an equal footing, and I felt that I'd yielded to that temptation, and, because he was ending prematurely, and it was better to leave it as an unsatisfactory, premature ending than to try and turn it into something else by praying. (Rachel)

Rachel felt that by praying at the beginning of the session (for the most loving of intentions), she was controlled by the client. He got something of her. Prayer was also then used to 'sanctify' an inappropriate ending that was difficult not to collude with because of the fact that it had been turned into 'something else' by prayer. Because of this experience, Rachel was reluctant to use prayer overtly with clients if she had to do the praying. However, Rachel felt that prayer could be used if a person wanted to express something in the counselling session that they felt they could not do in any other way.

If somebody wants to pray, then to let them, because that's something they want to express which perhaps they can't do in another way. You know, like people bring poems or pictures, that's fine. But for me to join in that way, I don't think is appropriate, because it's like bringing something in like your family concerns, or your experiences, and I think that helped me to see that, in future, I wouldn't bring myself in that way. (Rachel)

Amanda stated that quite a few Christian clients would assume that she would use prayer with them in her work. However, she did not see why she had to use it at all. Like any other intervention, she waited to see if its use was appropriate to the moment and the context of the session. Amanda also stated that she had used prayer with non-Christian clients as part of a creative ritual to aid 'completion', and many had found it helpful. However, she offered it in a way that the client could easily refuse, and prayer was not imposed on the client.

Anne was happy to pray with clients but felt that it had to be used cautiously. She preferred to leave prayer until the end of a session, even when clients asked her to pray in the session.

I have to say I don't do it unless they actually ask, but I have had Christian clients who have said to me 'Could you pray with me about this?', and I'm quite happy to do that, but I do think, actually, that it's something one has to be a bit careful with, because I have also had people who, as soon as it's got uncomfortable, 'Let's pray', and I think 'Well, no, we've actually got to stay with this discomfort', so I will do it, but I think it's got, you know, I might say 'Well, OK, yes, but let's leave it till the end', or you know, something like that, rather than actually use it as a kind of covering at the end, or a summing up at the end. (Anne)

Anne felt that it might set a precedent to pray in the session and then find it difficult to say 'no' if a client said that they wanted to pray 'now'. Anne also thought that it was important for the client to do some of the praying as a way of maintaining mutuality in the relationship.

Koenig and Pritchett (1998), Magaletta and Brawer (1998), Richards and Bergin (1997), Sperry (2001) and West (2000) refer to the importance of a formal assessment strategy for assessing clients' spirituality before deciding whether it is appropriate to include prayer in the therapeutic work. However, the experience of these counsellors indicates that the decision to integrate prayer is reliant on a less cognitive process. It is informed by the quality of attunement and connection between the client and counsellor. This 'intuitive' dimension is a major factor in determining how and if prayer should be introduced into the counselling relationship, even if prayer has not been included in the contract. This intuitive process is brought about through having a great relational sense of the client, and from having knowledge of how appropriate the introduction of prayer might be in respect of the client's spiritual beliefs and values. Even those counsellors who attribute this discernment to external sources, such as the 'Holy Spirit' (e.g. Ben), are able to recognise their responsibility in, and unconscious levels of awareness that inform, the decision to include prayer. For prayer to be 'right', it has to have a quality of 'naturalness' about it, if it is not to become incongruent and mechanistic. It must also be part of the client's culture, although one counsellor used prayer with non-Christians if the client believed in something beyond 'self'. It seems important in fostering the client's autonomy that prayer has an equal quality of naturalness for the client and for the counsellor, and that the client is able to give informed consent, and to refuse. So the notion of prayer is introduced with the quality of tentatively 'feeling your way' that emerges out of a sense of respect for the client. It also has to feel relevant (natural) to the context and 'moment' of what is being shared, and not interrupt the agenda and take the client away from experiencing the felt sense of the moment. Magaletta and Brawer (1998) stress the need for written consent forms, but interrupting the therapeutic process to sign consent forms seems to detract from the naturalness and attunement to the 'moment' that is stressed by the participants of this research, and prayer becomes something 'different' that needs special consent.

Some counsellors (e.g. Gemma) always prayed when the client requested it, but others (e.g. Amanda, Rachel and Donna) recognised that prayer could be used by some clients to manipulate the counsellor and to avoid facing up to difficult issues. This awareness is elaborated on by Webster (1992). In such cases, when their intuitive 'hunch' informed the counsellor that it may not be appropriate to comply with the request to pray, some counsellors felt able to challenge or withhold prayer (e.g. Amanda). Although this may be regarded as not respecting the client's autonomy, it is acting on the principle of beneficence as it is acting ultimately in the interests of the client based on the counsellor's professional assessment of the situation through systematic reflection and experience that informs the 'intuitive hunch'. This 'intuitive hunch' and sense of the client may even preclude the use of the word 'prayer' (e.g. Michael and Amanda) if it was felt to lead to intellectualisation or debate about language, rather than staying with the power and the simplicity of experiencing the 'felt' sense of prayer in the moment. There are many practical difficulties in praying: do both counsellor and client pray to maintain mutuality (Anne)? Is it acceptable to pray with clients of no faith (Amanda)? Is it acceptable to collude with prayer early in the relationship for the purposes of enhancing the therapeutic relationship (Rachel) in the short-term? Is it acceptable for the counsellor to be seduced by prayer (Rosie) if it is something that they themselves find useful? Should the counsellor pray with her eyes closed or open?

Boundaries and self-disclosure

In discussing the appropriateness of self-disclosure around issues of spirituality and prayer Emma recognised that the expectation of the counselling profession was that certain aspects of the counsellor's sense of self are brought to the therapeutic relationships, and certain aspects are deemed inappropriate to bring to the client. In working with this Emma stated:

> I subsume my spirituality into a more acceptable package, in terms of working with integrity, working ethically, working with care, and I try and integrate it that way, and resolve the gap. (Emma)

She felt that not all of her was 'out to tender' and was intrigued by people who came to her because she was a Christian. 'What does that label mean to them?' She acknowledged that to some clients sharing with them that she was a Christian might be facilitative, whilst to others it might be prohibitive in the sharing of some issues.

> I mean those are the whole issues around self-disclosure, and when do you use those therapeutically? When are they appropriate to give a bit of that and use it therapeutically, with some immediacy, as opposed to not? You need to balance that. But it's valid knowledge, in that each relationship with a client is very different, and very unique, but I think it has to be – I have to be, sort of, true to myself but I'm there for the client, not for me, so I don't enter into that, with me as my uppermost agenda, in that sense. (Emma)

Rosie felt uncomfortable about stating her faith affiliation through the written and verbal information that was given to clients. Although she wanted her clients to feel able to talk about spiritual issues (as she wanted them to feel able to talk about any issue), she felt that it was something that they 'sussed out' rather than something that she had to make explicit. She felt that this was done through a process of unconscious, non-verbal communication.

> It would feel uncomfortable, you know, be like, well, not quite like, but like saying which political party I belong to, or something. I mean it would seem very sort of in their face, that it wouldn't seem quite comfortable... My initial reaction is that you offer your skills and training and experience and the rest they have to kind of suss out, and you have to feel if there's a match, and so on, between you, which is part of the initial process, isn't it? But I have to say when they do actually bring it out, and we are able to share that, at whatever level...clients are able to talk about the spiritual part of their life and how it's affecting their problem, and so

on. I do find that very freeing and really appreciate those opportunities.
(Rosie)

It is interesting to see that Rosie found it 'freeing' when clients were able to
talk about spiritual issues. This sense of feeling more 'complete' as a
counsellor when spiritual issues were explored was also expressed by
Rachel.

> I mean, that is profoundly, that is very fulfilling, to combine everything
> like that, but it's still a therapeutic encounter, it's not spiritual direction,
> and that's what determines how it operates... It's a great pleasure when
> you can talk about the spiritual search openly with somebody, but it
> doesn't mean that not being able to do that means that – no, because what
> I'm finding is that I am more and more present, actually, with them.
> (Rosie)

Although Hannah re-experienced feelings of invigoration and excitement
from exploring spiritual issues with Christian clients, she was always left
with a deep sense of loss as, at one level, she would still like to have the
concrete faith that she once had and the sense of certainty that it once
carried for her. Rebecca was very open with her clients about her faith
system and saw that as necessary to her sense of integrity as a counsellor,
giving her clients an informed choice about whether they could work with
her or not, and giving her a chance to discern whether she could work
with the client. Anne, however, withheld her faith because she felt that it
might prevent openness in the session.

> I don't divulge it because my experience is that people who aren't
> Christians have all kinds of very inaccurate opinions about people who
> are, and I find it actually puts quite an agenda on the work, really, where
> they feel they've got to be ever so good for me, so they kind of damp
> down their language and sort of, don't like to tell me that actually Mum
> and Dad weren't married, or you know, that sort of thing, and I think
> actually it's not helpful... If they asked me, I would tell them, but if they
> don't ask, I don't say. (Anne)

Anne did recognise her dilemma of wanting to be fully herself in the
relationship, but having to deny an important part of herself.

The data reveal the dilemma that is faced by many practitioners about
what is appropriate self-disclosure and what is not appropriate. 'We learn
to be abstinent in our self-disclosure in order to allow space for the other to

express themselves...' (Rose 1999, p.57). Yet, Hammond, Hepworth and Smith (1977, p.215) state that when a counsellor authentically communicates aspects of their 'self' in a way that is relevant to the client, properly timed, used sparingly and discriminately, and communicated in a manner that does not put the spotlight on the counsellor, then self-disclosure may be helpful. Paulson, Everall and Stuart's (2001) research indicates that clients need to feel connected to their counsellors. Self-disclosure was not identified as a hindering experience but the counsellor seeming 'remote' and 'detached' was identified as being a hindering experience. This would seem to indicate that anything that enhances connection, such as indicating a similar frame of reference, attitudes and values, would be appropriate. Indeed, one of the categories – 'barriers to feeling understood' – identified 'talking to somebody who doesn't have a shared cultural experience' as a hindering experience. Therefore the research would seem to indicate the importance of self-disclosure in aspects of shared cultural experience. This is advocated in gay affirmative therapy as a way of enabling psychological contact, enhancing relationship and minimising isolation (Davies and Ackroyd 2002; Davies and Neal 1996). In the context of self-disclosing spiritual values West (2000), however, warns against going beyond simpler forms of self-disclosure. Such disclosure needs to be offered tentatively and in a manner that enables the client to work with them or reject them as appropriate (p.105). West's view resonates with Paulson et al.'s (2001) research that identified 'being concerned about the counsellor's religious agenda' as being another hindering experience. The literature seems to indicate that self-disclosure may be valid, as long as it is tentative and appropriate.

Culley (1991) offers the following guidelines: be brief, tailor your self-disclosure, understand your client first, be direct, be clear about your motives (pp.85–86). This dilemma is pertinent for the counsellors: what will self-disclosure of the counsellor's faith do to the client, or how will it impact on the relationship? Will it enable or inhibit? Is it better to allow an awareness of the counsellor's faith to emerge naturally in a way that is relevant to the context and the moment, or should one be 'up front' about it? Will clients pick up on it anyway through unconscious communication, so why is disclosure necessary? What is interesting is that many counsellors feel 'freer' and 'more complete' (more authentic and congruent) when their faith is disclosed, or when they have an opportunity to work with spiritual issues.

Prayer at the beginning of a session

Rebecca used to pray at the end of sessions with clients but she felt that it had changed the dynamic of the session for many clients. Instead, she now prayed with clients at the beginning of the session. Rather than prayer detract from what the client was bringing to the session, Rebecca experienced prayer at the beginning of the session as being a space where clients could get in touch with what the most important issue was for them to explore in the session, rather than simply talking about the first thing that entered their head.

> I will always ask if, you know, what would that person want? Do they want to pray? If they say absolutely not, then I would totally respect that, either at the beginning or at the end, and then I would say, you know, 'When do you feel is the best?', and it may be in contracting that, you know, in starting at the beginning there might be something that God will show me… And it's about asking the Lord to be present, and to clear out any grunge that may have been brought, so they can focus on what God wants them to bring. (Rebecca)

So prayer is a useful way of focusing the client on their 'point of pain', rather than using the session to discover the 'point of pain', leaving less time in the session to explore and experience it. Because prayer had been contracted for use at the beginning of the session, this did not mean that prayer always had to be used at the beginning of the session. Rebecca stated that she did not interrupt a client who came in and off-loaded, in order to pray.

> Sometimes people come in and they start, and will off-load a bit, and partway through I might say, 'Do you want to pray?' They may say yes, they may say no, that's OK. I mean, it's not because we have contracted to pray at the beginning of the session, say 'Hang on, got to stop now, going to pray', because that to me, then, is me-directed… I mean, obviously if somebody's in the flow of very painful stuff, I'm not going to say, 'Excuse me, stop, we need to pray'. There is no fixed timing as to when, if we've gone into already beginning the session as soon as the person comes in, because to me that's where we start. Often people come in and sit down and once they've kind of sat, you know, I may say, 'Shall we pray?' or 'Do you want to pray?', or whatever, and I have had people come in and say, 'Oh, can we pray before we start?', really kind of, quite, almost desperate.

So it's not fixed, it's not always me, it's not, you know, and it's not always them, it varies. (Rebecca)

In such prayer the content is not predetermined, the duration is not lengthy, and the issues that the client wants to look at (the point of pain) may well be evident.

Sometimes the client starts and I back it up. Sometimes I start and they will just say 'Amen', or they back it up... I'm not talking about half-an-hour's prayer. I'm talking probably two or three minutes maximum. So it really just is acknowledging God's presence, and it is because of him, you know, that actually we're sharing this space together... If the client has started, I mean, I usually find within the client's prayer, that the issues they want to look at have come in, you know – could be asking the Lord to help them to focus on the discomfort they're feeling, issues around sex, sexual orientation, issues around abuse, they'll bring it in. (Rebecca)

Hannah stated that she always begins the session with silence as a way of enabling her client to 'dis-identify' from whatever they have come with in order to become more reflective and more alert to the 'essence of their deepest self'.

I think the silence gives people an opportunity, and because I believe in Grace... I do think that if I/they can find a way in which to stop for a moment, and become willing, it's that saying yes again, even if it's at a not completely conscious level, that allows something else to happen, and that's the bit that's beyond us, really... It kind of opens a door somewhere... I don't know – it is the touch of God. I mean, I do believe – a part of me, I have to say it that way, there is a part of me that believes that the grand being, God, whatever words I use, is active in some sense, not simply a large process of which we are all a part. There's another part of me that believes that, but there is a part of me that believes that there are moments when I know it in my own life – the finger of God touches you, and the experience of that is sometimes a conscious experience, a knowledge of being graced, of being blessed, and sometimes not. (Hannah)

Shelagh also asked her clients if they could have a 'moment of quiet' to bring the main issues to be explored in the session into focus. Shelagh was aware of her own internal process during that moment of quiet. The space allowed her unconscious to speak and she often had an image that she sometimes shared with the client.

> Once I got this wonderful image of a beautiful tulip, and it was a purple tulip, but it had turned its head down. That's all I got, so I thought, 'Right, yes', and sure enough, there was you know, I thought we were getting on fine, but something had upset, and looking back, I could see the way this lady had walked into the room, without the bounce, but with, you know, definite 'Well, I'm here, because I'm here' attitude, but not that sort of sure thing that things were going to go OK, and there it was, this tulip, with its head bowed, not a very happy tulip at all! So it was useful – it made me more aware. (Shelagh)

Shelagh felt that that time was 'useful', and enabled her to have a deeper and more meaningful connection with the client, in which her intuition was at work. Even though her eyes were closed, she did not feel 'cut-off' from her client, unlike Amanda, but more deeply connected.

> They're sensing that I'm there for them, and the silence is not a cutting-off, it's actually a discovering for us both, where we're going to go. And certainly it feels like opening out – you can feel a settling down. And it helps them rather than sort of say how difficult it was to park, they will then come up with what it is they want to make use of their time. (Shelagh)

For Shelagh, intuition and spiritual awareness 'collapsed into each other' and are so similar that it is difficult to distinguish any difference. Amanda, however, had reservations about praying at the beginning of the session because she felt that it could restrict the expression of emotions that might be perceived as 'unacceptable' in a Christian context, e.g. anger. Rowena also felt that prayer would 'get in the way' at the beginning of the session, and could be used manipulatively by the client. This sense of prayer inhibiting emotions was challenged by Vivienne. She had experience of a client who prayed at both the beginning of the session and at the end. Prayer did not prevent her from getting angry in the sessions.

> I often felt, particularly the prayers at the beginning were very often her asking for grace – to be able to use the session well, and to be able to really take on board the few things I did say, I suppose. The end was usually both of us, I suppose, summing up what had happened in the session, and asking for healing, and asking for peace, and asking for gentleness and

forgiveness, and all those things, and those felt very good. And she was often very angry during the sessions, and scowling like a furious nine-year-old, I would say! And yet when she left, she was this gracious 40-year-old woman. (Vivienne)

Here, prayer helped her to return to some sense of dignity (her adult) when regression took place in the session. Prayer gave her the freedom to reach into the 'true' parts of herself and to be authentic, knowing that she would not 'lose it', but instead be able to regain her composure through prayer.

It is evident that there are two dimensions to praying at the beginning of a session. At a practical level prayer is regarded as an opportunity to 'centre' the client on their primary issue so that the session can usefully be focused on the 'point of pain', and on experiencing and exploring that primary issue. This avoids having to work through unnecessary narrative before the 'real work' begins. At another level, the 'prayer space' is an acknowledgement of the spiritual context of the work, in which the client can become 'alert to the essence of their deepest self' (Hannah) and for the 'unconscious to speak' (Shelagh). This enables both client and counsellor to engage in a more meaningful and deeper connection. Whilst some may prefer to explain this quality of contact in psychological terms (e.g. Wyatt and Saunders 2002) and to regard it simply as 'space', nevertheless the existential perception of this space and the intense level of connection that it creates is that it is a spiritual space which is 'prayer', even if no words are verbalised. For some counsellors (e.g. Rebecca) words are necessary; for others (e.g. Hannah and Shelagh) they are not. This may be related to the counsellor's orientation because both counsellors who used the space silently were both from a transpersonal orientation. It is interesting that very few counsellors used prayer at the beginning of a session. Rose (1999, 2002) suggests that if prayer is offered at the beginning of the session it may detract from the immediacy of the client. Whilst staying with the immediacy may be beneficial in some cases it is also clear that 'dis-identifyng' from that immediacy (Hannah) may also be therapeutically beneficial in order to connect with the deeper aspects of self. Whilst prayer can be used to avoid the true self (Webster 1992) the counsellors demonstrate how prayer is to enable clients to connect with 'the essence of their deepest self' (Hannah). There may be reservations about whether prayer inhibits the expression of certain emotions (e.g. Amanda), but that is something that the counsellor needs to be alert to and challenging of. The counsellors indicate that prayer can enable authenticity rather than prevent it. The counsellors also indicate that the practicality of prayer is that it should be centred on the client, and if verbal, it is a simple acknowledgement of what the client wants to bring (Rebecca). Lengthy prayer is not appropriate. Its content is not predetermined or mechanistic, and prayer needs to be focused on the client's needs (Rebecca).

Praying at times of client desperation

Ben gave an example of a client who had lost everything. All he had was his faith. The prayer seemed to uplift the client in his desperation.

> There was one particular case – a fellow who'd lost everything. He was in a husband and wife ministry. His wife walked out on him, and took their two children with her, so then he had to resign his post. Because he lost the tied house as well, she then put in a claim for colossal expenses, or settlement of whatever, and he said, 'I can see how easy it is for men to get within that distance of the gutter and lose everything – hitting the bottle, and just being total down-and-outs.' He said, 'I can just see, I came that close to it'. He'd felt that he couldn't see God at work in his life at all at this time, and was really at a loss, really, but he'd been really praying, and praying when it's hardest to pray, and he saw me as a sort of a, he couldn't feel a sense of God, yet he could see me as God-given to him in his time of need. He was sort of, just grabbing hold of this opportunity with both hands, which was really good, you know, to be a part of that, and he was coming up to a very difficult decision he had to make, and it was about another job situation, and something around his family, because she'd hidden the children from him, or something, and it just seemed appropriate at that point, because he was sort of, really desperate to know. I said, 'You've done a lot up to now, and you've been faithful, you've been praying. You can't quite see God in this, but just feel that you need the power of the Holy Spirit to see you through this next week. Can we pray about this now?', and he was right in there, 'Yes, definitely', and he said at the next session, 'I walked out of that session with a spring in my step. I just knew I had a greater strength on my side, to take me through that difficult week', so he was very grateful. (Ben)

At such a time, Ben described what he might have prayed as being along the lines of:

...calling on God to keep him strong in the situation, keep his, sort of, hand on the tiller, as it were, get his life back on track, and with his situation it would be giving him the courage and the – he needed to have a sort of, sense of peace and he needed to be firm, but not aggressive, so assertive not aggressive when dealing with his ex-wife, and there was a mother-in-law involved or something, they were keeping his children hidden from him. So he needed to have sort of, God's peace, in him as he was tackling the situation, and it was about praying for him to have a real sense of God's presence at this interview, because I think he felt he was battling on his own strength, and he just needed a bit more. So that would have been the substance of the prayer. (Ben)

This prayer took place towards the end of the fourth session, in an eight-session working relationship.

Michael had experience of working with a client who had experienced several traumatic events. During the counselling work the client experienced flashbacks and panic attacks in which she became breathless and dissociated. Michael used prayer as a way of calming her and claimed that the Alexander techniques that he would use now in such events could be regarded as prayer.

Whilst it has been evident from Chapter 5 that many counsellors pray covertly at times of client desperation, there were only two examples of how and why counsellors pray overtly with clients at difficult times. It is interesting that on both occasions it was male counsellors for whom this happened but that may be coincidental. In the example above (Ben), the counsellor prayed for courage and peace. The effect of the prayer was to re-establish the client's relationship with God, at a time when he had lost confidence in his spiritual resources. Prayer also enabled the client to have renewed hope and confidence in his ability because of an assurance of having 'a greater strength on my side'. The counsellor's offer 'to pray' could be regarded as having been inappropriately motivated by the counsellor's need to 'rescue' the client which may have detracted from the client's autonomy. However, prayer was offered with beneficence through acting in the best interests of his client at a time when the client's capacity for autonomy was diminished. Therefore it was appropriate. It is interesting that Michael used prayer as a means of working with symptoms (flashbacks, panic attacks, breathlessness and disassociation) because, arguably, techniques for minimising symptoms of anxiety are commonly found in most forms of counselling. As prayer carries similar anxiety-reducing traits (Helminiak 1982; McDonald 1999; Shapiro 1980) prayer is also appropriately offered through the ethical practice of non-maleficence (a commitment to avoiding harm to the client) and beneficence (a commitment to promoting the client's well-being).

Using prayer in a transpersonal way

Mary felt that the most important element of her client work was to help her clients to 'get in touch with their own inner wisdom'. She did this through the use of imaging.

> I reckon that talking to that image – a lion, a wise man, an eagle, a tree – talking and listening to what the image says back is actually very akin to prayer. (Mary)

The image was client-induced, not counsellor-imposed. This use of imaging enabled the client to reframe her experiences and move on from them. Mary describes this process as one of *redemption* – not in the Christian sense of 'Christ doing something for me', but 'It's something else that's within that is redeeming, if we find it or it finds us'. Mary vividly communicated this process as:

> The client didn't leave the hell to go to heaven, the hell turned into the heaven, and it seems that this is the kind of thing that wisdom does when you can access it... It somehow unplaits our neurosis and turns the very stuff of neurosis into stuff of redemption so that you don't have to get better, or change anything, you approach it differently... It's like shining a torch in a dark cellar – it's no longer dark... The dark is where we find the redeeming whatever it is – God if you like, in the shit...the going down and down into the dark and taking a light with us...to go in and in and back and back and discover things that eventually bring them back to the light... I would want to get them more aware of the light and kitted up properly for a descent, as it were, and then to take the lantern of light down with them, into the dark, and find all sorts of reassurances there, where their potential gets locked up. (Mary)

Specifying her methodology, Mary said:

> I would talk about a talisman, so if a person decided to go on an inner journey... I suggest that they find a talisman to take with them, holding it

in their inner hand, as it were, maybe a small animal, or maybe some small thing that will come with them, and whenever they get stuck or unhappy, I just say, 'What does the talisman feel about that, where would the talisman like to take you, what does the talisman say?' [The talisman] is a direct image of the other self. It's as near as we are going to get in that moment, to whatever it is. It speaks with the voice...this is something that knows more than you and I do... It very often leads them into places where, not so much that they resolve their difficulties that they begin to outgrow them. Like Jung said about the oak tree can get over the wall simply by growing...you don't dismember the wall, you just grow... It's a journey in depth...it's not about height. (Mary)

This methodology is something that is introduced by the counsellor. Mary stated that clients will often know that that is the way she works, and that is the reason why they come to her. Therefore, her clients will often be predisposed to working in this way. It is a method that is introduced tentatively through 'spot-imaging', i.e.

If they said something like, 'I remember I used to get under the table and my father used to kick me', I'd just say, 'Well, could you close your eyes and be under the table now?', and you do perhaps a five minutes thing on that, which is a way of spot-imaging, and then afterwards you can say, 'How did it feel doing that, you really went there, didn't you, and you were four years old, and is that the way you'd like to work a bit more?', and if they say no, then that's OK. (Mary)

Such a method can be used to introduce the transpersonal self, i.e. another 'overview' dimension to the 'here and now' of what is being worked with.

The observer, the wise compassionate observer of your life, who knows more than you know, which I suppose would be likely to constellate something of the image of God at that moment – wisdom, compassion, complete attention. (Mary)

There is a concreteness (a solidness or a realness) about what is revealed through such communication with that part of self (or God) which enables insights to be gained and lived. Hannah shared this way of working which she too regarded as prayer.

Sometimes I will ask them to invoke their wise being – to me, that's prayer, really – when they've found that wisest, deepest place for themselves, and have that kind of dialogue… I think any of the experiential work that we do that enables people to have a deeper experience of themselves, of their truer self, probably comes somewhere on the periphery of prayer as I would define it. (Hannah)

However, she felt that it was necessary to be careful with the language being used and to make sure that the client was aware of the symbolism used in the language so that they do not become confused by taking their experience literally.

I think there are dangers when it all becomes too literal, really. Symbols are meant to enable us to experience that level of being that's non-rational and less conscious, and profound, and meant to stay that way, really. I mean, I think if we use the symbol of a wise being, for instance, and a dialogue happens, that we have to treat that at a symbolic level, and then you use kind of common sense, and discernment, and discrimination in re-translating that back into everyday life, and I think it's that it's the confusion of levels that I see sometimes, in people who are just beginning – makes me wonder sometimes. (Hannah)

These two counsellors demonstrate that this way of working with the spiritual dimension (the overview dimension of self) is a powerful way of incorporating prayer in counselling. However, this level of work requires specific training that comes from the transpersonal approach to counselling. It is also interesting to see how both practitioners make use of quasi-religious imagery to make sense of their clients' experiences, e.g. light from darkness, redemption, 'the wise, compassionate observer of your life (i.e. God)'. The result of this approach is to establish insights about 'self' which have a solidity and which are meaningful at a profound level. However, the dangers are of using this type of approach with little or no training, of using language inappropriately, and of not enabling the client to be aware of the difference between the truth of the emerging insights and the symbolism of the experience (Hannah). From a phenomenological perspective this type of approach that involves relatedness and dialogue with the transpersonal 'other' is 'prayer'. From the existential awareness of the counsellors that employ its use it is prayer. It may be prayer to some clients but not to others. Other counsellors may frame this experience in wider philosophical and psychological genre. It is clear from the examples that are given that significant personal insight and healing/growth can be gained from this approach to prayer.

Using prayer in ritual

Prayer had been used by two counsellors as an important dimension of ritual. The use of prayer in ritual had brought about a 'resolution' and a sense of 'letting go'. Donna related an experience where a client wanted to burn names that she had called her father. Prayer was used in the ceremony of incineration.

> I know recently I had a client that had brought a list of names that she would attribute to her father, and found it very difficult to read them, and asked me to read it, and then we'd agreed that we would burn it. So it must have been around Bonfire Night, and we had a barrel here. We got it over the fence, and we had arranged to burn it, so we did that, and as we were burning it, she asked me, 'I feel like I want to say some words', and I asked her, 'What words would you like to say?' and she said she couldn't say the words, and could I say the words. I asked her what words she wanted me to say and she said, 'Words like you would say if you were praying'. So I said words, but that was again, instigated by her. But she didn't use the word prayer, she just said 'words'. Something had to be said about what was happening…she wanted something said over this burning mass of horror, really. (Donna)

Amanda related an occasion where a client planned a service that involved the local curate, as a way of 'ridding' herself of issues concerning her ex-husband.

> …she felt that in some way, in some sense she was still bound to her ex-husband, from whom she'd been divorced for many years, and what she wanted was a service, to ask to be set free from this binding that she felt she had with him, and what happened, she asked the curate at her church – a few miles from here, an Anglican church – and the three of us – the curate, herself and myself – were involved in this service in church, which obviously included different sorts of prayer and communion. So that was a completely different one – that is a one-off, but in that case the service was written by the client… I think we needed the priest there because she felt some sort of, I suppose, spiritual binding to this ex-husband, and the priest seemed the appropriate person to deal with

that…the curate came here and we talked about it, and planned it one week, and then the next week we went to the church and had the service… I saw her after that a couple of times. There was a sense that she had let go of her ex-husband…and she wrote down things which she needed to write, and they were put in a bowl on the table in the chapel, and then she burnt them. And then later, she took them down by the canal and let them go on the water – that was her idea, and she did that, and that really seemed to complete the freeing-up, you know, the freedom. (Amanda)

Amanda admitted that she felt attracted to the concept of ritual and by the powerful effect it had on clients. She did not process her client's need (paralleled with her own need?) to externalise their responsibility for letting go by exploring what was preventing them from letting go internally. Amanda stated that she sometimes used prayer with clients who were working through grief issues, especially those who had experienced a miscarriage or the loss of a child, as a way of offering up the child to God. This included non-Christian clients. Prayer was experienced as being helpful and enabling a sense of 'completion'. Prayer was accompanied by a ritual of lighting a candle, with the counsellor saying words like:

'I wonder if you would like me to pray?'… Almost always I'd offer, 'Would you like to light a candle for the baby, and would you like us to commit this child to God in prayer?', or similar words… Probably not the client praying, because I should think almost always, the client would be quite distressed…again, it might be a client who's not used to praying. (Amanda)

In introducing this use of prayer into the work, Amanda would cautiously say to the client: 'Some people have found this helpful, and I wonder if you feel this would be appropriate…' Although Amanda had never been refused, she felt that her clients were able to say 'no' because they had refused other types of work she had cautiously introduced. When challenged about whether prayer was something a client could refuse because it might be seen as sacrilege to refuse it, Amanda replied:

I can't say, because I haven't asked that… We do these things because it feels right, and I guess I'm working on a sort of, intuitive level, but I don't unpick it… (Amanda)

Amanda justified the use of prayer as being an 'added dimension' to her work but one on which she had not reflected much. However, she regarded overt prayer as being applicable to her work only as a method of completion and committal. To highlight this aspect of her work Amanda related a ritual in which prayer and 'naming' were used to aid completion.

> I had a client, quite a few years ago who was a GP-referred client, and hadn't had any experience, really, of any Christian experience or church, but she had a very sad obstetric history, and she'd lost six children, and we worked through this for a few sessions, and when we came to what felt to be, towards the end, she'd actually brought baby clothes that she'd knitted for these children, and had kept for many, many years. It must have been probably about 15 years after and she brought these clothes, and she lit a candle for each of these children, and she named them, and then we just committed them to God, with the names, into his keeping… Impossible to recall the exact words, but something like saying to God, acknowledging that these were his children and naming them and committing each of them by name to God for his keeping, and to allow the client, by name, to be able to let them go into his care… I would say that from that time she was much more at peace about this. She'd had quite a psychiatric history…but certainly she was in a far more peaceful frame of mind, a happier frame of mind, when we, you know, completed the work. And there were lots of other areas we worked on – she'd been abused as a child as well, so there was a lot of traumatic material, but this part of it really felt as if it had been completed, and I think that was the last time the children were mentioned… (Amanda)

Amanda stated that the client was prepared for this in the following way:

> It was prepared, probably, during the two previous sessions – there were weekly sessions – we talked about it, had she ever been to church, or was faith in God, or God ever part of her life, and how would she feel? And she seemed to think this was a good idea, and that she would like to bring all she had of these children, which was these clothes that she'd made for them. And she knew exactly how would it be if you lit a candle, and of course she had prepared, she had named these children before, she'd decided during, between the sessions, what she'd call these children, and so it was prepared…would she like to do it, and she was given time to think about it, and that's what she did. (Amanda)

Although using prayer in this way helped the client to feel more at peace with the issues it raises the question as to whether a client is able to talk about such issues again after such a powerful ritual because the message that such rituals could give is that the client 'should' now be whole – that 'completion' and 'resolution' of the issues 'should' have been made. The client may thus feel unable to bring their sense of continuing pain back to counselling. It is evident from Amanda's experience that her client did not talk about her six children again even though she continued to have counselling. This raises the question as to how realistic it is that the pain of losing six children could be ended through a ritual. Maybe the ritual could be seen by the client as the counsellor giving the message that this matter 'should' now be closed, or at worse, that the counsellor is tired of exploring the issue. Anne felt that it was important to pray that things be resolved 'for now' rather than raise the client's expectation that they would not feel any more pain after the ritual.

> Perhaps one ought to pray for it's been resolved for now. Taking the question at a sort of surface level, could they come back, I think some people would be able to come back, and some would find it very difficult. That would depend very much on them. And I think, also, it's part of – that kind of question sort of springs from the area which to me says all these things are a process and in fact we kind of spend our whole lives, sometimes, processing things, and it's OK for now, and then something happens and it comes up again, and you have to process it again, and each time, hopefully, it gets a bit easier. (Anne)

Anne felt that there was a tendency in some Christians to expect instant healing and not to accept responsibility for change. If the counsellor was not careful, they could collude with this expectation.

> Sometimes I have to say to people, 'Actually, this won't change until…you're the only one that – the only thing we can change in this room, really, is you, and you have to put your will into it as well'… I mean I have had experience with Christians coming to me for counselling, and actually they have absolutely no intention of changing, and in the end, that has to be brought into the work, that actually 'You're the one who has to change round here – God isn't going to override your free will, I'm afraid you have to do some of this as well'. (Anne)

Rowena felt that the use of prayer, after a cathartic experience, could be regarded as an act of 'sealing' the process. Rowena regarded healing as an ongoing process throughout life.

> It is usually after a client has been, had a very cathartic experience of being, re-living a memory, which has been painful; there've been lots and lots of tears – it could be then that I would offer prayer, which is usually towards the end of the session anyway…prayer a way of just bringing them back to a place of peace when they've been in a place of distress… I see that as a very important part of the process, certainly in gestalt, bringing things to a good enough ending, particularly if they've driven here, and they're on their own, and they're having to drive away…settling, sealing and protection, and in the prayer, I would always ask for God's protection as you leave this house, and you drive home, and I always say to the client, after the prayer, I go and sit back down there, I give them time to sort of gather themselves, and usually they sort of say something like, 'That was really very helpful, thank you', and I will then say, 'You've been on a long journey, you've got in touch with a lot of emotion, your reactions will be much slower, so take care as you drive home'… That's exactly what happened with a client who walked out of the door last week – she did a big piece of work here, and was very tearful and upset, and I asked her if she would like me to pray, and she said yes, and she was brought to a place that felt sort of settled, she has about 20-odd miles to drive home. When she arrived this week, she just said 'I feel a different person, I feel marvellous', and I experienced her as very different today… I think that was a combination of, I think it was more the piece of work that she did, anger as well as lots of tears, but for me, and she found it helpful, the prayer was the sort of sealing bit… I see it as the client having worked on a specific area in their life, that has brought healing for that specific incident, whatever it was, or often, it's layers…healing is an ongoing process. (Rowena)

Amanda used the 'empty-chair' technique when working with clients who had a need to express anger with God. Amanda felt that this fell within her definition of prayer. Fran related an occasion when she had prayed with a client using the laying on of hands and praying in tongues.

> I've got one client in particular, with whom prayer's been very important… She was in quite a bad state… As she described what had happened to her, there was an element of spiritual attack for her, in

that…well, her husband had dropped dead in front of her when they had been arguing, and her sense was that in everything adverse that happened was his attack on her, that he was getting back at her. He was saying to her 'Now look what you've done, right, I'm punishing you for this'… She'd bought a new car…but her car had gone wrong in that the heating control had gone wrong. It was a new car, and she said that when her husband was alive, the thing they used to argue about was the heating on the car – I mean, there were lots of examples of this… She and her husband had become Christians not long before, and I knew she'd been referred through her local Baptist church, so I knew that she was a Christian, so at the end of the session, I suggested that we prayed, and I said, 'Not only that, but I'm going to suggest that we actually kind of, sandwich our session between prayer – that we pray at the beginning as well'. I said, 'You've come here today, and I've been feeling quite disturbed and I just feel – we're both Christians, that it would be good to just make this time safe through prayer', and she said 'Oh that would be really good, that would be great', and so we decided to do that. However, I constantly forgot to pray when we met because I wasn't used to doing that and occasionally I would forget when she left as well! So we talked about this, and in the end I wrote a big notice 'Remember to pray'… I just wrote it for myself, to remind myself. Usually now I remember because we've got into the way of it. The other thing that happened with her was that she had some difficulty with her minister, her pastor, and I think it was because, understandably, he was very wary of being on his own with her… She had been sexually abused as a child, so she had a lot of difficulty with men, and was very quick to take this as a slight on her, and so we explored a little bit about why he might be doing that… Then she said that the elders in the church – she was feeling very vulnerable around – felt very criticised by them, for lots of reasons, which led to her feeling that some things she did were judged… It was really because she wanted to contact her husband. She felt that she would like to go to a medium and speak to him through this medium, and so she said that she had mentioned that at church and people were very condemnatory. I asked her why she thought they were being condemnatory about it, and she said, 'Well, apparently in the Bible it says you shouldn't do that', so we did actually look in the Bible to find out what the Bible said about it, which I've never done with a client before. It just seemed important to separate out the truth really, because truth was something that could become twisted for her. So we checked that out together, and she said, 'That's what I wanted them to do with me'. She said, 'I just wanted them to sit down with me and look at what the Bible says. Instead of which they dismissed me out of hand'. That then led on to the possibility of having hands laid on her for healing – I don't think I introduced it – I may have said 'Have you thought about going to a healing service?' – I may have said that, I think I probably did, and she, because we have healing services in our church, I think I probably asked if her church has a healing service, and she said that the elders do lay hands on people, but she said 'I wouldn't have them do that to me' and I said 'Because they're men?' and she said 'Yes, absolutely'. And so I said, 'Well, would you like me to do it?' And that was an immediate response, and felt a bit bold, but I just felt it was the right thing, and she said 'Oh yes please, I really would'. And so she knelt down and I just put my hands on her and prayed – and I do pray in tongues sometimes – and so I did that, and she said she felt a great experience of warmth and peacefulness, and that was that. I haven't done it since, and I haven't referred to it since. It felt appropriate in the moment, absolutely, but that's the only time I've done that. But it was, it felt a very good thing to do. I was pleased that I was able to follow my instinct there, and that's the only time I would do it, obviously. (Fran)

In this scenario, it is clear how an unusual set of circumstances culminated in an instinctive, but unusual, intervention that felt appropriate to the moment, creative and 'right' for this therapeutic relationship, this client, and this counsellor. It is interesting to see how Fran was glad to have done it but has never repeated the experience with another client. When asked how such circumstances affected boundaries, Fran stated that she may have become a Christian counsellor instead of a counsellor who is a Christian. However, she did not feel that she had become a priest. She stated that it was 'normal' for Christians to pray together. When asked if everything that felt normal was appropriate in counselling, she replied:

I am aware that when I suggest praying, most people, their eyes light up, their faces lighten and almost like a sort of relief, gratitude, all those emotions… It's a bond, I suppose, really, but because Christians actually belong to one another in a kind of family, that it's a sort of closeness, really. So it actually strengthens the working alliance. (Fran)

Fran felt that prayer enhanced her work with clients rather than detracted from any aspect of the work. She argued that prayer empowered people.

It's actually recognising that place of…interface between us, that God is in that interface, so it's actually recognising that and bringing him/it into the open, bringing it into consciousness, and our work is about making the unconscious conscious. (Fran)

Similar circumstances and feelings were expressed by Gemma who, on one occasion, had also prayed in tongues with a client. Gemma stated that she always asked the client's permission before praying with them. She had also recognised that a particular client knew about praying in tongues and prayed in tongues herself. She related the circumstances that occurred. Gemma stated that she believed in the concept of a 'devil' that she could discern through her client's eyes. In the following scenario she describes her client as being 'under attack' from something external to her. She firmly dismissed the idea that was put to her that it may simply be a psychological process and that praying in this way may prevent the client from taking responsibility.

There's one occasion I'll always remember. It was the last session I was having with a client who had come because she was having a lot of anxiety, and she was a Christian, but I wasn't counselling in an overtly Christian way. I was counselling her, but at the very end, she said to me, 'Just before I leave, would you pray for me?', so I said 'yes', and I started to pray, not in tongues, and I just prayed that the Lord would bless her, and take care of her, and fairly sort of, blanket prayer, in a way. When I'd finished she said to me, 'Every time you used the word Jesus I was blaspheming under my breath', so I knew that she was being attacked, so I said to her, 'Would you mind if I prayed in tongues with you on this?', and she said 'No, I would like that'. So I did, and the tongue was very strong, and I knew I was fighting with the Devil at that moment. So I would say I was praying in tongues strongly, I was standing up by this time, I asked if she minded, and after I'd finished, she left, basically. But I got a beautiful letter from her later, saying how after I'd prayed she was filled with peace and everything was now perfectly all right, so you know, I knew it was the Lord and Holy Spirit with us in the room. (Gemma)

Gemma stated that she had experienced times when she felt that her client was possessed with evil and that praying in tongues, whether overtly or under her breath, was her way of dealing with these evil spirits or the Devil.

Well, it's both... I believe it is the Devil, it is the demon, but it is also as you say, the distorted thought, which may not be the Devil at all. It might be just a psychological thing, and so it's sort of being able to – not only discern the spirits, but discern where they're coming from, and not to put more on them than they carry... I think even when they're taken over from outside, they still have a responsibility, although again you see, if they're not Christians, they – you're in another whole area, but I suppose I think, if a Christian – I mean, I think we all have evil spirits in us, we're none of us clear of that, but I think as Christians, if I personally suddenly start to feel really angry, or really whatever, negatively towards somebody, I have to ask myself whether this is just my psychology, or whether this is actually a spirit that I can rebuke, and bind in the name of Jesus. But if you're a Christian, you can do that, because you can wonder where this particular thing is coming from. But for a non-Christian, they're ignorant of it, and therefore, it can be either... If I'm very troubled by something, then I can rebuke the Devil in the name of Jesus, and if it's the Devil, it'll go, and if it isn't, then it's me just being troubled. And I can't always discern. (Gemma)

Only three of the counsellors talked about the 'devil' or 'evil'. Joanne talked about 'blessing' her clients frequently.

I often give them a hug as they go, and I will just put my hand on their head, and say something to them. (Joanne)

Again this has to be considered within the context that Joanne regarded her counselling work as being reparative. Joanne was also open to working in creative ways with her clients, and occasionally anointed her client with oil.

...if they are Christians, on the fringes as well, so I work with people's belief systems. I've got lots of other things I do...about six months ago I bought a little glass bottle – hand-painted bottle, and I put some oil in it, geranium oil, and it's just sitting in my room, my counselling room, and occasionally I use it to just anoint... So again, it's another aid, because I work with very early stuff, with the inner child... Well at the moment I've just been – a couple of clients, they just eat themselves around the nails, and so I've just rubbed the oil in. (Joanne)

Arguably, for some this may not be prayer. However, Joanne believed that it was the meaning that the client attached to the significance of the anointing that determined whether it was prayer to them. For her, every intervention was prayer because she believed that God was at the centre of her work as a counsellor. 'God is everywhere, I think – can't lock him up.' Joanne also related a client with whom she prayed. Praying in this way with clients enables them to 'take in' peace and 'get rid of' whatever is troubling them.

> ...because I was sort of looking at his posture, and I said 'Did you want me to pray for you?' So I put my hand on his head and where the pain finished in his back, and just prayed, and he commented himself that it wasn't a prayer of healing, it was the words he used about himself, which is that he wants to become strong...and sort of 'gave it out' or whatever... One of the other things I do, some Tai Chi, where you open yourself up and out, and I talk...if they're not Christians I talk about receiving the energy and taking it in and getting chi. But if they're Christians, I'll talk about taking God's peace and getting rid of whatever it is... (Joanne)

Joanne described some of her work as 'feeding' and 'affirmation'. In this context, she regarded prayer as being nutritional.

Ritual enables the recognition of emotion within a sanctioned milieu that provides secure boundaries in which to relive and experience emotional pain. This release of emotion halts the repression of emotional pain by facilitating the acknowledgement and expression of that which is painful. Ritual reinforces connection and attachment to others and it is this sense of connectedness that facilitates the cathartic response through which the painful emotions can be expressed and relived (Scheff 1979). Jacobs (1992, p.292) states that it is the attachment to the divine and to the significant others that gives ritual its power to engender potentially overwhelming feelings which are then resolved through a relational act of religious observance. Jacobs observes that the catharsis is enhanced when there is a relational framework in the ritual process that offers safety and protection. She suggests that religious rituals such as prayer play a significant role in reducing anxiety and isolation because the relational aspects of the ritual validate and give expression to the emotional reality of human experience (p.298). This is clearly evident in the use of prayer in ritual. All four counsellors (Donna, Amanda, Anne and Rowena) used ritual as a way of enabling catharsis which is described as: completion, resolution, letting go, ridding herself, committal, and 'sealing the process'. Ritual is sometimes used in some forms of counselling, especially in working through issues of grief and loss.

The issue that the data raises is one of client compliance. In Gubi (2002) I argue that in some forms of helping, prayer is used to 'exorcise' evil spirits (Collins 1988), and re-enact abuse issues (Bennett 1984) and as a formula for healing (McMinn 1996) with little respect or awareness of the client's needs. Prayer can be regarded as a 'quick fix' to emotional problems. The use of prayer in ritual can give the implicit message that once the client has engaged with the ritual, then wholeness, completion and resolution of the issues will ensue. In Amanda's case, it is clear that the client did not continue to talk about the loss of her six children after having performed the ritual of naming and committal. If prayer is to be used in ritual then it seems important for the counsellor to reinforce the client's autonomy by not encouraging the client to expect instant healing. Anne states that 'perhaps one ought to pray for its being resolved for now'. This 'for now' quality enables clients to have a more realistic expectation, and to continue to work on the issues if they recur. This resonates with Rowena who regards healing as 'an ongoing process throughout life'.

Rennie (1994) states that clients are reluctant to challenge their therapist because of issues of deference. They often have a fear of criticising their therapist, they desire to meet the therapist's perceived expectations, and they feel in debt to their therapist. Being deferential to the therapist can be the client's way of protecting and fostering the alliance. Because clients are extremely inclined to be deferential (Rennie 1994, p.436) it is important for the counsellor to facilitate an opportunity for the exploration of the client's process after the use of prayer in ritual and to be suspicious of complete closure rather than assume the 'success' of their intervention, especially if it may be inauthentic. It is not the purpose of this book to determine whether such concepts as 'devil', 'evil' and 'satanic attack' have any basis in reality or whether they are a useful metaphor for some underlying psychological process. From a phenomenological perspective the truth of these concepts is powerful for the counsellors who encounter such reality in their counselling work. The response in the examples above when counsellors believe they are facing evil is instinctive and tentative. It is respecting of the client's autonomy and acted out of the ethical principle of beneficence in that the counsellor is seeking to promote the client's well-being with her permission. It is clear that Fran has an understanding of the acceptability that performing such a ritual would have to the client. It is also evident that the performance of this type of ritual is rare, and is not routine and mechanistic. Although the ritual of 'praying in tongues' and 'laying on of hands' is unusual in counselling it is brought into the therapeutic relationship because of the appropriateness that the counsellor discerns from the 'felt sense' of the moment and the context of the issues being explored. It has an instinctive quality of naturalness for both the counsellor and the client. The result of the action was to leave the clients feeling 'at peace', 'fed' and 'affirmed'.

Silence as prayer

Michael stated that silence could be regarded as prayer, but only silence in which one is open to a sense of 'otherness' or there is a sense that there is an author behind events or a sense that there is something to be grateful for. Not all silence was prayer. Hannah felt that silence was a 'unitive' and prayerful experience. Hannah gave an account of how silence was used by a client – silence that had the quality of prayer.

> I have been working with somebody who – she's come to me as a therapy client, she's been working with me for about 18 months, and she came with everyday problems, really – her relationship wasn't the way she wanted it to be, she felt she wasn't doing what she wanted to do in her life, and we kind of worked with all that. But she is a committed Christian who's also struggling with not feeling at home in her church any more, etc., and she's moved quite a lot, in terms of growing, I feel, maturing, and she's been more and more drawn to silence. In the session about three weeks ago she was talking about that, and I suggested that she just let herself do that, if you feel drawn into silence, just allow yourself to go into the silence, and she just sat for about a quarter of an hour, and then when she brought her attention out again, she described what I'm certain was some kind of unitive experience – she felt her – the boundaries of her body dissolving till she'd become one with the room, and I just found that such an amazing experience, to be with somebody as they described that afterwards, and it was a very new and quite frightening experience for her... (Hannah)

Hannah also stated that the stillness of her presence in silence can enable clients to feel 'held' and 'contained'.

...if I'm very still inside I do become very still on the outside, and I can sit with anything. I can sit in a room with a lot going on amongst the students, and they feel very, very held by that, the fact that I can be very still. So maybe that's also true of clients, that there's something about inner silence that enables me to be very, very present, in a way that's very containing. (Hannah)

Although silence is covert, what is experienced from it has an overt presence in the counselling session and this form of prayer can be containing for the client.

These counsellors reveal the inherently diverse quality of silence. For some clients, silence can be a prayerful time of just being (Gubi 2001). The stillness of the counsellor in the silence can feel containing for a client whose inner process is disturbing (Hannah). The silence is prayer in that the client experiences being 'at one' (unitive) with something bigger (otherness) which has a cathartic effect of putting the client in touch with their internal process which can lead to further exploration. This is similar to what West (2003) describes as a 'spiritual silence' in which there is a feeling of being connected spiritually with each other and with something 'bigger'. This is a silence that fosters a connectedness to the sacred (Pargament 1997; Ulanov and Ulanov 1982) rather than silence that is used to enhance projection and transference as in some counselling approaches (e.g. the psychodynamic approach).

Prayer as a process of empowerment and release

Donna related her experience of a client in which she saw prayer as both an indication that the client was moving towards becoming a fully functioning person, and as part of her process of empowerment. Here, as the client gains in confidence and is more able to take responsibility, that process of empowerment can be seen in the client taking responsibility for the act of praying at the end of the session.

I was thinking about a client a long time ago, and how it seemed to work, how it seemed to become part of the process of her changing... I know that from our first interview she said at the end of the session she would like me to pray. I worked with her for a long time, and I – as she became more aware of who she was, she took over the prayer. I remember in supervision, talking about it. I would say each week, 'Would you like to say something?', almost like an ending, a blessing really, just what she wanted... As she sort of grew stronger, I would say, 'Would you like to?' – she was actually very, very spiritual, this lady, I would say I felt less spiritual than she did, but that was part of the issues, lack of confidence and everything, really. One day she said yes – I remember going to supervision and we talked about how prayer had become part of that process, almost. That move towards being fully functioning. As she became more like that, she was very open about it, and I wasn't doing it at all – she was. And she'd say 'What should we pray this week, about?', at the end. (Donna)

Michael felt that if his client was someone who was used to leading prayer in a church or in any other context then it would be empowering for them to pray for themselves and to have their voice heard. Michael also felt that if a client disclosed that she was praying for the counsellor then that might be a sign of empowerment. Amanda related an occasion in which the client asked her to pray with her for 'the gift of tears' after which she was able to cry.

This was a lady with a Christian faith, and this time the prayer was very specific. She was a very tight, tensed, lady – very low self-esteem, loads of trauma in her life, really, and she asked me to pray for the gift of tears, because she'd never been able to cry, and she'd never been able to love herself, and so we prayed specifically for that, but that was at her request... She was able to cry...it was lovely. It was very moving, actually, just to think about it, and it was quite a few years ago now. That was quite a moving moment...it was a release. (Amanda)

This ability to ask for prayer in this way enabled a shift in the client to occur that was releasing and empowering for the client.

It is evident in the literature that the use of prayer is not accepted as an appropriate therapeutic intervention because of its potential to disempower the client. Whilst an awareness of this dimension is ethically important it is interesting to discover the opposite view from those who have used prayer, that prayer can be empowering and releasing (cathartic). These therapeutic elements are evident in various ways: through the client moving from a place of needing the counsellor to 'do' the praying, to a place of wanting to pray herself (taking responsibility); through the client praying for the counsellor (although this could be regarded as the client needing to take responsibility for the counsellor) rather than just for herself (the development of mutuality); and through the ability to ask for prayer when it is needed (empowerment). All of these are signs of developing autonomy.

Using prayer to communicate with clients

Ben related an occasion where he used prayer to communicate something he felt otherwise unable to communicate with the client.

> There was a couple I was seeing, and they were both involved in the ministry in various ways, and she was getting very much into a sort of, 'careerist' mode, and trying to sort of, direct him in various ways which he didn't want to be directed, and they both came – well, she phoned up originally for help for him, but it became quite evident that it was a relationship thing, and I remember probably about halfway during one of the sessions with them, I just felt that God was directing me to pray for them both, and in that prayer, be almost directive to her, to how she was behaving. It was quite uncanny, because I'm not a directive sort of therapist, but there were certain words and parts of that prayer that were very much for her, because she was trying to manipulate him, and sort of, get up a career ladder of her own without being in tune with what God wanted for her life, and their life together. And that produced very good results because she – actually, the next session, she had markedly shifted her position, so it's a real evidence of – I'm sure that was a result of that. It was just the right time. (Ben)

In this relationship prayer was used to convey a message to the client. It is interesting that Ben was working with a manipulative client, and it was the manipulation that felt difficult for him. Yet, something of a parallel process was taking place in the session as Ben arguably used prayer to manipulate his client. Whilst acknowledging the directive and manipulative element of what he was doing through prayer, Ben justified his use of prayer as 'Holy Spirit-directed':

> …again, it's just knowing. It's just that awareness that it was, that I was Holy Spirit-directed to pray at that time, after seeking their permission – I always seek permission to pray at this point about your joint situation. So I was praying for him and what he was wanting to do, and her for what she was wanting to do, and how they were going to find this middle ground.

But within it there were these directive words towards her, so it's the knowing… It's difficult to describe that to the unbeliever without them really experiencing it. They've got to experience it to know, in a sense, so again, it's that knowing, I think… It was OK for them, and OK for me, and the expression on their faces was that this is God. (Ben)

This seems to come from an intuitive level – the 'knowing' level. Amanda also related an occasion in which she used prayer to communicate a message to her client.

I suppose in a way, I wanted to get a message through to the client because I felt she really ought not to be ending… I could see there was lots more work to be done… I think that was reinforcing what I'd already said. I had said, 'I think there's a lot more that you could work on', which she acknowledged but that wasn't the time. And maybe that wasn't the time for her, but…it was a genuine desire that somehow God would bring her to a place where that healing could be continued. Or indeed she could work through it on her own, which sometimes happens. (Amanda)

Here, prayer was used to reinforce the counsellor's hope for the client that she would continue to work on the issues. Lorna also used prayer to communicate her belief that the client is a 'wholesome and worthwhile person' although that belief will already have been communicated to the client through her way of being. Anne felt that it was ethically wrong to use prayer to 'plant' or communicate ideas that had not been discussed during the session.

I think the client has to lead the session, and I think in that sense, that does have to carry over into what's prayed about. If they've talked about it, I've done whatever I've done with it, and there's some sort of inner concord about the way forward, or whatever, or perhaps the fact there is no way forward as long as it's prayed about in that context, I think that's OK, but not to start introducing things at that stage… I think it's abusive to introduce something at that stage, at the end of the session, where they've got no comeback to say, and also when you're in a kind of, in that sort of transference, when you must feel quite – very powerful to them to start putting things on them that they haven't agreed to – I think it's abusive. (Anne)

Vivienne also felt that it was a 'cop-out' to use prayer to inform someone else about something – whether it was the client doing it, or the counsellor.

Whether it is ethical practice to use prayer to communicate with clients is unclear. Certainly two counsellors felt it was a 'cop-out' and ethically inappropriate to communicate or 'plant' ideas through prayer (Vivienne and Anne). One counsellor felt that it could be abusive (Anne). This view is reflected in the literature. However, prayer was used by three counsellors (Lorna, Ben and Amanda) to convey and 'sanctify' a belief that it is important to go with God's will for the client and that the client is a worthwhile person. This has the effect of enabling the client to rethink their position and come to a more growthful and insightful place (Ben and Amanda), which in both cases is also where the counsellor desires them to be. Prayer is also used to reinforce beliefs that the counsellor has about the client that have already been expressed but not necessarily heard in the session (Lorna and Amanda). Two of the counsellors (Ben and Amanda) argue philosophically that the 'intuitive knowing' that they had of their client gave them a sense of what was good for the client (and therefore of 'God') and that their intervention was justified by the shift that it brought about in the client. In many respects this is no different from the use of any other intervention because counsellors often assess the appropriateness of an intervention through a process of 'intuitive knowing' that is informed by training, theoretical awareness, awareness of 'self' and client, and from their professional experience. The effectiveness of their intervention is intuitively assessed on the effect that it has on the client and on their process. On the basis of this subjective assessment, resorting to prayer was useful, and its usefulness was determined by the way that the client presented in the next session (Ben). However, it could also be argued that it was the counsellor's desire and wish for the client that was being projected on to the client and not those of the client. It was the counsellor's values that determined what was beneficial for the client, not the client's values. The assumption is that there is something 'unethical' about such practice. But, such values and desires are present in all counselling.

It is generally accepted in most approaches to counselling that the client is the existential expert in their own world and it is ultimately they who are empowered to decide what is best for them. However, because of various factors in the client's process (e.g. the level of psychological awareness, their psychological blind-spots, their defences, their psychological fragility) the counsellor is often able to have an awareness and insight into the client's process before the client does and that the client is not necessarily aware of. This informs the counsellor's responses, interventions, method of challenge and facilitation of the client's process. So to a large extent it is the counsellor's values and desires which are appropriately trained, carefully monitored in supervision, greatly reflected upon, and sensitively practised, which influence the method of intervention and the maintenance of hope in the therapeutic alliance.

As it is not the conveying of such hopes and desires that is 'unethical' it must be something about the specific nature of 'prayer' that makes such practice inappropriate. Prayer is arguably a direct communication with God and therefore an indirect form of communication with the client. If this is the case then prayer is the antithesis of counselling which is about direct communication, characterised by trust and honesty (Gubi 2001, p.431). However, if 'God' is in all things, is at the centre of all people, and everything is connected, then prayer is a *direct* communication with both God *and the client.* It may be that prayer is difficult to challenge and that people are not encouraged to challenge what another person is praying. Prayer may also 'sanctify' (in the client's mind) what is being said, or be used to manipulate a client to comply with what the counsellor thinks is best for the client (Gubi 2002). This inability to challenge what is expressed in prayer could endanger the counselling relationship and it is important that the counsellor gives the client permission to challenge what is being prayed or to explore a client's inability to challenge and possibly not use prayer if that inability is evident. However, this danger is inherent in other counselling approaches where the counsellor shows direction and also in counselling approaches that profess to be non-directive, but this danger does not prevent the gestalt practitioner from inviting his client to partake in an experiment or cause the psychodramatist to withhold an effective activity. Potential issues of power and abuse exist in every counselling relationship and intervention. They need to be carefully monitored without precluding engagement in the process. Prayer need be no different nor more dangerous (Gubi 2001, p.431).

So it seems that it is not 'communication through prayer' that is unethical but the inappropriate nature and content of what is being communicated through prayer. Just as the nature of what is communicated through all counselling interventions is assessed as 'appropriate' from various psychological and culturally defined frameworks, the appropriateness of what is communicated through prayer must also be similarly defined, assimilated and translated through sensitive and reflexive practice that is congruent with the counselling orientation of the practitioner. There are many ways that counsellors communicate to their client that the client is a 'wholesome and worthwhile' person (Lorna). As well as those ways (e.g. accepting way of being, non-judgemental attitude, warmth, touch) why not also through prayer if it is meaningful for the client?

Processing the client's need to pray

Joyce felt that it was possible to step back with most clients and explore their need to pray.

> To reflect on it afterwards – yes, I think so. I think if a client asked in one session about praying, and that was happening, and then next time I think I would say, 'Well, what was it like when you prayed last time, and what did that mean to you?' Yes, I'd be wanting to process it. (Joyce)

However, she did recognise an occasion where she felt that exploring the client's need to pray would have felt disrespectful.

> With the old man priest, I don't think I would have done, and it's almost because it would have been like questioning something that he had never questioned – not to challenge or confront it in any way, but he would have – he'd gone through his life, spiritually I think, at quite a simple level, and I think at his stage of life and at that time, to have started to get him to reflect on his prayer life would have been disrespectful, in a way. (Joyce)

Gemma stated that prayer, when it took place, only happened at the end of sessions. When asked whether she felt able to process sensitively the client's need to pray at the beginning of the next session she stated that she always starts the session from where the client is at that time and 'it isn't usually questioning their need to pray'. Donna felt that she would talk with the client about their need to pray before she went ahead.

> I would look at what we were praying about. I'd probably ask why – what benefit would there be in it? I think we'd talk about it and I suppose I'd be interested in who was praying. Was I praying, or were they praying, or were we praying, was it out loud, was it in our heads – there'd be lots of questions to ask about it. (Donna)

However, Donna felt that it was the client who knew what was best for them and 'Who am I to actually say no?' Michael thought that it was important to reflect on the client's need to pray but felt that this could be done with subtlety.

> I think it is important to reflect on the client's need to do it, but I also think that psychodynamic practice can become extremely impudent, and unsatisfactory, in that sort of way, so I hope that I can wait, and tuck it away on the back burner, and see whether it emerges as an anxiety, and whether it can be tactfully alluded to, rather than sort of coming in with a sort of 'Why do you want to know that?' (Michael)

Some of the literature suggests that in order to ensure ethical practice in maintaining autonomy it is important for the client to be able to reflect on their process in the act of praying. This requires a sensitivity that allows the unfolding of meaning to the client's request (Webster 1992). Clients need to be sufficiently psychologically minded to be able to step back from an act of praying and reflect on their process. It may be difficult for some clients to do this as maintaining an act of mystery and reverence around something that is then psychologically explored involves different ways of thinking and could affect the nature of the client's belief (Gubi 2001, p.432). The possibility of reflecting on the client's process in prayer and the difficulties of doing that in a respectful way are evident. Some counsellors would explore their client's process in their 'need to pray' before prayer went ahead (Donna). Others would wait and let the exploration happen in a natural and unobtrusive way (Michael). Others would want to explore the client's process after prayer had happened (Joyce) and only then if it was appropriate to the client's agenda (Gemma). Joyce revealed that some of the factors that can determine whether the counsellor processes the need to pray with a client can depend on the counsellor's sense of the client, how they perceive the client may feel about the process, and what the counsellor perceives the level of the client's spirituality, or spiritual development, to be. There may also be something here about the age of the client and how they have experienced prayer over the course of a life-time. Looking at the client's process, in relation to prayer, may be disrespectful if prayer has developed as an instinctive part of the client over a long period of time. However, a reluctance to challenge aspects of the process of older clients may say more about the counsellor's agenda than the client.

Challenging clients' prayer

Some counsellors found it hard to challenge what clients were praying. Rosie stated that there might be an occasion where a client was praying, or requested prayer, and she did not feel able to go along with the request or with what was being prayed.

> There's a certain point, I think, beyond which you also have to be true to yourself as a worker, and not just being empathic and supportive, and all the other things, to the client, so yes, I think there could be a point at which I might have to say I wouldn't be happy with that, if the kind of prayer that they were wanting to offer up was something that I couldn't feel comfortable with. (Rosie)

Rosie likened it to a client requesting the counsellor to meet socially with her, where the counsellor may feel uneasy about the boundaries. Similarly a request made by the client to pray may feel uneasy for the counsellor.

> Well, if the kind of prayer that they were talking about was the kind of prayer to do something harmful to somebody, I mean that would almost – I mean, that's the kind of thing I was thinking, you know, invoking that kind of power. I mean, that's almost an ethical issue, isn't it, and I'm not sure whether there is anything I could be asked to engage in prayerfully that I would feel uncomfortable about that wouldn't be an ethical issue. But I don't like the idea of what you've just said, about the counsellor limiting what's possible in that way, but on the other hand, I do think we have – I have, I need my own integrity, and if there are some things, and I'm not clear what they are, that perhaps a code of ethics doesn't cover, that nevertheless is important for me, then I would, much as I feel discomfited by the way you expressed it, I would nevertheless hold to that. (Rosie)

Rosie acknowledged that it might be difficult to maintain a sense of integrity if the client was praying. There was no way of knowing what the client would pray for or the words they would use. She acknowledged that there was an element of risk but that if the client was praying, for example, for some kind of magical intervention, then she would sensitively challenge the client about their need for that after the prayer. Emma often felt like challenging clients if she sensed that clients were using prayer to side-step issues or avoid facing, or working through, difficult things, but she acknowledged a reluctance to challenge people in their prayer. Emma stated that she did not feel 'emboldened enough' to challenge a person in what they were praying. She felt that prayer was sacred to the person, and that it was not appropriate for her to intrude on that sacred experience. However, she described feeling as though she had had one hand tied behind her back as a therapist when the client prayed at times when she would rather they had worked for longer on a particular issue, and had worked through it for themselves. Prayer, somehow, closed access to that issue for her as a therapist. 'Now what am I going to do. Am I going to challenge God?!'

Emma felt that it was often inappropriate for her to challenge the client's need to pray. For her it depended on the relational depth (rapport), the level of work, and the strength of the therapeutic alliance. With some clients she felt able to challenge. With others, she held back because of her sensitivity to the client's belief structure, their interpretation of, and their relation to, God in terms of prayer. She was reluctant to 'unravel their spiritual knitting' (their belief constructs) yet she recognised that counselling was about enabling the client to unravel other aspects of self, for exploration and possible reconstruction – so why not prayer? Emma felt that she had no contract with her client to explore that aspect of self. Where spirituality was included in the contract she felt freer to 'explore meanings, and use of prayer, and that sort of thing'. Emma recognised that in all other areas of her therapeutic work she felt able to be congruent and able to challenge aspects of the work that she felt were dysfunctional in some way. However, with issues of spirituality she felt hesitant. In exploring this phenomenon Emma felt that her secular training had given her strong negative messages about exploring issues of spirituality. She stated that:

> It's interesting that I would have very little hesitation about exploring the congruence, and looking at that, and working with that, and yet when it comes to spiritual areas, somehow the rest is an open field – I can wander where I will, and the client will stop me if I've gone to an area they don't want, and we can explore that and move away. The spiritual bit almost feels like it's ring-fenced, and either there needs to be specific permission

given, in the initial contracting or whatever, or sort of, some gateway checking at the time. (Emma)

Emma felt conditioned by the secular culture of counselling to avoid issues of spirituality, or to work with, or challenge, spiritual interventions like prayer. She acknowledged the tension between counselling (as she saw it) as being a creative space in which the work was client-led and having to abide by the rules of the profession that overtly or covertly implied that certain aspects of the work must be avoided, or were not appropriate for exploration in counselling. This implied that there was a distinction between the psyche and the soul (spirituality). Work with the psyche belongs in counselling, and work with the soul does not. Ben also felt that he might have difficulty if someone was praying in a way in which it was evident that they were clearly abdicating their responsibility.

> If a client asks me to pray with them in the session, I think I would be suspicious, that they were perhaps abrogating their responsibilities, in a sense, or perhaps, saying that they're not going to work on this. They're just going to be open to God, which is OK on one level, but it's a bit like, I use the sort of analogy of someone sitting in an armchair staring out the window. 'Lord get me out this situation, get me a job so I can afford to eat', but stay in the armchair. You've got to do both. You've got to get out there as well as pray. I think if a client asked, then I would go with that, and if they were asking for guidance, and asking for help, and perhaps feeling weak at that point, and seeking my help to give them strength through prayer, then I would – that's OK. (Ben)

Donna felt that there was no need to challenge what clients were praying. She believed that the prayer would reflect the issues that were going on in the counselling relationship and it was those that could more appropriately be challenged. As those issues were worked through, the content of the prayer would change and become more 'healthy'.

> I think all the prayer would do would make you aware of what you were thinking, and make you aware of what was happening in the client's life, but I would imagine if they're like that in their prayer life, then they're going to be like that with you when they're talking about other things. So I think there'd be ample time to challenge that later. Certainly not in the prayer, I wouldn't dream of telling him his prayer. (Donna)

Donna did not view the act of non-challenging as 'colluding' with the prayer. She felt that the issues that were evident in the prayer could be challenged and explored through other parallel themes that would occur in the session, so collusion would be avoided.

> If I heard a client praying, having nothing, being helpless, being hopeless, then I would imagine that would parallel their life situation anyhow, that's why I can't see why it would collude... I believe that as the client changes, their prayer life changes. As they become more centred then their relationship changes with everybody else, and I'm sure with God, too. So their prayer life would actually be a good indicator of therapeutic change. (Donna)

Michael felt that it was very important to go along with what the client was praying even if it might cause some discomfort.

> I would see that as a cultural thing that they were bringing, and I would go with it as I would go with any cultural manifestation. I think it's very important – understanding Christianity as a culture. (Michael)

His experience was that in the initial stages of counselling it was important to stay in the client's cultural frame of reference and to let them couch things in a language that was familiar to them, to notice if the client is using prayer for indirect communication with the counsellor. He would hope that eventually he could encourage the client to say it directly to him rather than through prayer. Michael felt that some clients tended to 'spiritualise' or 'pietise' their issues and that it was important to let that happen, but to challenge it appropriately as the relationship progressed. He felt that clients who 'spiritualised' their issues, and who consequently saw their will as God's will (wish fulfilment), would pray in a way that would reveal this. He felt that it was the role of the counsellor to help the client to deconstruct such thinking if it was dysfunctional to help to bring the client to a more healthy place.

> One of the ways in which it is psychologically dysfunctional is that the theological understanding of the individual's personhood in its relationship with God is distorted so that on the one hand, what they're taught is that it's our task as Christians to allow God into our lives and one almost sort of arrives at a sense of the complete surrender of person or will, so that God's like a hand inside a glove puppet... I don't have a problem with that, but what then happens is that normal, everyday

expressions of human desire, such as 'I'd quite like a Mercedes-Benz, and that girl with platinum-blonde hair', gets read as God's will through wish-fulfilment, and if you go along with that as a counsellor, you just end up tied up in knots, not going anywhere. So it can be very tricky to get a sort of, purchase, really, on a person's unhappiness, because you can't appear within their understanding as an opponent of God. Nor would you want to, but you've got to somehow get hold of ways in which what they're reading as God is actually themselves, and not God... And one of the ways in which I find it's possible, sometimes, to deconstruct that, and bring things through into a new order of reality, is by not exercising my power over and against the client's, but actually just keeping quiet when I might normally speak, and becoming pensive and reflective in a way that, somehow, models a listening to God and opens the thing up into some new spirit of play and exploration, that sort of, begins to seduce a person away from rigid doctrinaire beliefs into something gentler. And there's a certain amount of cunning on my part, certain amount of active choice, but if it's – if anything really is going to happen between us, then all I'm doing is sort of, pushing something open and then we get into it together... I think what I am saying [to the client] is, 'Your self-righteousness is wrong, it's humbug, it's not going to contribute to your happiness, you're eating, you know, ersatz spiritual food. Let's go in search of the real stuff'. (Michael)

Michael regarded that process of reflection as prayer because it was quietly and patiently reflecting on what God (the author of events) really might want for the client.

...simply that I would pause, as I am with you now, not rush in with an easy answer, to say yes. Let's play with this together, you know, what do you think? That is prayer, because one is sort of saying, 'Well, I wonder what the author meant, or is meaning, by where we find ourselves'. (Michael)

For Michael, God is not a consumable, but is to be found in drawing the next breath. Anne likewise would not challenge the client's prayer even if it gave voice to the need for defences or magical interventions. Anne felt that the issues that were presented in prayer would occur in other ways during the session, and could more appropriately be challenged, or brought into conscious awareness.

> It might give me a clue of an area – I mean, it would be part of the session as far as I would hear that, hopefully, and think 'That's something that needs looking at', and my experience is that if there's something that needs looking at, it comes up again... I would kind of make a note here, and think, yes, OK, well, you know, let's look out for that when it comes up next time, and try and get hold of it. (Anne)

Rebecca said that on occasion clients wanted to use prayer as a distraction. If she discerned (instinctively felt) that this was happening, and the client requested that she pray at that point in the session, she might say something like:

> 'What is going on right now; yes, I'm happy to do that but I would like to know what's happening for you right now'. So I would check out the psychological process before...and do it. (Rebecca)

Rebecca likened it to a client who requests a hug from the counsellor. Before she could collude with the request, she would need to understand her client's process.

> Somebody might say, 'I really feel I need you to come and sit beside me and hold me', or something like that, and I would say, 'Well, I need to understand what's behind that'. (Rebecca)

Sometimes she might invite the client to stay with their process and, if it feels right for both of them, then they can pray at the end of the session. Prayer is not automatic, even when its use has been contracted.

Several writers (e.g. McMinn 1996; Webster 1992) elaborate on how clients can sometimes use prayer in therapeutically unhelpful ways. The experience of the counsellors reveals that the dilemma for the counsellor is to decide how far to collude with that practice and to decide if and when it can be appropriately challenged. Is it better to remain true to the counsellor's sense of integrity and to challenge the client over what was being prayed (Rosie) or is it better to go along with what is being prayed in the hope that the same concerns will emerge in other aspects of the work (Michael and Anne) when they could be challenged, or brought into conscious awareness, more appropriately? The nature of this dilemma is implicit in how prayer is viewed by the counsellor and the client. If prayer is regarded as a therapeutic intervention then it cannot be treated in a way that is different to how other therapeutic interventions are treated. If the 'sacredness' of prayer is regarded as being more important to the therapeutic context than the therapeutic value of prayer, then it may be less appropriate to challenge what is being said in prayer. It would seem disrespectful of the client's autonomy if prayer were interrupted by the counsellor in order to challenge the client. It may be more appropriate for a counsellor to congruently, but tentatively, say after the prayer, something like, 'I was noticing when you were praying that...' Through that way of being the counsellor is congruently able to share her insight and awareness with the client in order to further therapeutic exploration. However, my previous research (Gubi 2001) reveals that people are not generally encouraged to challenge the way that others pray, and that it may be quite difficult to maintain an act of mystery and reverence around something that is then psychologically explored.

Using prayer at the end of the session (committal)

Lorna used prayer only at the end of sessions. She stated that:

> I finish my counselling sessions with [some of my clients] by summing up the material of the session that came from them, in prayer. (Lorna)

The example that she provided of this is:

> I had a client who got some punishment in prison, loss of privileges, they call it, because he refused to strip for his strip-search, because some people on the unit had drugs, and they had to have a strip-search, and mandatory drugs tests, and he was punished because he wouldn't. So I know that he was sexually abused, physically abused, emotionally abused as a kid – he's spent most of his adult life in prison. And so, when it came to the end of the session where he'd shared the awful sense of shame that he felt at having to strip, the flashback to seeing his father stripping him before he abused him, being aware of his mum, who didn't come to his protection, very aware of why he's so violent, because it's his way of avoiding feelings, painful feelings. So in the summing-up prayer, I just said 'Johnny, will we finish with a prayer? Are you OK with that?', and he said 'Yes'. I said 'Well, we'll just relax for a moment then, and then we'll look back at what we've done in the session, and place it in the hands of God'. So both of us sat up with our backs against the back of the chair and our feet on the ground, and just focused on ourselves for a moment, and on our bodies, and the fact that we were going to tune in to God now that

it was the end of the session. So I started the prayer something like this – 'God, we bring to you, Johnny, and all the issues he has raised in this session, and we look back now at his being punished because he wouldn't strip and the painful feelings that this stripping brought up again for him, the fear that he felt, and the disappointment and sadness that his mum never intervened. Then you brought up about your violence being a response to all of this, even though you did recognise your responsibility to control your violent urges and behaviour as best you can. But you also said there are times when you just can't control it. So we placed all this in the hands of God knowing that on your own you feel really weak and vulnerable, even though there are lots of indications of your tremendous growth and seriously working on yourself, trying to integrate your past and become a more wholesome and worthwhile person, although in many of our lives you are already that. So we finish the session by saying thank you God, for Johnny. Amen.' (Lorna)

She believed that this helped her clients to place their difficulties into the hands of God. The context for her client work was in a prison – 'a place where the faith element arises much more easily than in other contexts'. In this setting, in which the prisoners have lost everything else, the one thing that many of them hold on to is their faith. It can enable them to connect with some sense of security, which perhaps originated from their childhood. In justifying its use, Lorna stated that using prayer is about 'recognising a dimension of the client and bringing it into the session.' In so doing, it is about acknowledging the whole being of the client, and not excluding one dimension of the client (i.e. their belief system or their spiritual dimension) from the sessions. Lorna did not believe that miracles would happen, through prayer, to change the external circumstances of her clients, and she sensitively challenged those clients who expected 'a kind of dial 999 God' to intervene. However, she stated that:

The kind of miracle that might happen as the result of prayer could be how we receive the inner strength to cope with reality... It's about reaching a place of inner peace and acceptance, rather than expecting the world to change. (Lorna)

Lorna believed that prayer heightens the awareness of a higher power within the client – that 'everything doesn't entirely depend on us'. She also believed that prayer helps her clients to discover a sense of meaning, purpose and direction in their lives, no matter how awful life is. The theological and philosophical basis for Lorna's work (and her life) is that God imbues everything. She believes in an 'incarnate God'. These beliefs enable her to hold the attitude of:

> God is in all human life. It's such an enriching concept…because if you get very obnoxious people in prison [who have committed] terrible crimes, one of the privileges that my position with them enables is that they are so trusting with you…and you see the lovely side of them, but it's terribly hidden…so it's a great privilege. When you meet the most hopeless cases, it's great to always have hope. Sometimes it's in faith only, but I believe there's always hope for people. (Lorna)

Lorna believed that this hope, which comes from her faith, rubs off on her clients. As in person-centred counselling, the valuing of clients comes from the counsellor's way of being with clients, not necessarily from the things she says but more from the way she is. So Lorna felt that her sense of her client's worth was picked up more non-verbally than verbally. Lorna did acknowledge, however, that she did tend to include 'messages of hope' when praying with clients. This is evident in Lorna's prayer with her client in the phrase *trying to integrate your past and become a more wholesome and worthwhile person, although in many of our lives you are already that.* Lorna described herself as a 'good news' person and that this emphasis of hope and valuing of her client pervades her work. 'I don't have it planned. Usually it just happens.' Lorna also believed in the death and resurrection patterns of life which are lived out in the counselling relationship.

> There are always little deaths and little resurrections. Sometimes there are very big deaths and big resurrections, so to me that is the good news of our faith. (Lorna)

Lorna believed that prayer:

> …enables someone to be more rooted in themselves, and to find out that they're not as hopeless as they might feel, so that it enables one to find a deeper sense of self. You see, I often say in the psychodynamic approach, that, you know, finding our own inner spirit and being led by our own spirit, that there's something about our spirit and the spirit of God being one… The more wholesome, and the more open to growth that we are, the more we become the people we are meant to be, you know, reach our potential, and so on. Come closer to reaching it, anyway, the happier we'll be, and the better our contribution to the world, and for me that's

> eschatology in the sense of eternity starting now...that we're not good little boys and girls in order to win heaven. We actually have some sort of heaven on earth, be it enormously flawed at times, but you know, the satisfaction and the joy we get in life, that's eternity starting here and now, we don't have to wait. (Lorna)

Lorna stated that the silence that can exist after praying with a client was a very powerful space.

> There's some sense that the client has got in touch with himself and sometimes it can be very traumatic issues that have been raised in the session, but at the end of the session he can be peaceful and silent without unease. Now that to me is wonderful reality. (Lorna)

She believed that the peace and calm at the end of the session was the result of prayer.

> The quieting of one's self, the focusing on God...maybe there's some subconscious realisation of being held by God...it's a mystery, isn't it. (Lorna)

Emma noticed that the few times that she has prayed with clients overtly in the session it has always been with female clients and at the end of the session as a form of conclusion. It has always been the clients who have instigated the prayer, not her. She felt that the reasons for this phenomenon were:

> There is the comfort factor, there is the point of connection, I think, with me as the therapist, and sometimes I have felt it almost, well, we've been here working together on this, now God, you either put your rubber stamp on it, or you do the work, please, and you take it forwards, or you endorse it. There's invariably in the prayer, something about asking for his guidance, asking for his help in things, but there's a transferring, sometimes, for God to sort of pick up the ropes and run with this, and make it so. The shadow side of that would be sometimes there's a slight side-stepping – 'Well I've been here and we've worked hard and we looked at some difficult things – now God – I've done my bit, so God would you get it sorted, please'. There's a little bit of transferring back, which is not how I would – I would rather stay with the client for a bit longer on that, and have them work that through for themselves. (Emma)

Prayer is being used by the client to ask God to endorse the work, to take it forward, to rubber-stamp it, to sort, and to mend. Fran only prayed at the end of a session as a way of putting the session into God's hands. She felt that the concept of committal was a Christian tradition that was common in the Church and praying with clients at the end of a session would be an opportunity for healing, guidance and comfort: 'People find it comforting to pray together...' To not offer prayer with clients who were Christian at the end of a session would feel like withholding something and would be unethical for Fran. In introducing prayer into the agenda Fran stated that she might do it in the following way:

> What I say to people is that we both love the same God. It makes sense to bring this, to bring him into our process, so to speak, to ask for his guidance on the work that we're doing, and his blessing, and healing. Those are all very good reasons for doing so, and it seems to me it would be really sad not to do that, given that we both have the same beliefs. (Fran)

Fran stressed that she would be tentative in bringing the concept of prayer to the client but acknowledged that she had never had a client who refused her. When challenged on whether clients would be able to say 'no' to her, or whether the way she introduced it might preclude them from saying 'no', Fran felt that she would instinctively pick up on any hesitation and not use prayer. When asked what the words of such a prayer might be, Fran offered the following content:

> I just pray as I always do in my own words, just talking to our heavenly Father, and possibly I might use phrases like, 'We make this commitment, commit our work to you', I might use a word like that, but I mean just really normal, everyday language. I would probably say 'Father we thank you for being with us in this work we've done today. We ask your blessing on [client's name] as she goes through the next week, and we ask for your continued guidance on what we're doing here, and thank you for your help' – something like that. Amen. In Jesus' name, I'd probably say. Because the name Jesus is powerful, so I do use that phrase.

Fran did not draw upon the material that was worked on in the session as a way of summarising the session. She stated that she summarised the session before she prayed. For her, prayer was very much about committal. This sense of committal was also evident in the work of Rosie.

I said, 'Can we put her in the palm of God's hand and leave her there?' So we weren't quite asking somebody to take it over and do something, but we were sort of the middle option of handing it over to God, and saying, 'We haven't quite sorted this out, we'll give it to you', but not with any expectation that miracles are going to be performed. (Rosie)

When challenged as to whether it was a good thing to introduce prayer at the end of a session because of its induced feelings of comfort and peace thus taking the client away from the feelings that they might be left with from the session, Fran stated:

I'm afraid I do work in the way I always reckon to bring my clients back to reality before they leave, and I do even ask questions to get their attention away from their distress, so I wouldn't see that as a bad thing, actually. It's just the way I work. They've got to go back into their everyday life, so I think that would be part of my boundaries, boundaries of the session, framework. (Fran)

Although Fran recognised that prayer could be viewed as a way of rescuing clients, she also felt that prayer could be challenging.

I can see that people might construe it as that – what I'm thinking is that I only do this with people who have a faith in God anyway, so I don't think it's rescuing them to actually remind them of where they stand, of you know, it's a reminder of the fact that our work is within a context of God's love, so I wouldn't think it's particularly rescuing really. But I can see that non-Christians might think that. (Fran)

Rosie did not consider it as rescuing but viewed it as 'freeing up' the client – of providing a 'cathartic liberation'.

She was saying that she has decided to be as freed up from the responsibility of trying to look after, and heal, this damaged child… It wasn't actually saying, 'Please make her better', but I was saying, I suppose, 'I don't think I can help you any more', and she was saying, 'And I don't think I can help this damaged part of me any more', so we give it over to someone else's safe keeping, really, I think. (Rosie)

In this way prayer can provide a release from the energy of 'having to heal' or 'do something with this' to enable the client to reach a point of acceptance and liberation through knowing that their woundedness is being looked after by God. Gemma stated that her clients only ever asked for prayer at the end of a session. She would not pray during the session because 'it might divert the client from where they are'. She described prayer as a 'finishing thing'. Michael disclosed that he would not bring any of the client's 'tender material' to the prayer but would customarily say words like:

> 'Thank you, thank you for the courage that's been on display, and thank you for the honesty that's been around', and something about a hope that the work will go somewhere, that the person will feel safe enough, prior to the next meeting. (Michael)

Amanda used prayer at the end of a session when the client was left in a difficult place.

> Sometimes, when the work has – is not ending in a good place, and it needs to continue on a, as a sort of holding prayer, I think, asking God to protect the client… (Amanda)

Amanda recognised that this process was partly for her own benefit – for putting her mind at rest that she had not caused the client any damage.

> I can't say if it has inhibited it, when they've gone away, but I suppose my concern for the client would be that when they went home, or went to work, or whatever they had to do, they would be really disturbed by what had happened in the session, and would not be able to continue through the rest of their week before they came back again… So I suppose, partly, it would be for me, wouldn't it – that I hadn't done them damage, yes. (Amanda)

Rowena stated that sometimes she had a strong sense of God being in the room. When she has that sense she sometimes feels 'nudged' to pray with a client at the end of a session. In those cases she sensitively asks the client if it would be acceptable for her to pray. In 15 years she had never been refused.

> If I'm working with a Christian, I think there is a sense of we have an understanding of where we are each coming from as we begin. And I don't actually pray with clients, Christian clients, very often at all. There are occasions when I feel led by a holy spirit, and it's usually quite a sort of nudge that I get, particularly if I use gestalt if they've been doing, perhaps, visualisation, where they've gone right back to a birth situation, or very young child, and they've been in touch with a lot of tears, I find I would

not do this, I would not offer prayer, other than to a client who is a Christian, and I always ask them. I would never pray during a session, I would just say at the end 'How would you feel if we prayed?' And they've never, in 15 years, said 'no'... So I would then say, 'Are you happy for me to move?', and I would move and come and kneel beside them here, and I would ask their permission, if it's all right for me to put a hand on their shoulder, and I would just pray, really, and I see that form of prayer as what I would call 'healing of the memories', where you bring Christ into whatever the situation was for the person, to bring healing, and I see that form of prayer as protection – it's a sort of sealing of the process that the client has gone through, and always they have a deep sense of peace and having moved when I've prayed for them. (Rowena)

Rowena stated that she was reticent about using prayer because it could be intrusive and invasive. It needed to be introduced sensitively.

I'm just aware of needing to be very, very sensitive, as to when I do ask a client if they would like me to pray. I don't have any misgivings. I don't have any doubts. I don't have any reservations. I hope I am so sufficiently listening to God that when I do offer prayer, it is done in a very sensitive way. (Rowena)

There is little in the counsellors' experiences that raises ethical issues because prayer is used by the counsellors to aid fidelity and autonomy and promote beneficence and non-maleficence. For some counsellors prayer at the end of a session is a way of: reinforcing the work that the client engaged in, a way of conveying messages of hope and affirmation, a way of heightening awareness of a higher power, a way of helping a client to be at peace in themselves, a point of connection and of feeling upheld by something greater, a way of sanctifying the work as being worthwhile, a cathartic liberation of feelings to enable acceptance to be reached, a place of comfort, but also of challenge, and a place to leave tender material in a place of safety with a feeling of being 'looked after'. This use of prayer is evident in the literature (Gubi 1999, 2001; Rose 1996, 1999, 2002). Prayer as a way of committal seems to have a more natural place in the session because it is less intrusive to the process of the session. This is demonstrated by how no counsellors have been refused prayer at this point in the session. However, it is clear that prayer has to be introduced sensitively, even at this point in the session (Rowena). There is an issue about whether prayer is sometimes used by some counsellors (e.g. Fran and Amanda) out of a response to their own need to leave clients in a place of comfort. This may take the client away from the feelings when it may be more beneficial to leave a client in contact with the experience. However, it is unethical to leave clients in a traumatised state (non-maleficence) and prayer may be a helpful way of enabling clients to be in a more peaceful state before they leave the session. The literature indicates the danger that prayer has of introducing connotations of magic, victimhood and helplessness, and in using prayer at the end of a session as a place to 'dump and run' (Gubi 2001). However, the wording of the prayers above reveal: a sense of hope in that the client is able to be in touch with a deeper sense of self, a sense of being blessed, a sense of 'being with' something greater, a sense of entrusting – a 'handing over', a sense of safety and protection, and a sense of ongoing healing. None of the examples of the prayers that were offered indicated a request for miracles and instant healing. Instead they echo the belief in a supportive God of hope whose healing is brought about by that sense of being encompassed and held in a place of safety and connection (love). This reinforces the therapeutic work in which the client has responsibility for healing, change and acceptance. This form of prayer can be empowering to the client. There is also no evidence from the counsellors who use prayer in their work that 'dumping and running' has taken place through prayer.

Praying at the end of the counselling relationship

Joyce stated that she always asks all of her clients how they want to end the counselling relationship. On one occasion she had asked this question of a client who decided that she wanted to pray.

> I'd said to her the week before, 'How would you like to spend your last session? I'll leave it for you to decide'. I often say that to people… At the end of the last session she said, 'I've brought you a present' and she opened the bag and in the bag was a little blue glass container with a candle in it, and she put it on the table, and she said, 'I want us to pray'. Then she took out a little holy picture with a prayer on the back, and she put that down beside it, and she lit the candle, and she got down on her knees, and I thought 'Oh blimey! Here we go again – really synchronistic!' and it was really strange, because – I don't know if you know CAT

[cognitive analytic therapy] and the goodbye letter? I often do that with people as a goodbye, and we swop letters – they write a letter to me and I write a letter to them and we read it out and exchange the letters, and anyway, she started to pray. She was down on her knees and I was sitting on my chair, feeling a bit uncomfortable, and she started praying and thanking God for bringing me to her, or bringing her to me, or finding me, or whatever, and the work we'd done and so on…, and then when she ended, I thought 'This doesn't feel right, it doesn't feel equal'. So I said to her, 'Well, you know, I'd like to pray if that's all right', and she said 'yes'. I held her hands, and I said – I started thanking God for bringing Samantha, and talking about her talents and her personality and the things I noticed about her, and how she'd struggled through, and I realised that actually what I was doing was like a CAT letter and halfway through, I realised that what I'd done was, I'd changed. I was no longer praying to God. I was praying to her. I was talking to her directly, and I was saying, you know, 'Thank you for sharing' and all this, and I was saying it to her, and suddenly I realised that felt better, because it didn't feel quite right to be thanking God out there, it was like in here, in her… It was me talking to her, and you know, I often talk about people having this God-spot, I don't know whether I say God-spot or God-centre. (Joyce)

In this scenario Joyce understood the client's process as having a need to sanctify and formalise the work with prayer. It is interesting to see how the counsellor made the experience authentic for herself after experiencing initial discomfort by praying to the God-centre of the client rather than to a God outside of the client. This was experienced as talking to the client herself and the content was similar to what the counsellor would write in a goodbye letter to the client as practised in cognitive analytic therapy.

It almost seemed like she wanted to formalise it, like doing it this way actually gave it a kind of an elevated status. Just saying those things to me wasn't enough, but to put it within a kind of framework of being holy in some way made it better for her… I don't think she thinks she's good enough. I think she needs the church or the ritual as a kind of vehicle because she's not enough in herself… The formalisation of the words into prayer form gave her something…that was meaningful, on another level…it's like a crystallisation…and focusing, and it reaches a different spot. (Joyce)

So prayer can be a way of formalising the end of the counselling relationship, of sanctifying the work, and of making the work meaningful at a spiritual or more 'elevated' level.

The example that is given above comes from a counsellor (Joyce) who did not use prayer at any other time in the therapeutic encounter with her client. It was therefore remembered specifically in the context of 'ending' because of its uniqueness and because of the issues that it raised for the counsellor. Many of the counsellors who use prayer to 'end' may more regularly use prayer as 'committal' and would not regard prayer in the context of 'ending' as being different from prayer in the context of committal. However, none of the literature specifically mentions prayer in the context of ending except Dobbins (2000). The main focus of the literature on prayer is on the effect of prayer on the therapeutic relationship and on encouraging strategic and process awareness. The literature does not refer specifically to 'ending', possibly because it may be felt that prayer no longer has an impact on an ongoing therapeutic relationship, or because prayer is assumed to be less unethical, and less dangerous, at an ending stage. However, it is likely that prayer will have an impact on what is taken away from the therapeutic relationship. The way that prayer is implemented at this stage is also important. Dobbins (2000) states that prayer can be used in ending as a way of consolidating therapeutic gain. This is also the purpose of the 'goodbye letter' that Joyce makes reference to. In cognitive analytic therapy the goodbye letter enables the client to leave with a reminder of both the journey that has been made and of what has been learnt and encountered (Ryle and Cowmeadow 1992). Through prayer the client was able to formalise the ending in a way that made the work more spiritually meaningful, in which gratitude to God, and to the counsellor, for what had been learnt and encountered, could be expressed. Because the prayer was mutual, and the communication was directly to the God-centre of the client, it enabled 'closure' and termination of the work at a spiritual level for both counsellor and client.

Summary

It has been important to enable the voice of counsellors whose work includes prayer to be heard in as authentic a way as possible and their experiences make a strong case for the possibility of considering the integration of prayer in mainstream counselling. Ethical difficulties that are reflected in the literature do not appear to be insurmountable dilemmas in practice, providing that there is appropriate reflexiveness, awareness, and sensitivity of the client, that there is a quality of naturalness and authenticity in the counsellor's way of being, and that both client and counsellor are open to the practice of prayer. Prayer, if handled with the same care as any other intervention, has a place in ethical mainstream counselling practice.

CHAPTER 7

Meeting the Challenge

Whether people like it or not, it is clear that prayer occurs in and influences mainstream counselling and psychotherapy practice and can be integrated in an appropriate and ethical manner by practitioners who are 'open' to its use.

Considerations for the practice of prayer in counselling

The purpose of this book is not to formulate a model for using prayer, but it is possible to ascertain considerations for good practice as various themes have emerged which can provide some guidance in the use of prayer in counselling. These considerations for good practice are underpinned by an awareness of potential ethical issues, an awareness of how prayer can be integrated ethically, an awareness of the quality and characteristics of the prayer being used, and a considered awareness of issues of tension and difficulty for the counsellor.

Developing an awareness of potential ethical issues

The first consideration for good practice is the development of an awareness of potential ethical issues. This awareness is important in preventing the counsellor from colluding with defences and resistance. However, the ethical difficulties, although cautionary, are not prohibitive if prayer is integrated appropriately into practice. Similarly, a good counsellor knows of potential risks when entering into a therapeutic relationship, but an awareness of the potential risks enables her to facilitate more appropriately without withholding the therapeutic opportunity. Whilst the ethical difficulties may seem insurmountable at a theoretical level, the mainstream counsellors whose work includes prayer have carefully reflected on the issues and have reached a place of understanding of the issues where they have found the use of prayer to be less implicated with ethical dilemmas than the literature suggests.

How prayer is integrated ethically

The second consideration for good practice is an awareness of how prayer can be integrated ethically. The literature suggests that the counsellor should conduct a formal assessment of the client's spiritual history (Magaletta and Brawer 1998; Richards and Bergin 1997; West 1998, 2000). This enables the counsellor to communicate an acceptance of the client's spirituality and gain a better sense of the client's world and spiritual practice. It is clear that some counsellors do formalise the use of prayer as a possible intervention and are open in their disclosure about their spirituality. However, many counselling approaches (particularly humanistic approaches) do not conduct 'formal assessments' at the contracting stage of the relationship. In such cases counsellors use pre-contact information or a symbolic environment (often discreet religious symbols in the room or on jewellery) to communicate acceptance of spirituality. Clients who are in touch with their own spirituality can often become aware of the counsellor's openness to spirituality through the counsellor's presence, way of being, and unconscious communication. Instead of a formalised procedure, the integration of prayer seems to rely more on a sensitive awareness of the client's needs and an intuitive sensing of the appropriateness of the situation and the client. It is likely that the counsellor has informally gained a sense of her client's coping strategies and spirituality as the relationship has unfolded. So the integration of prayer is more often informed by the quality of attunement and connection between counsellor and client. The integration of prayer is therefore more likely to be a relational and intuitive process based on an awareness of the appropriateness of prayer for the client. Prayer must not be mechanistic and routine (except perhaps in the provision of silence at the beginning of the session) or attributed to external sources (e.g. the Holy Spirit) except where such attribution actually stems from discernment that comes from the counsellor's conscious awareness.

The quality and characteristics of the prayer

The third consideration for good practice is an awareness of the quality and characteristics of prayer. Prayer must have a quality of naturalness about it, with the notion of prayer being introduced with the tentative quality of 'feeling your way' that emerges out of a sense of respect for the client. The prayer has to feel relevant to the context and the 'moment' of what is being shared, and must not interrupt the agenda or take the client away from experiencing the 'felt sense' of the moment. Prayer has to respect the client's autonomy and attention needs to be paid to potential issues of deference (Rennie 1994) and compliance. In checking out issues of deference and compliance it is important to gain the client's consent, although to gain formal written consent, as Magaletta and Brawer (1998) suggest, might detract from the intimacy of the moment and lead to an intellectualisation of the phenomenon in which the simplicity and power of the experience is lost. It is important that the client is able to refuse prayer and it seems important that the counsellor is reflexive about her clients never refusing prayer to ascertain honestly if her method of introducing prayer can enable a client to refuse.

If prayer occurs with the counsellor's eyes closed the counsellor may more fully engage with the prayer experience itself but she may miss having a sense of the client's way of being as he prays. The use of silence at the beginning of a session is the most appropriate form of prayer at this stage of the session as it enables the client to gain stillness and a focus for the work. It provides a spiritual space which facilitates the client in focusing on their point of pain and on the essence of their deepest self (authenticity) which allows the unconscious to speak. The prayerful space also acknowledges the spiritual context of the work in a subtle way. Praying with words may inhibit the expression of certain emotions. Lengthy prayer and routine, mechanistic prayer are not appropriate. Any verbal prayer needs to be focused on the client's needs and be a simple acknowledgement of what the client wants to bring.

Praying at times of client desperation may take the client away from experiencing the aloneness and the fear of the experience. However, after that has been experienced and explored, prayer at these times may be beneficent at a time when the client's autonomy has been diminished. Meditative prayer may also be appropriate at times when the client is experiencing panic as such prayer carries anxiety-reducing traits (Helminiak

1982; McDonald 1999; Shapiro 1980). The use of ritual to aid completion, resolution, a letting go, and a committal, can also be an appropriate place for prayer to be integrated in counselling. However, it is important that the client does not expect instant healing from the ritual, but is able to continue to work on the issues as and when they recur. It is also important that the counsellor checks out that the client does not feel that the counsellor would be disappointed if healing or closure did not occur. This can enhance the client's authenticity. Practices such as the 'laying on of hands' and 'speaking in tongues' are rare practices. However, they do occur and are existentially powerful to those who encounter them. It is important that this type of ritual is not routine or mechanistic, and that the counsellor reflects carefully on her need to introduce such practice. Again, such practice needs to have a sense of naturalness about it for both counsellor and client. It also needs to emerge from a discernment of the 'felt sense' of the moment.

Silence that fosters a connectedness to the sacred (Pargament 1997; Ulanov and Ulanov 1982) is a less controversial, but nevertheless overt, use of prayer. Whilst prayer has the potential to disempower the client, prayer also has the potential to empower the client. This can be seen in the client taking responsibility for the praying, in the way that the content of prayer changes over time, and in the ability of the client to ask for prayer. All of these can be regarded as signs of developing autonomy.

Some of the common uses of prayer in counselling were at the end of a session or the termination of a counselling relationship. Using prayer at these times is less intrusive to the therapeutic process of the session. This use of prayer to convey messages of hope and affirmation reinforces the therapeutic work in which the client has responsibility for healing, change, and/or acceptance. Prayer for intervention which introduces connotations of magic (e.g. instant healing and miracles), victimhood and helplessness is not appropriate. The use of prayer to 'dump and run' (Gubi 2001) is also not appropriate. Using prayer to end the counselling relationship can act as a way of consolidating the therapeutic gain (Dobbins 2000), enabling closure and termination of the work at both a practical and a spiritual level.

Issues of tension and difficulty for the counsellor

The fourth consideration for good practice is an awareness of the possible areas of tension and difficulty for the counsellor. Whether prayer can be used to communicate with the client emerged as a contentious issue. The literature suggests that prayer should not be used to impose or communicate the counsellor's values to the client (Magaletta and Brawer 1998; McMinn 1996; Rose 1993, 1996, 1999, 2002; Webster 1992) because the client may be unable to challenge what is being prayed, and the use of prayer in this way is open to manipulation and abuse. However, certain values that are compatible with the counselling values (e.g. the client is a person of worth and of value) may be appropriately imparted and sanctified through prayer. Prayer may also be a useful medium through which the client is more able to hear the counsellor's insight and awareness of the client and of her process. Rather than being an indirect communication with the client, which may be regarded as the antithesis of counselling (Gubi 2001), prayer can be regarded as a direct communication with the client if God is at the centre of the client.

Some counsellors were reluctant to enable their clients to explore their motivation for, and act of, praying. However, if prayer is to be integrated into mainstream counselling practice it must not be treated any differently from any other intervention in counselling. Exploration of whatever happens is an implicit part of therapy and prayer is no different. Some counsellors explore the client's need to pray before the prayer. Others wait and let the exploration happen in a natural and unobtrusive way. Others explored the client's process after the prayer. Out of respect for the client it was important to travel alongside the client through the prayer (even if the content did not feel comfortable for the counsellor) and then to unpick the process therapeutically, or appropriately challenge the client by sensitively, congruently, but tentatively sharing the counsellor's insights and awareness of the client to further therapeutic exploration. If prayer is to be used as a therapeutic intervention it must not assume a 'sacredness' that excludes it from the way that other counselling interventions are worked with. Even though it has been argued that prayer is different from other interventions (McMinn 1996) prayer must be subjected to the same ethical considerations as other interventions, and whatever is used in counselling must be open to exploration. From an ethical perspective, prayer cannot be treated any differently from any other intervention in the context of counselling and psychotherapy.

Self-disclosure of the counsellor's spirituality was also identified as an area of potential tension. Disclosure of the counsellor's spirituality can enable a more profound connection for clients who want to explore spiritual issues, because exploring spiritual material is often problematic for clients (West 2000, 2002). However, the sharing of spiritual beliefs may lead to an unhelpful transference phenomenon (Hinksman 1999) or inappropriately influence the counselling agenda. Even when counsellors make their faith explicit to their client, the use of prayer is still not often used in counselling.

Implications for training

Many counselling practitioners are still largely unwilling to look beyond the paradigms of particular counselling approaches and the cultural norms of mainstream counselling (Gubi 2002). There is a misguided belief that counselling and psychotherapy are informed by purely scientifically informed processes and that everything that is used in counselling must also be scientifically informed. However, counselling is multi-disciplinary and informed both by the counsellor's experience of life and by the client's experience, as well as by training and reflexive reading. Neither the counsellor's nor the client's experience is confined to a chosen therapeutic meta-perspective, and counsellors need to be more open to 'seeing' what is happening (McLeod 2001) and be prepared to be appropriately creative in working with the phenomenon that the client presents. Training therefore needs to challenge these cultural norms within the counselling culture itself that prohibit acceptance of what is of value to the client.

Webster (1992) states that fear is what prevents the cultural acceptance of prayer in counselling. Many battle with the assumptions which they have inherited from their training that religious and spiritual matters do not belong in counselling. This has led to a sense of 'guilt' about using an intervention that is life-enhancing. It has also nurtured a culture of secrecy that does not have permission to be talked about, except to researchers such as myself or in selective workshops where spirituality is on the agenda. Training is the place to challenge these unhelpful assumptions and to explore generically the ethical implications of all interventions, creating a framework that informs ethical practice. Magaletta and Brawer (1998) argue that 'educating for competence' is an ethical requirement. Training should include the broadening of the counsellor's personal perspective of prayer and spirituality in a way that will enable greater openness to the prayer practice of others. West (2000, pp.131–133) suggests that a training programme should contain nine elements that give the trainee the opportunity to examine their own prejudices and biases around spirituality and develop their knowledge and understanding about spirituality. Whilst a training course should not necessarily include a module on 'how to pray' with clients, training courses must foster an openness to the spiritual dimension of counselling and an openness to how strategies, like prayer, can enhance the therapeutic process. A good training course will already impart the skills and attitudes that are necessary to work sensitively and exploratively with whatever a client brings, and students will be aware of what constitutes ethical practice. So a training in prayer types and methods is not advocated here as it is by some (e.g. McMinn 1996) – merely an openness to prayer as a legitimate counselling intervention when working with the spiritual dimension of the client, and a commitment to the quality of 'naturalness' that is reflected in the language and content of the prayer. This process comes more easily to a spiritually attuned counsellor, and so training courses could encourage their trainees to engage in useful spiritual practices such as that advocated by Thorne (1994, 1998, 2002). It may also be helpful for counsellors to examine their understanding of prayer and grow in such a way as to free themselves in extemporary prayer, whilst being conscious of the language and assumptions that are being communicated in prayer within the context of counselling. However, such an awareness of language is intrinsically the same as being aware of how the counsellor communicates with the client – an awareness of language and communication that is already imparted in good counsellor training courses.

Implications for supervision

Supervision, likewise, needs to foster an openness to the experience of 'the other'. This includes the other's practice of prayer. Webster (1992), Ten Eyck (1993), and Magaletta and Brawer (1998) all stress the importance of good clinical supervision when using prayer in counselling, but the importance of good supervision is necessary for all counselling, not just counselling in which prayer is integrated. Bringing issues of prayer in counselling to supervision is highly problematic. My survey (Gubi 2004) suggests that 59 per cent of British Association for Counselling and Psychotherapy (BACP) Accredited Counsellors and 91 per cent of Churches Ministerial Counselling Services (CMCS) Approved Counsellors have used/use prayer either covertly or overtly to influence their counselling work. Those figures suggest that spirituality is an implicit part of many counsellors' practice, yet 35 per cent of BACP Accredited Counsellors and 22 per cent of CMCS Approved Counsellors who have used overt prayer in their counselling practice have not explored its use in supervision. This is because many counsellors do not feel free to explore their practice of prayer due to a fear of not being understood, being judged, losing respect and credibility, being thought of as transgressing, exposure by the supervisor, a lack of trust in how the supervisor will treat the disclosure, and condemnation and dismissal of something that is important and precious to the counsellor. Much of this says something about the counsellors as well as the supervisors, but the experience of many of the counsellors who use prayer is of the supervisor being 'shocked' at the revelation, and of how supervisors from particular modalities (e.g. the psychodynamic) seem to be less open to what their supervisee brings, and can instil 'fear' in their supervisee. This leaves supervisees finding creative ways of separating out certain aspects of their work to explore among several supervisors or avoiding exploring some parts of their practice with anyone – neither of which is ethically satisfactory.

Like training, the implication of this is in examining cultural bias and assumptions to enable supervisors to explore what aspects of their supervisees they are not open to hearing. Whilst hearing about the use of prayer may cause some supervisors to have concern about their supervisees' practice, not hearing those aspects of their supervisees' work would be even more unethical and dangerous. Because so much of supervision is based on trust, supervisors also need to examine how they convey to their supervisees that it is acceptable to bring all of their work, including the spiritual, and to challenge sensitively those counsellors who do not feel that they have to bring matters of prayer to supervision because of a reluctance to theorise and rationalise the prayer dimension of counselling. Because some counsellors do not bring prayer issues to supervision as they only bring issues of concern to supervision, again this indicates that supervisors need to challenge sensitively supervisees on what aspects of their work they do not bring to supervision, including the good aspects of their work. The relationship between supervisor and supervisee also needs to be honestly examined. These issues for exploration are already clearly a part of good practice for supervision and are intrinsic in most supervision theory (e.g. Carroll 2001; Hawkins and Shohet 2000; Page and Wosket 2001). However, it appears that the theory becomes more problematic when translated into practice.

The central implication for supervision is in creating a culture of openness to all aspects of the counselling process without judgement, where the supervisee feels accepted, able and open to explore all aspects of the work with the same supervisor. This prevents unethical practice and enables consistency of work.

Personal reflections

In the introduction I stated that this book has been something of a personal journey, in that I set out to answer some personal questions. What I have discovered is that prayer does have a place in ethical practice. What stops me from integrating prayer in my own practice is 'me'. To do so means that I have to question some cherished beliefs and assumptions that have been instilled in me from my training as a counsellor. I have discovered how difficult and frightening it is to be open to another's spirituality at times, even when I have a strong spirituality of my own. I have discovered that the boundary between prayer and counselling is an existential and epistemological boundary that is firmer the more the difficulties are that are advanced in my mind, and less firm the more open I am to the practice of others and to the potential of my own counselling practice. The boundary consists of that which I carry in my mind as a prejudice and as a fear even though that fear is not necessarily the reality of practice. Where is the limit for me in the interface between acceptance (which can never be wholly unconditional) and my respecting of others' needs when I'm taken to that zone where my comfort is decreased and my fear is intensified? Can I increase the flexibility of my constructs without losing my sense of self as a person or my integrity as a practitioner, in order to accommodate 'the other' within the norms of ethical practice? That is our challenge.

References

Ai, A.L, Dunkle, R.E., Peterson, C. and Bolling, S.F. (1998) 'The role of private prayer in psychological recovery among midlife and aged patients following cardiac surgery.' *The Gerontologist 38*, 5, 591–601.

Alcoholics Anonymous (1981) *Twelve Concepts for World Service.* New York: AA World Services Inc.

Allinson, J. (1966) 'Recent empirical studies of religious conversion experiences.' *Pastoral Psychology 17*, 21–33.

American Psychological Association (1992) 'Ethical principles of psychologists and code of conduct.' *American Psychologist 47*, 1597–1611.

Ames, E.S. (1910) *The Psychology of Religious Experience.* Boston: Houghton Mifflin.

Arieti, S. (1967) *The Intrapsychic Self.* New York: Basic Books.

Armer, J.H. (1994) 'Coping strategies identified as "utilized" and "helpful" by relocated rural elders.' *Clinical Gerontologists 14*, 55–60.

Ashby, J.S. and Lenhart, R.S. (1994) 'Prayer as a coping strategy for chronic pain patients.' *Rehabilitation Psychology 39*, 3, 205–209.

Astin, J.A., Harkness, E. and Ernst, E. (2000) 'The efficacy of distant healing: A systematic review of randomised trials.' *Annals of Internal Medicine 132*, 11, 903–910.

Aviles, J.M., Whelan, E., Hernke, D.A., Williams, B.A., Kenny, K.E., O'Fallon, M. and Kopecky, S.L. (2001) 'Intercessory prayer and cardiovascular disease progression in a coronary care unit population: A randomized controlled trial.' *Mayo Clinic Proceedings 76*, 1192–1198.

BACP (2002) *Ethical Framework for Good Practice in Counselling and Psychotherapy.* Rugby: British Association for Counselling and Psychotherapy.

Baines, E. (1994) 'Caregiver stress in the older adult.' *Journal of Community Health Nursing 4*, 257–263.

Barnum, B. (1998) *Spirituality in Nursing from Traditional to New Age.* New York: Springer.

Bearon, L.B. and Koenig, H.G. (1990) 'Religious cognitions and use of prayer in health and illness.' *The Gerontologist 30*, 249–253.

Beck, F.O. (1906) 'Prayer: A study in its history and psychology.' *American Journal of Religious Psychology and Education 2*, 107–121.

Bennett, R. (1984) *How to Pray for Inner Healing.* Eastbourne: Kingsway.

Benor, D.J. (1993) *Healing Research.* Volumes 1–4. Munich: Helix Verlag.

Benson, H. (1996) *Timeless Healing: The Power and Biology of Belief.* New York: Scribner.

Bernardi, L., Sleight, P., Bandinelli, G., Centetti, S., Fattorini, L., Wdowczyc-Szulc, J. and Lagi, A. (2001) 'Effect of rosary prayer and yoga mantras on automatic cardiovascular rhythms: comparative study.' *British Medical Journal 323*, 1446–1449.

Bloom, A. and LeFebvre, G. (2002) *Courage to Pray*. New York: SVS Press.

Borysenko, J. and Borysenko, M. (1994) *The Power of the Mind to Heal: Renewing Body, Mind and Spirit*. Carson, CA: Hay House.

Brown, L.B. (1994) *The Human Side of Prayer. Birmingham, Alabama: Religious Education Press.*

Brown-Saltzman, K. (1997) 'Replenishing the spirit by meditative prayer and guided imagery.' *Seminars in Oncology Nursing 13*, 4, 255–259.

Browner, W.S. and Goldman, L. (2000) 'Distant Healing: An unlikely hypothesis (Editorial).' *American Journal of Medicine 108*, 6, 507–508.

Brueggemann, W. (1993) *Praying the Psalms*. Winona, MN: St Mary's Press.

Buber, M. (1970) *I and Thou.* Edinburgh: Clark.

Bullis, R.K. (2001) *Sacred Calling, Secular Accountability: Law and Ethics in Complementary and Spiritual Counselling*. Philadelphia, PA: Brunner-Routledge.

Bunker, D.E. (1991) 'Spirituality and the four Jungian personality types.' *Journal of Psychology and Theology 19*, 1, 26–34.

Byrd, R.C. (1988) 'Positive therapeutic effects of intercessory prayer in coronary care unit population.' *Southern Medical Journal 81*, 826–829.

Canda, E.R. (1990) 'An holistic approach to prayer for social work practice.' *Social Thought 16*, 3–13.

Capps, D. (1982) 'The psychology of petitionary prayer.' *Theology Today 39*, 130–141.

Carr, W. (1997) *Handbook of Pastoral Studies*. London: SPCK.

Carrington, P. (1977) *Freedom in Meditation*. Garden City, NY: Anchor/Doubleday.

Carrington, P. and Ephron, H. (1975) 'Meditation as an Adjunct to Psychotherapy.' In Arieti, S. (ed.) *New Dimensions in Psychiatry: A World View*. New York: Wiley.

Carroll, M. (2001) *Counselling Supervision: Theory, Skills and Practice*. London: Cassell.

Carson, V. and Huss, K. (1979) 'Prayer, an effective therapeutic and teaching tool.' *Journal of Psychiatric Nursing 17*, 34–37.

Chamberlain, T.J. and Hall, C.A. (2000) *Realized Religion – Research on the Relationship between Religion and Health*. Philadelphia, PA: Templeton Foundation Press.

Clarke, T.E. (1983) 'Jungian types and forms of prayer.' *Review for Religions 42*, 5, 661–676.

Clebsch, W. and Jaekle, C. (1964) *Pastoral Care in Historical Perspective*. New York: Harper Torchbooks.

Clinebell, H.J. (1963) 'Philosophical–religious factors in the etiology and treatment of alcohol.' *Journal of Studies on Alcohol 24*, 473–488.

Coe, G.A. (1916) *The Psychology of Religion*. Chicago, IL: University of Chicago Press.

Collins, G.R. (1988) *Christian Counseling – A Comprehensive Guide*. Milton Keynes: Word Publishing.

Collipp, P.J. (1969) 'The efficacy of prayer: a triple-blind study.' *Medical Times 69*, 201–204.

Cox, R.J. (2000) *Relating Different Types of Christian Prayer to Religious and Psychological Measures of Well-being*. Unpublished PhD thesis, Boston University, USA.

Craigie, F.C and Tan, S.Y. (1989) 'Changing resistant assumptions in Christian cognitive-behavioural therapy.' *Journal of Psychology and Theology 17*, 93–100.

Crocker, S.F. (1984) 'Prayer as a model of communication.' *Pastoral Psychology 33*, 2, 83–92.

Cronan, T.A., Kaplan, R.M., Posner, L., Blumberg, E. and Kozin, F. (1989) 'Prevalence of the use of unconventional remedies for arthritis in a metropolitan community.' *Arthritis and Rheumatism 32*, 1604–1607.

Culley, S. (1991) *Integrative Counselling Skills in Action.* London: Sage.

Cutten, G.B. (1908) *The Psychological Phenomena of Christianity.* New York: Charles Scribner's Sons.

Davies, D. (1998) 'The six necessary and sufficient conditions applied to working with lesbian, gay and bisexual clients.' *Person-Centred Journal 5*, 2, 111–120.

Davies, D. and Ackroyd, M. (2002) 'Sexual Orientation and Psychological Contact.' In Wyatt, G. and Saunders, P. (eds) *Contact and Perception.* Ross-on-Wye: PCCS.

Davies, D. and Neal, C. (1996) *Pink Therapy.* Milton Keynes: Open University Press.

Davis, T.N. (1986) 'Can prayer facilitate healing and growth?' *Southern Medical Journal 79*, 6, 733–735.

Deikman, A.J. (1966) 'Deautomatization and the mystic experience.' *Psychiatry 29*, 324–338.

Dmochowski, M.A. (1991) *A Theological and Psychodynamic Examination of the Role of Petition in the Development of Personal Prayer Life.* Unpublished Ph.D. thesis, The Catholic University of America.

Dobbins, R.D. (2000) 'Psychotherapy with Pentecostal Protestants.' In P.S. Richards and A.E. Bergin (eds) *Handbook of Psychotherapy and Religious Diversity.* Washington, DC: American Psychological Association.

Doniger, S. (ed.) (1953) *Psychological Aspects of Prayer.* Great Neck, NY: Pastoral Psychology Press.

Dossey, L. (1993) *Healing Words – the Power of Prayer and the Practice of Medicine.* San Francisco, CA: HarperCollins.

Duncan, B. (1993) *Pray Your Way – Your Personality and God.* London: Darton, Longman and Todd.

Dunn, K.S. and Horgas, A.L. (2000) 'The prevalence of prayer as a spiritual self-care modality in elders.' *Journal of Holistic Nursing 18*, 4, 337–351.

Elkins, D., Anchor, K.N. and Sandler, H.M. (1979) 'Relaxation training and prayer behavior as tension reduction techniques.' *Behavioral Engineering 5*, 81–87.

Elkins, D.N., Hedstrom, L.J., Hughes, L.L., Leaf, J.A. and Saunders, C. (1988) 'Towards a humanistic–phenomenological spirituality.' *Journal of Humanistic Psychology 28*, 4, 5–18.

Ellens, J.H. (1977) 'Communication theory and petitionary prayer.' *Journal of Psychology and Theology 5*, 48–54.

Ellinson, C.G. and Taylor, L.M. (1996) 'Turning to prayer: Social and situational antecedents of religious coping among African-Americans.' *Review of Religious Research 38*, 111–131.

Feltham, C. (2005) Book review of West (2004) 'Spiritual Issues in Therapy.' *Counselling and Psychotherapy Research 5*, 1, 34–35.

Fingarette, H. (1958) 'The ego and mystic selflessness.' *Psychoanalytic Review 45*, 5–40.

Finney, J.R. and Malony, H.N. (1985a) 'An empirical study of contemplative prayer as an adjunct to psychotherapy.' *Journal of Psychology and Theology 13*, 284–290.

Finney, J.R. and Malony, H.N. (1985b) 'Contemplative prayer and its use in psychotherapy: A theoretical model.' *Journal of Psychology and Theology 13*, 172–181.

Finney, J.R. and Malony, H.N. (1985c) 'Empirical studies of Christian prayer: A review of the literature.' *Journal of Psychology and Theology 13*, 104–115.

Foskett, J. and Lynch, G. (2001) 'Pastoral counselling in Britain: an introduction.' *British Journal of Guidance and Counselling 29*, 4, 373–379.

Francis, L.J. and Astley, J. (2001) *Psychological Perspectives on Prayer*. Leominster: Gracewing.

Freud, S. (1927) *The Future of an Illusion* (Robson-Scott, W.D., transl.) New York: H. Liveright.

Freud, S. (1963) *Civilization and Its Discontents*. New York: Basic Books.

Fry, P.S. (1990) 'A factor analytic investigation of home-bound elderly individuals' concerns about death and dying, and their coping responses.' *Journal of Clinical Psychology 46*, 737–748.

Fukuyama, M.A. and Sevig, T.D. (1999) *Integrating Spirituality into Multicultural Counselling*. London: Sage.

Galton, F. (1872) 'Statistical inquiries into the efficacy of prayer.' *Fortnightly Review 18*, 125–135.

Galton, F. (1883) *Inquiries into Human Faculty and Its Development*. London: Macmillan.

Garzon, F.L. (2005) 'Inner Healing Prayer in "Spirit-Filled" Christianity.' In R. Moodley and W. West (eds) *Integrating Traditional Healing Practices into Counseling and Psychotherapy*. Thousand Oaks, CA: Sage.

Gass, K.A. (1987) 'Coping strategies of widows.' *Journal of Gerontological Nursing 13*, 29–33.

Gay, V.P. (1978) 'Public ritual versus private prayer: psychodynamics of prayer.' *Journal of Religion and Health 17*, 4, 244–260.

Goddard, N.C. (1995) 'Spirituality as integrative energy: a philosophical analysis as requisite precursor to holistic nursing practice.' *Journal of Advanced Nursing 22*, 808–815.

Goehring, M.M. (1995) 'Listening prayer: the unseen and unheard real.' *Journal of Psychology and Christianity 14*, 4, 318–329.

Goleman, D. (1971) 'Meditation as meta-therapy: Hypotheses towards a proposed fifth state of consciousness.' *Journal of Transpersonal Psychology 3*, 1–25.

Greenberg, D. and Witztum, E. (1994) 'The influence of cultural factors on Obsessive Compulsive Disorder: Religious symptoms in a religious society.' *Israel Journal of Psychiatry and Related Services 31*, 3, 211–220.

Greyson, B. (1997) 'Distance healing of patients with major depression.' *Journal of Scientific Exploration 10*, 447 (abstract).

Gubi, P.M. (1995) *What is Christian Counselling? A Study of the Aims, Assumptions and Methodology of Christian Counsellors*. Unpublished MA dissertation, University of Nottingham, UK.

Gubi, P.M. (1999) *Prayer and Psychotherapy – an Exploration of the Therapeutic Nature of Christian Prayer and Its Possible Use with Christian Clients in Secular Psychotherapy.* Unpublished MTheol dissertation, University College Chester (University of Liverpool), UK.

Gubi, P.M. (2000) *Prayer and Psychotherapy – An Exploration of the Therapeutic Nature of Christian Prayer and Its Possible Use with Christian Clients in Secular Psychotherapy.* Paper presented to the 6th BAC Annual Research Conference, University of Manchester, UK.

Gubi, P.M. (2001) 'An exploration of the use of prayer in mainstream counselling.' *British Journal of Guidance and Counselling 29,* 4, 425–434.

Gubi, P.M. (2002) 'Practice behind closed doors – challenging the taboo of prayer in mainstream counselling culture.' *Journal of Critical Psychology, Counselling and Psychotherapy 2,* 2, 97–104.

Gubi, P.M. (2003a) Book review of Rose, J. (2002) 'Sharing Spaces? Prayer and the Counselling Relationship.' *Counselling and Psychotherapy Journal 14,* 1, 42.

Gubi, P.M. (2003b) *Integrating Prayer and Counselling: An Enquiry into Mainstream Counsellors Whose Work Includes Prayer.* Unpublished PhD thesis, University of Manchester, UK.

Gubi, P.M. (2004) 'Surveying the extent of, and attitudes towards, the use of prayer as a spiritual intervention among British mainstream counsellors.' *British Journal of Guidance and Counselling 32,* 4, 461–476. Also available at www.informaworld.com

Hammond, D.C., Hepworth, D.H. and Smith, V.G. (1977) *Improving Therapeutic Communication.* San Francisco, CA: Jossey-Bass.

Hardy, A. (1979) *The Spiritual Nature of Man.* Oxford: Clarendon.

Harkness, E.F., Abbot, M.C. and Ernst, E. (2000) 'A randomised trial of distant healing for skin warts.' *American Journal of Medicine 108,* 6, 448–452.

Harris, W., Gowda, M., Kolb, J., Strychacz, C., Vacek, J., Jones, P., Forker, A., O'Keefe, J. and McCallister, B. (1999) 'A randomised, controlled trial of the effects of remote intercessory prayer on outcomes in patients admitted to the coronary care unit.' *Archives of Internal Medicine 159,* 2273–2278.

Harvey, J.H., Stein, S.K., Olsen, N. and Roberts, R.J. (1995) 'Narratives of loss and recovery from a natural disaster.' *Journal of Social Behavior and Personality 10,* 313–330.

Hawkins, P. and Shohet, R. (2000) (2nd edition) *Supervision in the Helping Professions.* Milton Keynes: Open University Press.

Hawley, G. and Irurita, V. (1998) 'Seeking comfort through prayer.' *International Journal of Nursing Practice 4,* 9–18.

Hay, D. (1982) *Exploring Inner Space: Scientists and Religious Experience.* Oxford: Mowbray.

Hay, D. and Nye, R. (2006) (2nd edition) *The Spirit of the Child.* London: Jessica Kingsley Publishers.

Head, J. (2002) *Mental Health, Religion and Spirituality.* London: Quay Books.

Heiler, F. (1932) *Prayer: A Study in the History and Psychology of Religion.* (McComb, S., transl.). New York: Oxford University Press.

Helminiak, D.A. (1982) 'How is meditation prayer?' *Reviews for Religion 41,* 5, 774–782.

Hinksman, B. (1999) 'Tranference and Countertransference in Pastoral Counselling.' In G. Lynch (ed.) *Clinical Counselling in Pastoral Settings.* London: Routledge.

Hodge, A. (1931) *Prayer and Its Psychology.* London: SPCK.

Hood, R.W., Spilka, B., Hunsberer, B. and Gorsuch, R. (1996) (2nd edition) *The Psychology of Religion – An Empirical Approach*. New York: Guilford Press.

Horton, W.M. (1931) *A Psychological Approach to Theology*. New York: Harper and Brothers.

Hurding, R.F. (1985) *Roots and Shoots – a Guide to Counselling and Psychotherapy*. London: Hodder and Stoughton.

Jacobs, J.L. (1992) 'Religious Ritual and Mental Health.' In J.F. Schumaker (ed.) *Religion and Mental Health*. Oxford: Oxford University Press.

James, W. (1902) *The Varieties of Religious Experience – A Study in Human Nature*. London: Longmans, Green and Co.

Jenkins, C. (2006) *A Voice Denied: Clients' Experience of the Exclusion of Spirituality in Counselling and Psychotherapy*. Unpublished PhD thesis, University of Manchester, UK.

Johnson, P.E. (1945) *Psychology of Religion*. New York: Abingdon-Cokesbury.

Johnson, P.E. (1953) 'A psychological understanding of prayer.' *Pastoral Psychology 4*, 36, 33–39.

Johnson, W.B. and Ridley, C.R. (1992) 'Sources of gain in Christian counseling and psychotherapy.' *Counseling Psychologist 20*, 1, 159–175.

Joyce, C.R.B. and Welldon, R.M.C. (1964) 'The objective efficacy of prayer.' *Journal of Chronic Disorders 18*, 367–377.

Kaplan, M.S., Marks, G. and Mertens, S.B. (1997) 'Distress and coping among women with HIV infection: Preliminary findings from a multiethnic sample.' *American Journal of Orthopsychiatry 67*, 80–91.

Kaye, J. and Robinson, K.M. (1994) 'Spirituality among caregivers.' *IMAGE: Journal of Nursing Scholarship 26*, 218–221.

Keefe, F.J. and Dolan, E. (1986) 'Pain behavior and pain coping strategies in low back pain and myofascial pain dysfunction syndrome patients.' *Pain 24*, 49–56.

King, D.E. and Brunswick, B. (1994) 'Beliefs and attitudes of hospital inpatients about faith healing and prayer.' *Journal of Family Practice 39*, 4, 349–352.

King-Spooner, S. and Newnes, C. (eds) (2001) *Spirituality and Psychotherapy*. Ross-on-Wye: PCCS.

Koenig, H.G., Cohen, H.J. and Blazer, D.G. (1992) 'Religious coping and depression among hospitalised medically-ill men.' *American Journal of Psychiatry 149*, 1, 693–700.

Koenig, H.G. and Pritchett, J. (1998) 'Religion and Psychotherapy.' In Koenig, H.G. (ed.) *Handbook of Religion and Mental Health*. California: Academic Press.

Kris, E. (1936) 'The psychology of caricature.' *International Journal of Psychoanalysis 17*, 285–303.

Lange, M.A. (1983a) *Prayer and Psychotherapy: Beliefs and Practice*. Unpublished DPsych thesis, Rosemead School of Psychology, California, USA.

Lange, M.A. (1983b) 'Prayer and psychotherapy: beliefs and practice.' *Journal of Pastoral Counseling 2*, 3, 36–49.

Larson, D.B. (1993) *The Faith Factor: Vol. 2. An Annotated Bibliography of Systematic Reviews and Clinical Research on Spiritual Subjects*. Washington, DC: National Institute for Healthcare Research.

Lawrence, R. (1993) *How to Pray When Life Hurts*. London: Scripture Union.

Leech, K. (1980) *True Prayer: An Introduction to Christian Spirituality*. London: Sheldon Press.

Leibovici, L. (2001) 'Effects of remote, retroactive intercessory prayer on outcomes in patients with bloodstream infection: randomised controlled trial.' *British Medical Journal 323*, 1450–1451.

Leyser, Y. (1994) 'Stress and adaptation in orthodox Jewish families with a disabled child.' *American Journal of Orthopsychiatry 64*, 376–385.

Lilliston, L. and Brown, P.M. (1981) 'Perceived effectiveness of religious solutions to personal problems.' *Journal of Clinical Psychology 37*, 118–122.

Lilliston, L., Brown, P.M. and Schliebe, H.P. (1982) 'Perceptions of religious solutions to personal problems of women.' *Journal of Clinical Psychology 38*, 546–549.

Lindgren, K.N. and Coursey, R.D. (1995) 'Spirituality and serious mental illness: a two-part study.' *Psychosocial Rehabilitation Journal 18*, 3, 93–111.

London, P. (1985) (2nd edition) *The Modes and Morals of Psychotherapy*. New York: Hemisphere.

Lyall, D. (1995) *Counselling in a Pastoral and Spiritual Context*. Buckingham: Open University Press.

Lynch, G. (ed.) (1999) *Clinical Counselling in Pastoral Settings*. London: Routledge.

Lynch, G. (2000) 'Pastoral counselling in the new millennium.' *Counselling 11*, 6, 340–342.

Lynch, G. (2002) *Pastoral Care and Counselling*. London: Sage.

Macquarrie, J. (1972) *The Faith of the People of God*. London: SCM Press.

Magaletta, P.R. and Brawer, P.A. (1998) 'Prayer in psychotherapy: A model for its use, ethical considerations and guidelines for practice.' *Journal of Psychology and Theology 26*, 4, 322–330.

Maher, M.F. and Hunt, T.K. (1993) 'Spirituality reconsidered.' *Counseling and Values 38*, 21–28.

Mallory, M. (1977) *Christian Mysticism: Transcending Techniques*. Amsterdam: Van Gorcum Assen.

Maltby, J., Lewis, C.A. and Day, L. (1999) 'Religious orientation and psychological well-being: The role of the frequency of personal prayer.' *British Journal of Health Psychology 4*, 4, 363–378.

Martin, J.E. and Carlson, C.R. (1988) 'Spiritual Dimensions of Health Psychology.' In Miller, W.R. and Martin, J.E. (eds) *Behavior Therapy and Religion*. Newbury Park, CA: Sage.

Matthews, D.A. (1998) *The Faith Factor – Proof of the Healing Power of Prayer*. London: Penguin.

Matthews, D.A., Marlowe, S.M. and MacNutt, F.S. (2000) 'Effects of intercessory prayer on patients with rheumatoid arthritis.' *Southern Medical Journal 93*, 12, 1177–1186.

Maupin, E.W. (1965) 'Individual differences in response to a Zen meditation exercise.' *Journal of Consulting Psychology 29*, 139–145.

May, G.G. (1993) *Simply Sane: The Spirituality of Mental Health*. New York: Crossroads Publishing Company.

McCullough, M.E. (1995) 'Prayer and Health: Conceptual issues, research review, and research agenda.' *Journal of Psychology and Religion 23*, 1, 15–29.

McCullough, M.E. and Larson, D.B. (1999) 'Prayer.' In W.R. Miller (ed.) *Integrating Spirituality into Treatment – Resources for Practitioners.* Washington, DC: American Psychological Association.

McDonald, D. (1999) 'Body language and spirituality.' *Search – A Church of Ireland Journal,* spring issue.

McLeod, J. (2001) *Qualitative Research in Counselling and Psychotherapy.* London: Sage.

McMinn, M.R. (1996) *Psychology, Theology and Spirituality in Christian Counseling.* Wheaton, IL: Tyndale House.

Mearns, D. and Cooper, M. (2005) *Working at Relational Depth in Counselling and Psychotherapy.* London: Sage.

Mearns, D. and Thorne, B. (2000) *Person-Centred Therapy Today: New Frontiers in Theory and Practice.* London: Sage.

Miller, W.R. (ed.) (1999) *Integrating Spirituality into Treatment – Resources for Practitioners.* Washington, DC: American Psychological Association.

Moodley, R. and West, W. (eds) (2005) *Integrating Traditional Healing Practices into Counselling and Psychotherapy.* Thousand Oaks, CA: Sage.

Moore, J. and Purton, C. (eds) (2006) *Spirituality and Counselling: Experiential and Theoretical Perspectives.* Ross-on-Wye: PCCS.

Moss, B. (2005) *Religion and Spirituality.* Lyme Regis: Russell House.

Neser, W.B., Husaini, B.A., Linn, J.G. and Whitten-Stovall, R. (1989) 'Health care behaviour among Black and White women.' *Journal of Health and Social Policy 1,* 75–89.

Nicholls, V. (ed.) (2002) *Taken Seriously: The Somerset Spirituality Project.* London: Mental Health Foundation.

O'Connor, J.E. (1975) 'Motives and expectations in prayer.' *Review for Religious 34,* 3, 403–408.

O'Donohue, J. (1997) *Anam Cara – Spiritual Wisdom from the Celtic World.* London: Bantam Books.

O'Donohue, J. (1998) *Eternal Echoes – Exploring our Hunger to Belong.* London: Bantam Books.

Ohaeri, J.U., Shokunbi, W.A., Akinlade, K.S. and Dare, L.O. (1995) 'The psychosocial problems of sickle cell disease sufferers and their methods of coping.' *Social Science and Medicine 40,* 955–960.

O'Laoire, S. (1997) 'An experimental study of the effects of distant, intercessory prayer on self-esteem, anxiety, and depression.' *Alternative Therapies in Health and Medicine 3,* 6, 38–53.

O'Murchu, D. (1994) 'Spirituality, recovery and transcendental meditation.' *Alcoholism Treatment Quarterly 11,* 1 and 2, 169–184.

Ornstein, R.E. (1971) 'The techniques of Meditation and Their Implications for Modern Psychology.' In C. Naranjo and R.E. Ornstein (eds) *On the Psychology of Meditation.* New York: Viking Press.

Otis, L.S. (1974) 'If well-integrated but anxious, try TM.' *Psychology Today*, November issue, 45–46.

Page, S. and Wosket, V. (2001) *Supervising the Counsellor: a Cyclical Model.* London: Routledge.

Palmer, R.F., Katerndahl, D. and Morgan-Kidd, J. (2004) 'A randomized trial of the effects of remote intercessory prayer: Interactions with personal beliefs on problem-specific outcomes and functional status.' *Journal of Alternative and Complementary Medicine 10*, 3, 438–448.

Pargament, K.I. (ed.) (1992) *Religion and Prevention in Mental Health: Research, Vision, and Action.* Binghamton, NY: Haworth Press.

Pargament, K.I. (1997) *The Psychology of Religion and Coping.* New York: Guilford.

Parker, W.R. and St John, E. (1957) *Prayer Can Change Your Life.* Carmel, NY: Guideposts.

Paulson, B.L., Everall, R.D. and Stuart, J. (2001) 'Client perceptions of hindering experiences in counselling.' *Counselling and Psychotherapy Research 1*, 1, 53–61.

Payne, I.R., Bergin, A.E. and Loftus, P.E. (1992) 'A review of attempts to integrate spiritual and standard psychotherapy techniques.' *Journal of Psychotherapy Integration 2*, 171–192.

Payne, L. (1991) *Restoring the Christian Soul through Christian Prayer.* Wheaton, IL: Crossway Books.

Pearsall, P.K. (2001) 'On a wish and a prayer: Healing through distant intentionality.' *Hawaii Medical Journal 60*, 255–256.

Phillips, D.Z. (1965) *The Concept of Prayer.* London: Routledge and Kegan Paul.

Poloma, M.M. and Pendleton, B.F. (1991). 'The effects of prayer and prayer experiences on measures of general well-being.' *Journal of Psychology and Theology 19*, 1, 71–83.

Potts, R.G. (1996) 'Spirituality and the experience of cancer in an African-American community: Implications for psychosocial oncology.' *Journal of Psychosocial Oncology 14*, 1–19.

Pratt, J.B. (1930) *The Religious Consciousness.* New York: MacMillan.

Prince, R. and Savage, C. (1972) 'Mystical States and the Concept of Regression.' In J. White (ed.) *The Highest State of Consciousness.* Garden City, NY: Anchor/Doubleday.

Propst, R.L. (1988) *Psychotherapy in a Religious Framework: Spirituality in the Emotional Healing Process.* New York: Human Sciences Press.

Relton, H.M. (1925) 'The Psychology of Prayer and Religious Experience.' In O. Hardman (ed.) *Psychology and the Church.* London: MacMillan.

Rennie, D.L. (1994) 'Clients' deference in psychotherapy.' *Journal of Counseling Psychology 41*, 4, 427–437.

Richards, D.G. (1991) 'The phenomenology and psychological correlates of verbal prayer.' *Journal of Psychology and Theology 19*, 4, 354–363.

Richards, P.S. and Bergin, A.E. (1997) *A Spiritual Strategy for Counselling and Psychotherapy.* Washington, DC: American Psychological Association.

Richards, P.S. and Bergin, A.E. (ed.) (2003) *Spiritual Strategies: Case Studies.* Washington, DC: American Psychological Association.

Roberts, L., Ahmed, I. and Hall, S. (2001) *Intercessory Prayer for the Alleviation of Ill Health (Cochrane Review)*. The Cochrane Library. Issue 3. Available at: www.update-software.com/abstracts/ab000368.htm (accessed 3 August 2007).

Rogers, C.R. (1951) *Client-Centred Therapy*. Boston, MA: Houghton Mifflin.

Rogers, C.R. (1980) *A Way of Being*. Boston, MA: Houghton Mifflin.

Rose, J. (1993) *The Integration of Prayer and Practice in the Counselling Relationship*. Unpublished MSc dissertation, Roehampton Institute of Higher Education (University of Surrey), UK.

Rose, J. (1996) *A Needle-Quivering Poise – Between Prayer and Practice in the Counselling Relationship*. Edinburgh: Contact Pastoral Trust (Monograph No. 6).

Rose, J. (1999) 'Pastoral Counselling and Prayer.' In Lynch, G. (ed.) *Clinical Counselling in Pastoral Settings*. London: Routledge.

Rose, J. (2002) *Sharing Spaces? Prayer and the Counselling Relationship*. London: Darton, Longman and Todd.

Rossiter-Thornton, J.F. (2000) 'Prayer in psychotherapy.' *Alternative Therapies 6*, 1, 125–128.

Rowan, J. (1993) *The Transpersonal, Psychotherapy and Counselling*. London: Routledge.

Ryle, A. and Cowmeadow, P. (1992) 'Cognitive-Analytic Therapy.' In W. Dryden (ed.) *Integrative and Eclectic Therapy – A Handbook*. Milton Keynes: Open University Press.

Sacks, H.L. (1979) 'The effect of spiritual exercises on the integration of self-system.' *Journal for the Scientific Study of Religion 18*, 46–50.

Sajwaj, T. and Hedges, D. (1973) 'A note on the effects of saying grace on the behavior of an oppositional retarded boy.' *Journal of Applied Behavior Analysis 6*, 711–712.

Saudia, T.L., Kinney, M.R., Brown, K.C. and Young-Ward, K. (1991) 'Health locus of control and helpfulness of prayer.' *Heart and Lung 20*, 60–65.

Scheff, T.J. (1979) *Catharsis in Healing, Ritual and Drama*. Berkeley, CA: University of California Press.

Schneider, S. and Kastenbaum, R. (1993) 'Patterns and meanings of prayer in hospice caregivers: An exploratory study.' *Death Studies 17*, 471–485.

Schreurs, A. (2002) *Psychotherapy and Spirituality: Integrating the Spiritual Dimension into Therapeutic Practice*. London: Jessica Kingsley Publishers.

Schumaker, J.F. (ed.) (1992) *Religion and Mental Health*. Oxford: Oxford University Press.

Seamands, D. (1985) *Healing of Memories*. Wheaton, IL: Victor Books.

Segal, Z.V., Williams, J.M.G. and Teasdale, J.D. (2001) *Mindfulness-based Cognitive Therapy for Depression: A New Approach to Preventing Relapse*. New York: Guilford Press.

Selbie, W.B. (1924) *The Psychology of Religion*. Oxford: Oxford University Press.

Shafranske, E.P. and Gorsuch, R.L. (1984) 'Factors associated with the perception of spirituality in psychotherapy.' *Journal of Transpersonal Psychology 16*, 231–241.

Shafranske, E.P. and Malony, H.N. (1990) 'Clinical psychologists' religious and spiritual orientations and their practice of psychotherapy.' *Psychotherapy 17*, 1, 72–78.

Shapiro, D.H. (1980) *Meditation: Self-regulation and Altered States of Consciousness*. Hawthorne, NY: Aldine.

Shea, J. (1991) 'Taking care of yourself spiritually.' *Praying 45*, 13–15.

Shelly, J.A. (ed.) (1983) *Spiritual Dimensions of Mental Health.* Downers Grove, IL: InterVarsity Press.

Sicher, F., Targ, E., Moore, D. and Smith, H. (1998) 'A randomised double-blind study of the effect of distant healing in a population with advanced AIDS.' *Western Journal of Medicine 169,* 6, 356–363.

Simon, R. (1989) 'The spiritual program – its importance for mental health.' *Studies in Formative Spirituality 10,* 157–170.

Simpson, R. (1995) *Exploring Celtic Christianity – Historic Roots for Our Future.* London: Hodder and Stoughton.

Smith, J.A. (1996) 'Beyond the divide between cognition and discourse: using interpretative phenomenological analysis in health psychology.' *Psychology and Health 11,* 261–271.

Smith, J.A., Jarman, M. and Osborne, M. (1999) 'Doing Interpretative Phenomenological Analysis.' In M. Murray and K. Chamberlain (eds) *Qualitative Health Psychology: Theories and Methods.* London: Sage.

Sodestrom, K.E. and Martinson, I.M. (1987) 'Patients' spiritual coping strategies: A study of nurse and patient perspectives.' *Oncology Nursing Forum 14,* 41–46.

Sperry, L. (2001) *Spirituality in Clinical Practice – Incorporating the Spiritual Dimension in Psychotherapy and Counseling.* Philadelphia, PA: Brunner Routledge.

Steere, D. (1997) *Spiritual Presence in Psychotherapy – A Guide for Caregivers.* New York: Brunner/Mazel.

Steinberg, M. (1975) *Basic Judaism.* New York: Harcourt Brace Jovanovich.

Stern, R.C., Canda, E.R. and Doershuk, C.F. (1992) 'Use of non-medical treatment by cystic fibrosis patients.' *Journal of Adolescent Health 13,* 612–615.

Stewart, D.W. and Shamdasani, P.N. (1990) *Focus Groups: Theory and Practice.* London: Sage.

Still, A. (2001) 'The Immanence of Transcendence in Psychotherapy.' In S. King-Spooner and C. Newnes (eds) *Spirituality and Psychotherapy.* Ross-on-Wye: PCCS.

Stolley, J.M., Buckwalter, K.C. and Koenig, H.G. (1999) 'Prayer and religious coping for caregivers of persons with Alzheimer's disease and related disorders.' *American Journal of Alzheimer's Disease 14,* 3, 181–191.

Stolz, K.R. (1923) *The Psychology of Prayer.* New York: Abingdon Press.

Strauss, A. and Corbin, J. (1990) *Basics of Qualitative Research – Techniques and Procedures for Developing Grounded Theory.* London: Sage.

Strong, A.L. (1909) *The Psychology of Prayer.* Chicago, IL: University of Chicago Press.

Strunk, O. (1959) *Readings in the Psychology of Religion.* New York: Abingdon Press.

Surwillo, W.W. and Hobson, D.P. (1978) 'Brain electrical activity during prayer.' *Psychological Reports 43,* 135–143.

Sutton, T.D. and Murphy, S.P. (1989) 'Stressors and patterns of coping in renal transplant patients.' *Nursing Research 38,* 46–49.

Swinton, J. (2001) *Spirituality and Mental Health Care – Rediscovering a Forgotten Dimension.* London: Jessica Kingsley Publishers.

Tacey, D. (2004) *The Spirituality Revolution: The Emergence of Contemporary Spirituality.* Hove: Brunner-Routledge.

Tan, S.-Y. (1996) 'Religion in Clinical Practice: Implicit and Explicit Integration.' In E.P. Shafranske (ed.) *Religion and the Clinical Practice of Psychology.* Washington, DC: American Psychological Association.

Ten Eyck, C.C.R. (1993) *Inner Healing Prayer: The Therapist's Perspective.* Unpublished EdD thesis, University of South Dakota, USA.

Thorne, B. (1991) *Person-Centred Counselling – Therapeutic and Spiritual Dimensions.* London: Whurr.

Thorne, B. (1994) 'Developing a Spiritual Discipline.' In D. Mearns (ed.) *Developing Person-Centred Counselling.* London: Sage.

Thorne, B. (1998) *Person-Centred Counselling and Christian Spirituality – The Secular and the Holy.* London: Whurr.

Thorne, B. (2001) 'The prophetic nature of pastoral counselling.' *British Journal of Guidance and Counselling 29,* 4, 435–445.

Thorne, B. (2002) *The Mystical Path of Person-Centred Therapy: Hope Beyond Despair.* London: Whurr.

Thouless, R.H. (1923) *An Introduction to the Psychology of Religion.* Cambridge: Cambridge University Press.

Tuckwell, G. and Flagg, D. (1995) *A Question of Healing – The Reflections of a Doctor and a Priest.* London: Fount.

Ulanov, A. and Ulanov, B. (1982) *Primary Speech: A Psychology of Prayer.* Atlanta, GA: John Knox Press.

Ulanov, A. and Ulanov, B. (1992) 'Prayer and Personality: Prayer as Primary Speech.' In C. Jones, G. Wainwright, and E. Yarnold, (eds) *The Study of Spirituality.* London: SPCK.

Valentine, C.H. (1929) *Modern Psychology and the Validity of Christian Experience.* London: SPCK.

Watts, F. and Williams, M. (1988) *The Psychology of Religious Knowing.* London: Geoffrey Chapman.

Webster, J.P. (1992) *Verbal Prayer in Psychotherapy: A Model for Pastoral Counsellors.* Unpublished STD thesis, San Francisco Theological Seminary, USA.

Weil, S. (1963) *Gravity and Grace.* London: Routledge and Kegan Paul.

Welford, A.T. (1947) 'Is religious behavior dependent upon effect or frustration?' *Journal of Abnormal and Social Psychology 42,* 310–319.

West, W.S. (1995) *Integrating Psychotherapy and Healing – An Inquiry into the Experiences of Counsellors and Psychotherapists Whose Work Includes Healing.* Unpublished PhD thesis, University of Keele, UK.

West, W.S. (1998) 'Therapy as a Spiritual Process.' In C. Feltham (ed.) *Witness and Vision of the Therapists.* London: Sage.

West, W.S. (2000) *Psychotherapy and Spirituality – Crossing the Line Between Therapy and Religion.* London: Sage.

West, W.S. (2001) 'The use of forgiveness in counselling.' *British Journal of Guidance and Counselling 29,* 4, 415–423.

West, W.S. (2002) 'Being present to our clients' spirituality.' *Journal of Critical Psychology, Counselling and Psychotherapy 2*, 2, 86–93.

West, W.S. (2003) 'Spiritual Case Study (Matthew).' In P.S. Richards and A.E. Bergin (eds) *Spiritual Strategies: Case Studies.* Washington, DC: American Psychological Association.

West, W.S. (2004) *Spiritual Issues in Therapy: Relating Experience to Practice.* Basingstoke: Palgrave Macmillan.

White, B.F. and MacDougall, J.A. (2001) *Clinician's Guide to Spirituality.* New York: McGraw-Hill.

Willows, D. and Swinton, J. (2000) *Spiritual Dimensions of Pastoral Care.* London: Jessica Kingsley Publishers.

Wimberly, E.P. (1990) *Prayer in Pastoral Counseling: Suffering, Healing and Discernment.* Louisville, KY: Westminster/John Knox Press.

Wirth, D.P. and Barrett, M.J. (1994) 'Complementary healing therapies.' *International Journal of Psychosomatics 41*, 61–67.

Wirth, D.P. and Cram, J.R. (1994) 'The psychophysiology of non-traditional prayer.' *International Journal of Psychosomatics 41*, 68–75.

Woodmansee, M.F. (2000) *Mental Health and Prayer: An Investigation of Prayer, Temperament, and the Effects of Prayer on Stress When Individuals Pray for Others.* Unpublished PsyD thesis, Spalding University, USA.

Worsley, R. (2004) 'Integrating with Integrity.' In P. Saunders (ed.) *The Tribes of the Person-centred Nation: An Introduction to the Schools of Therapy Related to the Person-centred Approach.* Ross-on-Wye: PCCS.

Wosket, V. (1999) *The Therapeutic Use of Self: Counselling Practice, Research and Supervision.* London: Routledge.

Wyatt, G. and Saunders, P. (eds) (2002) *Contact and Perception.* Ross-on-Wye: PCCS.

Yarnold, E. (1992) 'The Theology of Christian Spirituality.' In C. Jones, G. Wainwright, and E. Yarnold (eds) *The Study of Spirituality.* London: SPCK.

Yungblut, J.R. (1991) *Rediscovering Prayer.* Shaftesbury: Element.

Zeidner, M. (1993) 'Coping with disaster: The case of Israeli adolescents under threat of missile attack.' *Journal of Youth and Adolescence 22*, 89–108.

Subject Index

Author Index

Author Index